Nobility, Tragedy, and Naturalism

Education in Ancient Greece

 THE BURGESS
HISTORY OF WESTERN EDUCATION SERIES

Nobility, Tragedy, and Naturalism
Education in Ancient Greece

Edited by J. J. Chambliss
Rutgers University

Burgess Publishing Company

426 South Sixth Street • Minneapolis, Minn. 55415

Copyright © 1971 by Burgess Publishing Company
Printed in the United States of America
Library of Congress Catalog Card Number 75-130629
SBN 8087-0332-3

Preface

THIS IS THE INITIAL VOLUME in The Burgess History of Western Education Series. The aim, in presenting it, is, first, to take certain ideas as a point of departure for studying education in ancient Greece; and, second, to set them forth as ideas having an integrity that has left an enduring mark in the history of western education. It consists of selections that are organized to show that the ideas of nobility, tragedy, and naturalism, in their development in Greek culture, were manifested in educational thought and practice.

The twofold intent that has guided the preparation of this volume is also to be characteristic of forthcoming volumes, some of which are in preparation. Each volume of the series will focus on certain seminal periods in the history of western education, such as ancient Greece, medieval Europe, the Enlightenment, and the nineteenth century. Each book will illustrate ways in which various ideas, in their influence upon educational thought and practice, had an integrity of their own growing out of their peculiar historical conditions and were the kind of ideas that have endured. As the series grows, those interested in studying the history of education will have the opportunity to make selections from several source books depending upon individual interest and variety of needs.

The volumes of the series are intended for use by students in courses such as History of Education and History of Educational Thought; they could be required by instructors who prefer to use books of readings, either alone or as companions to text books. Also, the volumes will provide supplementary readings for courses in Philosophy of Education, Social Foundations of Education, Cultural Foundations of Education, and for certain courses in Social and Intellectual History. The series is appropriate for students in undergraduate courses, as well as in first-year graduate courses.

OCTOBER 1, 1970   J. J. CHAMBLISS

Contents

Introduction

THE purpose of this book is to illustrate one of the enduring contributions of the Greeks to the history of education—the development of a way of thinking about education. It is a way of thinking that envisions a life in which man will strive to live as a part of nature rather than apart from it and one in which he will learn how to make the most of his potentialities, while understanding what his limitations are and the futility of trying to overreach them. A literature of educational thinking was created that articulated and criticized various conceptions of the relationship between the ideal of human excellence and the process by which this ideal might be attained in reality.

The origins of Greek educational thinking developed from a poetic, knightly, nonintellectual culture to a self-critical, sophisticated, somewhat enlightened one. Chronologically, the development took place from the period of the construction of Homer's *Iliad* and *Odyssey* about 850-750 B.C., through an increasingly artistic and enlightened fifth century (the poets Aeschylus, Sophocles, Euripides,

and Aristophanes; the historian Thucydides; the Athenian statesman Pericles; and the Sophists, the first professional teachers), and
culminated in the rhetoric of Isocrates and the philosophy of Plato
and Aristotle in the fourth century.

The scope of this book of readings is limited to illustrating some
expressions of Greek culture which had a significant bearing on the
development of educational thinking from Homer to Aristotle.
While it is not intended to be a comprehensive survey of Greek
education, it is intended to show students something of the fertility
of the Greek mind and of the educational ideas which took shape
in its development. Insofar as it does this, its main thrust is intro-
ductory rather than conclusive; suggestive rather than definitive;
illustrative rather than comprehensive; and limited rather than
extensive.

Two kinds of sources constitute the selections included. Transla-
tions of Greek writers—Pindar, Aeschylus, Sophocles, Euripides,
Thucydides, Aristophanes, Plato, Isocrates, and Aristotle—account
for eleven of the fifteen selections. The remaining four readings are
taken from studies of Greek thought, rather than from the Greek
authors themselves. First of all, Werner Jaeger's introduction to his
Paideia is so suggestive as to the place of the Greeks in the history of
education that it has been chosen as the point of departure here.
Since extensive selections would be required to capture something
of Homer's educational significance, two interpretive pieces are included instead—one by Giambattista Vico and the other by H. I.
Marrou. In the case of the Sophists, little remains of their writings;
consequently, H. I. Marrou's attempt to give them a fair historical
hearing is presented.

PART I

The Place of the Greeks in the History of Education

I N *Paideia: The Ideals of Greek Culture,* completed in German in the 1930s and later translated into English, Werner Jaeger provides exceptional insight for studying the development of educational ideas treated in this book. His introduction to the study of *Paideia,* which might be translated as "the ideals and the means by which the Greek character took shape," calls to our attention certain aspects of the process by which the Greek cultural ideals were developed; the remainder of our book illustrates more fully some of those aspects which Jaeger calls to mind.

In his text of *Paideia* itself, Jaeger sets forth the thesis that the history of the idea of *Paideia* may be taken as the most fundamental context for the study of the development of various aspects of Greek culture—such as art, law, politics, and philosophy. This is especially interesting to students of the history of education, for, in the most profound sense, Jaeger illustrates that the history of the Greek attempt to find a relationship between the ideal and the means by which men might live according to their nature is an *educational*

3

history. Furthermore, the origins of the various arts and sciences themselves are to be found in the history of the Greek effort to solve *educational* questions.

1. Paideia: The Ideals of Greek Culture

Werner Jaeger

The revolutionary, epoch-making position held by the Greeks in the history of education cannot be explained in a few sentences. The purpose of this book is to give an account of their culture, their *paideia,* and to describe its peculiar character and its historical development. It was not a sum of several abstract ideas; it was Greek history itself, in all its concrete reality. But the facts of Greek history would long ago have sunk into oblivion if the Greeks had not moulded them into a permanent form — the expression of their highest will, of their resistance to change and destiny. At the earliest stage of their development they had no clear conception of the nature of this act of will. But as they moved into ever clearer vision, along their historical path, the ever present aim of their life came to be more and more vividly defined. It was the creation of a higher type of man. They believed that education embodied the purpose of all human effort. It was, they held, the ultimate justification for the existence of both the individual and the community. At the summit of their development, that was how they interpreted their nature and their task. There is no reasonable ground for the assumption that we could understand them any better through some superior insight, psychological, historical, or social. Even the majestic works of archaic Greece can best be understood in this light, for they were created by the same spirit. And it was ultimately in the form of paideia, 'culture,' that the Greeks bequeathed the whole achievement of the Hellenic mind to the other nations of antiquity. Augustus envisaged the task of the Roman empire in terms of Greek culture. Without Greek cultural ideals, Greco-Roman civilization would not have been a historical unity, and the culture of the western world would never have existed.

We are accustomed to use the word culture, not to describe the ideal

From *Paideia: The Ideals of Greek Culture,* Volume 1, by Werner Jaeger, translated by Gilbert Highet. Copyright 1939, 1967 by Oxford University Press, Inc. Reprinted by permission. By permission also from Basil Blackwell, Publisher, Oxford. This selection is from the Introduction, pp. xvi-xviii, and does not include the author's notes.

which only the Hellenocentric world possesses, but in a much more trivial and general sense, to denote something inherent in every nation of the world, even the most primitive. We use it for the entire complex of all the ways and expressions of life which characterize any one nation. Thus the word has sunk to mean a simple anthropological concept, not a concept of value, a consciously pursued *ideal*. In this vague analogical sense it is permissible to talk of Chinese, Indian, Babylonian, Jewish or Egyptian culture, although none of these nations has a word or an ideal which corresponds to real culture. Of course every highly organized nation has an educational system; but the law and the prophets of the Israelites, the Confucian system of the Chinese, the Dharma of the Indians are in their whole intellectual structure fundamentally and essentially different from the Greek ideal of culture. And ultimately the habit of speaking of a number of pre-Hellenic 'cultures' was created by the positivist passion for reducing everything to the same terms: an outlook which applies hereditary European descriptions even to non-European things, and neglects the fact that historical method is falsified by any attempt to apply our conceptions to a world foreign to them. The circular reasoning to which almost all historical thought is liable begins with that basic error. It is impossible to do away with it entirely, because we can never escape from our own inborn ways of thinking. But we can at least solve the fundamental problems of history, and one of them is to realize the cardinal distinction between the pre-Hellenic world and the world that begins with the Greeks—the world in which a cultural ideal was first established as a formative principle.

Perhaps it is not great praise to say that the Greeks created the ideal of culture. In an age which is in many respects tired of civilization, it may even be a disparagement so to describe them. But what we call culture today is an etiolate thing, the final metamorphosis of the original Greek ideal. In Greek terms, it is not so much paideia, as a vast disorganized external apparatus for living, κατασκευὴ τοῦ βίου. It seems, in fact, that the culture of the present cannot impart any value to the original Greek form of culture, but rather needs illumination and transformation by that ideal, in order to establish its true meaning and direction. And this realization of and return to the archetype implies a mental attitude closely akin to the Greek—an attitude which recurs in Goethe's philosophy of nature, though probably without direct historical descent from Greece. Inevitably, towards the end of a historical period, when thought and custom have petrified into rigidity, and when the elaborate machinery of civilization opposes and represses man's heroic qualities, life stirs again beneath the hard crust. At such times, a deep-seated historical instinct drives men not only to go back to the resources of their own national culture, but also to live once more in that earlier age when the spirit of Greece (with which they have so much in common) was still fervently alive, and from its ardent life was creating the forms which eternalized its ardour and its genius. Greece is much more than a mirror to reflect the civilization of today, or a symbol of our rationalist consciousness of selfhood. The creation of any ideal is surrounded by all the secrecy and wonder of birth; and, with the increasing danger of degrading even the highest by daily use, men who realize the deeper values of the human spirit must turn more and more to the original forms in which it was first embodied, at the dawn of historical memory and creative genius.

We have said that the world-wide historical importance of the Greeks as educators was derived from their new awareness of the position of the individual in the community. When compared with the ancient East, they differ from it so fundamentally that their ideals seem to blend with those of modern Europe. Hence it is easy to conclude that the Greek ideal was the modern one of individualistic freedom. And in fact there could be no sharper contrast than that between the modern man's keen sense of his own individuality, and the self-abnegation of the pre-Hellenic Orient, made manifest in the sombre majesty of Egypt's pyramids and the royal tombs and monuments of the East. As against the Oriental exaltation of one God-king far above all natural proportions (which expresses a metaphysical view of life totally foreign to us) and the Oriental suppression of the great mass of the people (which is a corollary of that quasi-religious exaltation of the monarch), the beginning of Greek history appears to be the beginning of a new conception of the value of the individual. And it is difficult to refrain from identifying that new conception with the belief—which Christianity did most to spread—that each soul is in itself an end of infinite value, and with the ideal proclaimed during and after the Renaissance, that every individual is a law to himself. And how could the individual's claim to value and importance be justified, without the Greek recognition of the value of human character?

Historically it must be admitted that, since at the summit of their philosophical development the Greeks formulated and tried to solve the problem of the individual's place in the community, the history of personality in Europe must start with them. Roman civilization and the Christian religion each made some contribution to the question, and the mingling of these three influences created the modern individual's sense of complete selfhood. But we cannot clearly and fundamentally understand the position of Greek thought in the history of culture by starting from the modern point of view; it is far better to attack the question by considering the peculiar character of the Greek mind.

The variety, spontaneity, versatility, and freedom of individual character, which seem to have been the necessary conditions that allowed the Greek people to develop so rapidly in so many different ways, and which strike us with amazement in every Greek author from the earliest to the latest times, were not deliberately cultivated subjective qualities in the modern sense. They were natural, inborn. And when the Greeks who possessed them consciously realized their own individuality, they did so indirectly—by discovering objective standards and laws which, as soon as recognized, gave them a new certainty of thought and action. From the Oriental standpoint it is impossible to understand how the Greek artists contrived to represent the human body in free untrammelled motions and attitudes, not by the external process of copying a number of casually selected positions, but by learning the universal laws governing its structure, balance, and movement. Similarly, the distinguished and effortless ease of the Greek mind was produced by their lucid realization of the fact (concealed from earlier nations) that the world is governed by definite and comprehensible laws. They had an innate sense of the natural. The concept of 'nature,' which they were the first to work out, was without doubt produced by their peculiar mentality. Long before they conceived it, they had looked at the world with the steady gaze that did not see any part of it as separate and cut off from the rest, but always as an element in a living whole, from which it derived its position and its meaning. We call this the organic point of view, because it sees individual things as elements in a living whole. This sense of the natural, mature, original, and organic structure of life is closely connected with the Greek instinct to discover and formulate the laws governing reality—the instinct which appears in every sphere of Greek life, in their thought, their speech, their action, and all their art.

The characteristic Greek method of constructing and looking at a work of art was first and foremost an aesthetic instinct, based on the simple act of sight, not on the deliberate transference of an idea to the realm of artistic creation. It was relatively late in their history, in the classical period of the fifth and fourth centuries, that they idealized art, and blended an intellectual attitude with a physical and aesthetic act. Of course, when we say that their aesthetic sense was natural and unconscious, we have not explained why the same thing which is true of plastic art is also true of literature, where artistry does not depend on sight, but on the interplay of language and emotion. In Greek literature we find the same principles of form as in Greek sculpture and architecture. We speak of the plastic or the architectonic qualities of a poem or a prose work. Yet the qualities so described are not structural values *imitated* from sculpture or architecture, but *analogous* standards in language and its structure. We use these metaphors only because we grasp the structural principles of a statue or a building more vividly, and hence more quickly. The literary forms used by the Greeks, with all their manifold variety and elaborate structure, grew organically out of the transference of the bare simple forms in which men express themselves in language, to the ideal sphere of art and style. In the art of oratory too, their ability to carry out a complex plan and create an organic whole out of many parts proceeded purely and simply from a natural perception, increasingly sharpened, of the laws which govern feeling, thought, and speech—the perception which finally (grown abstract and technical) created logic, grammar, and rhetoric. In this respect we have had much to learn from the Greeks, and what we have learnt from them is the rigid and unalterable set of forms which still govern literature, thought, and style.

This applies even to the Greek mind's most miraculous creation, the most eloquent witness to its unique structure—philosophy. In philosophy the force which produced the forms of Greek art and thought is most visibly displayed. It is the clear perception of the permanent rules which underlie all events and changes in nature and in human life. Every people has produced a code of laws; but the Greeks always sought for one Law pervading everything, and tried to make their life and thought harmonize with it. They are the philosophers of the world. The *theoria* of Greek philosophy was deeply and inherently connected with Greek art and Greek poetry; for it embodied not only rational thought, the element which we think of first, but also (as the name implies) vision, which apprehends every object as a whole, which sees the *idea* in everything—namely, the visible pattern. Even when we know the dangers of generalizing, and of interpreting the earlier stage by the later, we cannot help realizing that the Platonic idea—a unique and specifically Hellenic intellectual product—is the clue to understanding the mentality of the Greeks in many other respects. In particular, the tendency to formalize which appears throughout Greek sculpture and painting sprang from the same source as the Platonic idea. The connexion was noted even in antiquity, and has often been observed since; but the same holds good of Greek oratory, and in fact of the basic intellectual attitude of the Greeks throughout. For instance, the earliest natural philosophers, with their efforts to see the cosmos as a whole governed by one law, are a complete contrast to the calculating, experimental, empirical scientists of modern times. They did not work by summarizing a series of separate results and systematizing them into an abstract conclusion, but went much further, and interpreted each isolated fact from a general conception which gave it position and meaning as part of a whole. It was this tendency, too, to construct universal patterns which distinguished Greek music and mathematics from those of earlier nations, so far as they are known today.

The unique position of Hellenism in the history of education depends on the same peculiar characteristic, the supreme instinct to regard every part as subordinate and relative to an ideal whole—for the Greeks carried that point of view into life as well as art—and also on their philosophical sense of the universal, their perception of the profoundest laws of human nature, and of the standards based on them which govern the spiritual life of the individual and the structure of society. For (as was realized by Heraclitus, with his keen insight into the nature of the mind) the universal, the *logos,* is that which is common to all minds, as law is to all citizens in the state. In approaching the problem of education, the Greeks relied wholly on this clear realization of the natural principles governing human life, and the immanent laws by which man exercises his physical and intellectual powers. To use that knowledge as a formative force in education, and by it to shape the living man as the potter moulds clay and the sculptor carves stone into preconceived form—that was a bold creative idea which could have been developed only by that nation of artists and philosophers. The greatest work of art they had to create was Man. They were the first to recognize that education means deliberately moulding human character in accordance with an ideal. "In hand and foot and mind built foursquare without a flaw"—these are the words in which a Greek poet of the age of Marathon and Salamis describes the essence of that true virtue which is so hard to acquire. Only this type of education deserves the name of culture, the type for which Plato uses the physical metaphor of *moulding* character. The German word *Bildung* clearly indicates the essence of education in the Greek, the Platonic sense; for it covers the artist's act of plastic formation as well as the guiding pattern present to his imagination, the *idea* or *typos.* Throughout history, whenever this conception reappears, it is always inherited from the Greeks; and it always reappears when man abandons the idea of training the young like animals to perform certain definite external duties, and recollects the true essence of education. But there was a special reason for the fact that the Greeks felt the task of education to be so great and so difficult, and were drawn to it by an impulse of unparalleled strength. That was due neither to their aesthetic vision nor to their 'theoretic' mentality. From our first glimpse of them, we find that Man is the centre of their thought. Their anthropomorphic gods; their concentration on the problem of depicting the human form in sculpture and even in painting; the logical sequence by which their philosophy moved from the problem of the cosmos to the problem of man, in which it culminated with Socrates, Plato, and Aristotle; their poetry, whose inexhaustible theme from Homer throughout all the succeeding centuries is man, his destiny, and his gods; and finally their state, which cannot be understood unless viewed as the force which shaped man and man's life—all these are separate rays from one great light. They are the expressions of an anthropocentric attitude to life, which cannot be explained by or derived from anything else, and which pervades everything felt, made, or thought by the Greeks. Other nations made gods, kings, spirits: the Greeks alone made men.

We can now define the specific character of Hellenism, in contrast to the Orient. By discovering man, the Greeks did not discover the subjective self, but realized the universal laws of human nature. The intellectual principle of the Greeks is not individualism but 'humanism,' to use the word in its original and classical sense. It comes from *humanitas:* which, since the time of Varro and Cicero at least, possessed a nobler and severer sense in addition to its early vulgar sense of humane behaviour, here irrelevant. It meant the process of educating man into his true form, the real and genuine human nature. That is the true Greek paideia, adopted by the Roman statesman as a model. It starts from the ideal, not from the individual. Above man as a member of the horde, and man as a supposedly independent personality, stands man as an ideal; and that ideal was the pattern towards which Greek educators as well as Greek poets, artists, and philosophers always looked. But what is the ideal man? It is the universally valid model of humanity which all individuals are bound to imitate. We have pointed out that the essence of education is to make each individual in the image of the community; the Greeks started by shaping human character on that communal model, became more and more conscious of the meaning of the process, and finally, entering more deeply into the problem of education, grasped its basic principles with a surer, more philosophical comprehension than any other nation at any other period in history.

The ideal of human character which they wished to educate each individual to attain was not an empty abstract pattern, existing outside time and space. It was the living ideal which had grown up in the very soil of Greece, and changed with the changing fortunes of the race, assimilating every stage of its history and intellectual development. This was not recognized by the classicists and humanists of earlier generations than ours—they left history out of account and construed the 'humanity,' the 'culture,' or the 'mind' of Greece or of classical antiquity as the expression of an absolute and timeless ideal. Of course the Greek nation bequeathed to its successors a great number of imperishable and immutable discoveries in the realm of the spirit. But it would be a most dangerous misconception of what we have described as the Greek will to shape individual character on an ideal standard, if we imagined that the standard was ever fixed and final. Euclidean geometry and Aristotelian logic are even now permanent sets of principles for the operation of the mind, and cannot possibly be put aside. Yet even these intellectual laws, universally valid, and purged of all temporal content, were created by Greek science; are, when viewed with a historical eye, Greek through and through; and do not exclude the co-existence of other mathematical and logical principles of thought and observation. And this is still more true of the other works of the Greek mind, which still bear the stamp of the age and nation that made them, and are directly connected with a definite historical situation.

The Greek critics who lived at the beginning of the Roman empire were the first to describe the masterpieces of the great age of Greece as 'classical' in the timeless sense—partly as formal patterns for subsequent artists to imitate, partly as ethical models for posterity to follow. At that time, Greek history had become part of the life of the world-wide empire of Rome, the Greeks had ceased to be an independent nation, and the only higher ideal which they could still follow was the preservation and veneration of their own tradition. So they were the first to develop the classicist theology of the mind—a legitimate description of that peculiar type of humanism. Their aesthetic *vita contemplativa* was the original form of the modern humanist's and scholar's life. Both lives were based on the same principle, an abstract timeless conception of the mind as a realm of eternal truth and beauty high above the troubled destinies of any one nation. Similarly, the German humanists of Goethe's time regarded the Greeks as the perfect manifestation of true human nature in one definite and unique historical epoch—an attitude nearer to the rationalism of the 'age of enlightenment' than to the new historical outlook which their doctrines actually encouraged.

A century of historical research, waxing while classicism waned, now separates us from that point of view. If today we counter the opposite danger—a boundless and aimless passion for viewing everything as history, a night in which all cats are grey—by returning to the permanent values of classical antiquity, still we can never again set them up as timeless idols. They cannot display the standards implicit in their meaning, and their irresistible power to transform and mould our lives, except as forces working within a definite historical milieu—just as they did in the era when they were created. We cannot any longer read or write histories of Greek literature *in vacuo,* cut off from the society which produced it and to which it was addressed. The Greek mind owes its superior strength to the fact that it was deeply rooted in the life of the community. All the ideals made manifest in its work were drawn, by the men who created them and reduced them to aesthetic form, from that powerful suprapersonal life. The man revealed in the work of the great Greeks is a political man. Greek education is not the sum of a number of private arts and skills intended to create a perfect independent personality. No one believed that it was, until the decline of Hellenism, when the Greek state as such had vanished—the age from which modern pedagogy is directly derived. It is easy to understand why the German classicists, living in an unpolitical age, followed that belief. But our own intellectual interest in the state has opened our eyes to the fact that in the best period of Greece mind without state was as impossible as a state without minds. The greatest works of Hellenism are memorials of a unique sense of the state, which developed uninterruptedly from the heroic age of Homer's epics to Plato's educational state, in which the individual and the community fight their last duel in the territory of philosophy. Any future humanism must be built on the fundamental fact of all Greek education—the fact that for the Greeks humanity always implied the essential quality of a human being, his political character. It is a mark of the close connexion between the productive artistic and intellectual life and the community that the greatest of the Greeks always felt they were its servants. This attitude is well known in the East also: it seems to be most natural in a state where life is organized by severe quasi-religious rules. Yet the great men of Greece came forward not to utter the word of God, but to teach the people what they themselves knew, and to give shape to their ideals. Even when they spoke in the form of religious inspiration, they translated their inspiration into personal knowledge and personal form. But personal as it might be in shape and purpose, they themselves felt it fully and compellingly social. The Greek trinity of poet, statesman, and sage ($\pi o \iota \eta \tau \acute{\eta} \varsigma$, $\pi o \lambda \iota \tau \iota \kappa \grave{o} \varsigma$, $\rho o \phi \acute{o} \varsigma$) embodied the nation's highest ideal of leadership. In that atmosphere of spiritual liberty, bound by deep knowledge (as if by a divine law) to the service of the community, the Greek creative genius conceived and attained that lofty educational ideal which sets it far above the more superficial artistic and intellectual brillance of our individualistic civilization. That is what lifts classical Greek literature out of the category of pure aesthetics, in which many have vainly tried to understand it, and gives it the immeasurable influence on human nature which it has exercised for thousands of years.

The art of the Greeks, as it was at its greatest periods and in its noblest masterpieces, plays the strongest part in that influence upon us. In fact, we need a history of Greek art, considered as a reflection of the ideals which dominated Greek life from time to time. It is true of Greek art as well as of Greek literature that until late in the fourth century it is principally the expression of the spirit of the community. Who can understand, for instance, the athletic ideal evoked by Pindar's hymns of victory, without knowing the statues of the Olympic victors, which show us its physical incarnation, or the images of the gods that embody all the Greeks felt about the physical and spiritual perfection possible to man? The Doric temple is unquestionably the mightiest monument left by the Dorian character and the Dorian ideal of severely subordinating each individual part to a rigidly compact whole. It has still a vast power to make historically present the vanished life which it eternalizes and the religious faith by which it was inspired. But the true representatives of paideia were not, the Greeks believed, the voiceless artists—sculptor, painter, architect—but the poets and musicians, orators (which means statesmen) and philosophers. They felt that the legislator was in a certain respect more akin to the poet than was the plastic artist; for both the poet and the legislator had an educational mission. The legislator alone could claim the title of sculptor, for he alone shaped living men. Often as the Greeks compared the act of education with the work of the plastic artist, they themselves despite their artistic nature hardly ever thought that a man could be educated by looking at works of art, as Winckelmann did. They considered that the only genuine forces which could form the soul were words and sounds, and—so far as they work through words or sounds or both—rhythm and harmony; for the decisive factor in all paideia is active energy, which is even more important in the culture of the mind than in the *agon* which exercises physical strength and agility. According to the Greek conception, fine art belonged to a different category. Throughout the whole classical period it kept its place in the sphere of religion, from which it had originated. Essentially, a picture or a statue was an *agalma,* an ornament. That does not apply to the heroic epic, and from the heroic epic educational energy flowed into every other type of poetry. Even where poetry was closely connected with religion, its roots were deeply sunk in the soil of social and political life; and that applies to works in prose even more than to poetry. Thus, the history of Greek culture coincides in all essentials with the history of Greek literature: for Greek literature, in the sense intended by its original creators, was the expression of the process by which the Greek ideal shaped itself. Moreover, we have practically no literary evidence but poetry to help in understanding the centuries preceding the classical period, so that even for a history of Greece in the factual sense, the only subject which can really be discussed is that process as depicted in poetry and art. It was the will of history that nothing else should survive of all the life of that age. We cannot trace the culture of the Greeks through those centuries except by studying the ideal which they shaped and cultivated.

.   .   .

PART **II**

The Ideal of Noble Birth in Epic and Ode

I. Homer: "The Educator of Greece"

IN the Homeric writings, the passages of relevance to our work are difficult to set forth briefly in a way that makes their significance clear. We have therefore selected our readings from two studies of Homer. The first is taken from a recent, in fact the first, translation into English of the Italian Giambattista Vico's *New Science,* written in the first half of the eighteenth century. This was a pioneering work on the nature and method of scientific social theory. The second is taken from a work of the twentieth century, H. I. Marrou's *A History of Education in Antiquity,* first published in an English translation in 1956.

Jaeger's statement "The Greek mind owes its superior strength to the fact that it was deeply rooted in the life of the community," takes on particular meaning when one views it in the light of Vico's discussion of the origins and nature of "poetic wisdom" and its relation to "philosophic wisdom." Specifically, Vico relates the Homeric epics to the development of Greek philosophy. It is not the intention here to discuss the question of the origins of the Homeric writings for its own sake, but rather to employ Vico's discussion of "the discovery of the true Homer" as a hypothesis for the place of Homer in the development of the Greek mind and its influence on educational ideals. Of special significance for our purpose is Vico's distinction between poetry and philosophy and his treatment of poetry as the source of philosophy; that is to say, "poetic wisdom" as expressed by Homer predates philosophy but is no less concerned with wisdom. In fact, poetic wisdom is a different sort of wisdom from philosophic wisdom and indeed is the source from which the latter sprang. Vico's fundamental thesis that Homeric poetry expressed a certain way of life, a kind of mind and character which was to help shape the ideals of the Greeks, might well suggest how deeply rooted the poetic wisdom was in the life of the Greek peoples. Further, it suggests the deep penetration of poetic wisdom in the development of later philosophic wisdom; so that an aristocratic Plato, in his criticisms of Homer, would come to oppose what Vico calls "the vulgar wisdom of the lawgivers who founded the human race."

Plato called Homer the educator of Greece; H. I. Marrou, in the second selection on Homer, epitomizes the substance of Homer's knightly hero in discussing his place in the origins of classical education. It is noteworthy that Marrou, like Vico before him, emphasizes the "nonphilosophical" character of Homer's poetry. Marrou finds Homer's poetic wisdom portrayed in the style of life, in the ethical context in which his heroes act. Homer was not, according to Marrou, an intellectualized "handbook of morality," or a source from which a compendium of scientific knowledge should be composed (as certain Sophists were to do with Homer). In Vico's terms, Homer "the sublime poet," was not a "sublime metaphysician"; the substance of his poetry "submerges the mind into the senses." Later scientists and philosophers who found sciences and philosophies in Homer must have put them there themselves. Both Vico and Marrou expressed the idea that Homer was an enduring source of wisdom; so much so that post-Homeric artists, scientists, and philosophers of culture found themselves emulating, combatting, intellectualizing, or otherwise finding a place for Homer in their more civilized and sophisticated ways of treating ideals. However varied were the reactions to the Homeric ideals, his influence was such that no serious writers on education in Greek antiquity could entirely escape his influence.

2. New Science

Giambattista Vico

BOOK II: POETIC WISDOM

Throughout this book it will be shown that as much as the poets had first sensed in the way of vulgar wisdom, the philosophers later understood in the way of esoteric wisdom; so that the former may be said to have been the sense and the latter the intellect of the human race. What Aristotle said of the individual man is therefore true of the race in general: *Nihil est in intellectu quin prius fuerit in sensu.* That is, the human mind does not understand anything of which it has had no previous impression (which our modern metaphysicians call "occasion") from the senses. Now the mind uses the intellect when, from something it senses, it gathers something which does not fall under the senses; and this is the proper meaning of the Latin verb *intelligere.*

.   .   .

Hence poetic wisdom, the first wisdom of the gentile world, must have begun with a metaphysics not rational and abstract like that of learned men now, but felt and imagined as that of these first men must have been, who, without power of ratiocination, were all robust sense and vigorous imagination. This metaphysics was their poetry, a faculty born with them (for they were furnished by nature with these senses and imaginations); born of their ignorance of causes, for ignorance, the mother of wonder, made everything wonderful to men who were ignorant of everything. Their poetry was at first divine, because they imagined the causes of the things they felt and wondered at to be gods. . . . At the same time they gave the things they won-

Reprinted from Thomas Goddard Bergin and Max Harold Fisch: *The New Science of Giambattista Vico.* Copyright© 1970 by Cornell University. Copyright© 1961 by Thomas Goddard Bergin and Max Harold Fisch. Copyright 1948 by Cornell University. Used by permission of Cornell University Press. This selection is from *Book II: Poetic Wisdom,* pp. 70, 74-75, 76-77, 77-79, 241.

dered at substantial being after their own ideas, just as children do, whom we see take inanimate things in their hands and play with them and talk to them as though they were living persons.

In such fashion the first men of the gentile nations, children of nascent mankind, created things according to their own ideas. But this creation was infinitely different from that of God. For God, in his purest intelligence, knows things, and, by knowing them, creates them; but they, in their robust ignorance, did it by virtue of a wholly corporeal imagination. And because it was quite corporeal, they did it with marvelous sublimity; a sublimity such and so great that it excessively perturbed the very persons who by imagining did the creating, for which they were called "poets," which is Greek for "creators." Now this is the threefold labor of great poetry: (1) to invent sublime fables suited to the popular understanding, (2) to perturb to excess, with a view to the end proposed: (3) to teach the vulgar to act virtuously, as the poets have taught themselves; as will presently be shown. Of this nature of human institutions it remained an eternal property, expressed in a noble phrase of Tacitus, that frightened men vainly "no sooner imagine than they believe."

In this fashion the first theological poets created the first divine fable, the greatest they ever created: that of Jove, king and father of men and gods, in the act of hurling the lightning bolt; an image so popular, disturbing, and instructive that its creators themselves believed in it, and feared, revered, and worshiped it in frightful religions. Whatever these men saw, imagined, or even made or did themselves they believed to be Jove; and to all of the universe that came within their scope, and to all its parts, they gave the being of animate substance. This is the civil history of the expression "All things are full of Jove." . . . But for the theological poets Jove was no higher than the mountain peaks. The first men, who spoke by signs, naturally believed that lightning bolts and thunderclaps were signs made to them by Jove; whence from *nuo,* to make a sign, came *numen,* the divine will, by an idea more than sublime and worthy to express the divine majesty. They believed that Jove commanded by signs, that such signs were real words, and that nature was the language of Jove. The science of this language the gentiles universally believed to be divination, which by the Greeks was called theology, meaning the science of the language of the gods.

Thus, in accordance with what has been said about the principles of the poetic characters, Jove was born naturally in poetry as a divine character or imaginative universal, to which everything having to do with the auspices was referred by all the ancient gentile nations, which must therefore all have been poetic by nature. Their poetic wisdom began with this poetic metaphysics, which contemplated God by the attribute of his providence; and they were called theological poets, or sages who understood the language of the gods expressed in the auspices of Jove; and were properly called divine in the sense of diviners, from *divinari,* to divine or predict. Their science was called Muse, defined by Homer as the knowledge of good and evil; that is, divination, on the prohibition of which God ordained his true religion for Adam. Because they were versed in this mystic theology, the Greek poets, who explained the divine mysteries of the auspices and oracles, were called *mystae,* which Horace learnedly renders "interpreters of the gods." . . .

All the things here discussed agree with that golden passage on the origins of idolatry: that the first people, simple and rough, invented the gods "from terror of present power." Thus it was fear which created gods in the world; not fear awakened in men by other men, but fear awakened in men by themselves. Along with this origin of idolatry is demonstrated likewise the origin of divination, which was brought into the world at the same birth. The origins of these two were followed by that of the sacrifices made to procure or rightly understand the auspices.

That such was the origin of poetry is finally confirmed by this eternal property of it: that its proper material is the credible impossibility. It is impossible that bodies should be minds, yet it was believed that the thundering sky was Jove. And nothing is dearer to poets than singing the marvels wrought by sorceresses by means of incantations. All this is to be explained by a hidden sense the nations have of the omnipotence of God. From this sense springs another by which all peoples are naturally led to do infinite honors to divinity. In this manner the poets founded religions among the gentiles.

All that has been so far said here upsets all the theories of the origin of poetry from Plato and Aristotle down to Patrizzi, Scaliger, and Castelvetro. For it has been shown that it was deficiency of human reasoning power that gave rise to poetry so sublime that the philosophies which came afterward, the arts of poetry and of criticism, have produced none equal or better, and have even prevented its production. Hence it is Homer's privilege to be, of all the sublime, that is, the heroic poets, the first in the order of merit as well as in that of age. This discovery of the origins of poetry does away with the opinion of the matchless wisdom of the ancients, so ardently sought after from Plato to Bacon's *De sapientia veterum.* For the wisdom of the ancients was the vulgar wisdom of the lawgivers who founded the human race, not the esoteric wisdom of great and rare philosophers. Whence it will be found, as it has been in the case of Jove, that all the mystic meanings of

lofty philosophy attributed by the learned to the Greek fables and the
Egyptian hieroglyphics are as impertinent as the historical meanings they
both must have had are natural.

.   .   .

We have shown that poetic wisdom justly deserves two great and sovereign tributes. The one, clearly and constantly accorded to it, is that of having founded gentile mankind, though the conceit of nations on the one hand
and that of scholars on the other, the former with ideas of an empty magnificence and the latter with ideas of an impertinent philosophical wisdom,
have in effect denied it this honor by their very efforts to affirm it. The other,
concerning which a vulgar tradition has come down to us, is that the wisdom of the ancients made its wise men, by a single inspiration, equally
great as philosophers, lawmakers, captains, historians, orators, and poets,
on which account it has been so greatly sought after. But in fact it made or
rather sketched them such as we have found them in the fables. For in these,
as in embryos or matrices, we have discovered the outlines of all esoteric
wisdom. And it may be said that in the fables the nations have in a rough
way and in the language of the human senses described the beginnings of
this world of sciences, which the specialized studies of scholars have since
clarified for us by reasoning and generalization. From all this we may conclude what we set out to show in this [Second] Book: that the theological
poets were the sense and the philosophers the intellect of human wisdom.

BOOK III: DISCOVERY OF THE TRUE HOMER

The complete absence of philosophy which we have shown in Homer, and
our discoveries concerning his fatherland and his age, arouse in us a strong
suspicion that he may perhaps have been quite simply a man of the people.
This suspicion is confirmed by Horace's observation in his *Art of Poetry*
concerning the desperate difficulty of creating fresh characters or persons
of tragedy after Homer, on account of which he advises poets to take their
characters from Homer's poems. . . .

To Horace's difficulty we must add two others of wider scope. For one
thing, how is it that Homer, who came first, was such an inimitable heroic
poet, while tragedy, which was born later, began with the crudeness familiar to everybody and which we shall later describe more in detail? And for
another, how is it that Homer, who preceded philosophy and the poetic and

Reprinted from Thomas Goddard Bergin and Max Harold Fisch: *The New Science of
Giambattista Vico.* Copyright© 1970 by Cornell University. Copyright© 1961 by Thomas
Goddard Bergin and Max Harold Fisch. Copyright 1948 by Cornell University. Used by
permission of Cornell University Press. This selection is from *Book III: Discovery of the
True Homer,* pp. 254-57, 257-58, 259-63, 270-71, 272-73. (The notes are not included here.)

critical arts, was yet the most sublime of all the sublime poets, and that after the invention of philosophies and of the arts of poetry and criticism there was no poet who could come within a long distance of competing with him? . . .

The reason cannot be found elsewhere than in the origin of poetry, as discovered above in the Poetic Wisdom, and consequently in the discovery of the poetic characters in which alone consists the essence of poetry itself. . . . The Old Comedy took arguments or subjects from real life and made plays of them just as they were, as the wicked Aristophanes once did with the good Socrates, thus bringing on his ruin. But tragedy puts on the scene heroic hatred, scorn, wrath, and revenge, which spring from sublime natures which naturally are the source of sentiments, modes of speech, and actions in general that are wild, crude, and terrible. Such arguments are clothed with an air of marvel, and all these matters are in closest conformity among themselves and uniform in their subjects. Such works the Greeks could produce only in the time of their heroism, at the end of which Homer must have come. This is shown by the following metaphysical criticism. The fables, which at their birth had come forth direct and proper, reached Homer distorted and perverted. As may be seen throughout the Poetic Wisdom above set forth, they were all at first true histories, which were gradually altered and corrupted, and in their corrupt form finally came down to Homer. Hence he must be assigned to the third age of the heroic poets. The first age invented the fables to serve as true narratives, the primary and proper meaning of the word *mythos,* as defined by the Greeks themselves, being "true narration." The second altered and corrupted them. The third and last, that of Homer, received them thus corrupted.

But, to return to our purpose, for the reason assigned by us to this effect, Aristotle in his *Poetics* says that only Homer knew how to invent poetic falsehoods. For his poetic characters, which are incomparable for the sublime appropriateness which Horace admires in them, were imaginative universals, as defined above in the Poetic Metaphysics, to which the peoples of Greece attached all the various particulars belonging to each genus. To Achilles, for example, who is the subject of the *Iliad,* they attached all the properties of heroic valor, and all the feelings and customs arising from these natural properties, such as those of quick temper, punctiliousness, wrathfulness, implacability, violence, the arrogation of all right to might, as they are summed up by Horace in his description of this character. To Ulysses, the subject of the *Odyssey,* they attached all the feelings and customs of heroic wisdom; that is, those of wariness, patience, dissimulation, duplicity, deceit, always preserving propriety of speech and indifference of action, so that others may of themselves fall into error and may be the causes of their own deception. And to these two characters, according to kind, they attached those actions of particular men which were conspicuous enough to arouse and move the still dull and stupid Greeks to note them and refer them to their kinds. These two characters, since they had been created by an entire nation, could only be conceived as naturally uniform (in which uniformity, agreeable to the common sense of an entire nation, alone consists the decorum or beauty and charm of a fable); and, since they were created by powerful imaginations, they could not be created as anything but sublime. Hence derive two eternal properties of poetry: one that poetic sublimity is inseparable from popularity, and the other that peoples who have first created heroic characters for themselves will afterward apprehend human customs only in terms of characters made famous by luminous examples.

In view of what we have stated, the following philosophical proofs may be assembled. First of all, the one numbered above among the axioms which states that men are naturally led to preserve the memories of the institutions and laws that bind them within their societies. The truth understood by Castelvetro, that history must have come first and then poetry, for history is a simple statement of the true but poetry is an imitation besides. Yet this scholar, though otherwise most acute, failed to make use of this clue to discover the true principles of poetry by combining it with the other philosophical proof which follows next. Inasmuch as the poets came certainly before the vulgar historians, the first history must have been poetic.

The fables in their origin were true and severe narrations, whence *mythos,* fable, was defined as *vera narratio.* But because they were originally for the most part gross, they gradually lost their original meanings, were then altered, subsequently became improbable, after that obscure, then scandalous, and finally incredible. . . .

The poetic characters, in which the essence of the fables consists, were born of the need of a nature incapable of abstracting forms and properties from subjects. Consequently they must have been the manner of thinking of entire peoples, who had been placed under this natural necessity in the times of their greatest barbarism. It is an eternal property of the fables always to enlarge the ideas of particulars. On this there is a fine passage in Aristotle in which he remarks that men of limited ideas erect every particular into a maxim. The reason must be that the human mind, which is indefinite, being constricted by the vigor of the senses, cannot otherwise express its almost divine nature than by thus enlarging particulars in imagination. It is perhaps on this account that in both the Greek and the Latin poets the images of gods and heroes always appear larger than those of men.

Since poetic characters are of this nature, their poetic allegories, as we have shown above throughout the Poetic Wisdom, must necessarily contain historical significations referring only to the earliest times of Greece.

Such histories must naturally have been preserved in the memories of the communities of the peoples, in virtue of our first philosophical proof; for, as the children of the nations, they must have had marvelously strong memories. . . . In that human indigence, the peoples, who were almost all body and almost no reflection, must have been all vivid sensation in perceiving particulars, strong in referring them to their imaginative genera, and robust memory in retaining them. It is true that these faculties appertain to the mind, but they have their roots in the body and draw their strength from it. Hence memory is the same as imagination, which for that reason is called *memoria* in Latin. . . . Memory thus has three different aspects: memory when it remembers things, imagination when it alters or imitates them, and invention when it gives them a new turn or puts them into proper arrangement and relationship. For these reasons the theological poets called Memory the mother of the Muses. . . .

By the very nature of poetry it is impossible for anyone to be at the same time a sublime poet and a sublime metaphysician, for metaphysics abstracts the mind from the senses, and the poetic faculty must submerge the whole mind in the senses; metaphysics soars up to universals, and the poetic faculty must plunge deep into particulars.

In virtue of the axiom that he who has not the natural gift may by industry succeed in every [other] capacity, but that in poetry success by industry is completely denied to him who lacks the natural gift, the poetic and critical "arts" serve to make minds cultivated but not great. For delicacy is a small virtue and greatness naturally disdains all small things. Indeed, as a great rushing torrent cannot fail to carry turbid waters and roll stones and trunks along in the violence of its course, so his very greatness accounts for the low expressions we so often find in Homer. But this does not make Homer any the less the father and prince of all sublime poets. For we have seen that Aristotle regarded the Homeric lies as without equal, which is equivalent to Horace's opinion that his characters are inimitable.

He is celestially sublime in his poetic sentences, which must be conceived of true passions, or in virtue of a burning imagination must make themselves truly felt by us, and they must therefore be individualized in those who feel them. Hence maxims of life, as being general, were defined by us as sentences of philosophers; and reflections on the passions themselves are the work of false and frigid poets. The poetic comparisons taken from wild and savage things are certainly incomparable in Homer. The frightfulness of the Homeric battles and deaths gives to the *Iliad* all its marvelousness. But these sentences, comparisons, and descriptions could not have been the natural product of a calm, cultivated, and gentle philosopher.

For in their customs the Homeric heroes are like boys in the frivolity of their minds, like women in the vigor of their imaginations, and like turbulent youths in the boiling fervor of their wrath, and therefore it is impossible that a philosopher should have conceived them so naturally and felicitously. The ineptitudes and indecencies are effects of the awkwardness with which the Greek peoples had labored to express themselves in the extreme poverty of their language in its formative period. And even if the Homeric poems contained the most sublime mysteries of esoteric wisdom, as we have shown in the Poetic Wisdom that they certainly do not, the form in which they are expressed could not have been conceived by a straightforward, orderly, and serious mind such as befits a philosopher.

The heroic language was a language of similes, images, and comparisons, born of the lack of genera and species, which are necessary for the proper definition of things, and hence born of a necessity of nature common to entire peoples.

It was by a necessity of nature that the first nations spoke in heroic verse. Here too we must admire the providence which, in the time when the characters of common script were not yet invented, ordained that the nations should speak in verses so that their memories might be aided by meter and rhythm to preserve more easily the histories of their families and cities.

These fables, sentences, and customs, this language and verse, were all called heroic, and were current in the times to which history has assigned the heroes, as has been fully shown above in the Poetic Wisdom. Hence all the aforesaid were properties of entire peoples and consequently common to all the individual men of these peoples. In virtue, therefore, of the very nature from which sprang all the aforesaid properties, which made Homer the greatest of poets, we denied that he was even a philosopher. Further we showed above in the Poetic Wisdom that the meanings of esoteric wisdom were intruded into the Homeric fables by the philosophers who came later.

But, as esoteric wisdom appertains to but few individual men, so we have just seen that the very decorum of the heroic poetic characters, in which consists all the essence of the heroic fables, cannot be achieved today by men most learned in philosophy, in the art of poetry, and in the art of criticism. It is for this decorum that Aristotle and Horace give the palm to Homer, the former saying that his lies are beyond equal and the latter that his characters are inimitable, which comes to the same thing.

.   .   .

The reason why the Greek peoples so vied with each other for the honor of being his fatherland, and why almost all claimed him as citizen, is that the Greek peoples were themselves Homer. That the reason why opinions as to his age vary so much is that our Homer truly lived on the lips and in the memories of the peoples of Greece throughout the whole period from the Trojan War down to the time of Numa, a span of 460 years. And the blindness and the poverty of Homer were characteristics of the rhapsodes, who, being blind, whence each of them was called *homeros*, had exceptionally retentive memories, and, being poor, sustained life by singing the poems of Homer throughout the cities of Greece; and they were the authors of these poems inasmuch as they were a part of these peoples who had composed their histories in the poems.

Thus Homer composed the *Iliad* in his youth, that is, when Greece was young and consequently seething with sublime passions, such as pride, wrath, and lust for vengeance, passions which do not tolerate dissimulation but which love magnanimity; and hence this Greece admired Achilles, the hero of violence. But he wrote the *Odyssey* in his old age, that is, when the spirits of Greece had been somewhat cooled by reflection, which is the mother of prudence, so that it admired Ulysses, the hero of wisdom. Thus in the time of Homer's youth the peoples of Greece found pleasure in coarseness, villainy, ferocity, savagery, and cruelty, while in the time of his old age they found delight in the luxury of Alcinous, the joys of Calypso, the pleasures of Circe, the songs of the Sirens, the pastimes of the suitors, and the attempts, nay the siege and the assaults, on the chastity of Penelope: two sets of customs which, conceived above as existing at the same time, seemed to us incompatible. This difficulty was enough to cause the divine Plato to declare, in order to solve it, that Homer had foreseen by inspiration these nauseating, morbid, and dissolute customs. Yet in this way he merely made of Homer a stupid founder of Greek civility, for, however much he may condemn, he nevertheless teaches these corrupt and decadent customs which were to come long after the nations of Greece had been founded, to the end that, by an acceleration of the natural course of human institutions, the Greeks might hasten on toward corruption.

In this fashion we show that the Homer who was the author of the *Iliad* preceded by many centuries the Homer who was the author of the *Odyssey*. And we show that it was from the northeastern part of Greece that the Homer came who sang of the Trojan War, which took place in his country, and that it was from the southwestern part of Greece that the Homer came who sang of Ulysses, whose kingdom was in that region.

Thus Homer, lost in the crowd of the Greek peoples, is justified against all the accusations leveled at him by the critics, and particularly [against those made] on account of his base sentences, vulgar customs, crude comparisons, local idioms, licenses in meter, variations in dialect, and his having made men of gods and gods of men.

.   .   .

But more than ever to Homer belong by right the two great pre-eminences which are really one: that poetic falsehoods, as Aristotle says, and heroic characters, as Horace says, could be created only by him. On this account Horace avows himself to be no poet because he lacks the skill or the wit to maintain what he calls the colors of works, *colores operum,* which means the same thing as the poetic untruths of Aristotle's phrase, for in Plautus we find *obtinere colorem* in the sense of telling a lie that under every aspect has the appearance of truth, which is what a good fable must be. In addition to these, all those other pre-eminences fall to him which have been ascribed to him by all the masters of the art of poetry, declaring him incomparable in his wild and savage comparisons, in his cruel and fearful descriptions of battles and deaths, in his sentences filled with sublime passions, in the expressiveness and splendor of his style. All these were properties of the heroic age of the Greeks, in which and throughout which Homer was an incomparable poet, just because, in the age of vigorous memory, robust imagination, and sublime invention, he was in no sense a philosopher.

Wherefore neither philosophies, arts of poetry, nor arts of criticism, which came later, could create a poet who could come anywhere near to rivaling Homer. And, what is more, his title is assured to the three immortal eulogies that are given him: first, of having been the founder of Greek polity or civility; second, of having been the father of all other poets; and third, of having been the source of all Greek philosophies. . . . The philosophers did not discover their philosophies in the Homeric fables but rather inserted them therein. But it was poetic wisdom itself whose fables provided occasions for the philosophers to meditate their lofty truths, and supplied them also with means for expounding them.

3. Education in Homeric Times

H. I. Marrou

THE KNIGHTLY CULTURE

This is the fundamental fact underlying the original features of the educational tradition of classical Greece. Greek culture was originally a privilege reserved for an aristocracy of warriors. Here we see the culture in its nascent state; for these Homeric heroes are not brutal old soldiers, prehistoric

From *A History of Education in Antiquity,* by H. I. Marrou, © 1956 Sheed & Ward Inc., New York. This selection is from Part I, Chapter I, Education in Homeric Times, pp. 5-13. Marrou's notes are included, but not his "additional notes." His references make use of the following abbreviations: *Il., Iliad; Od., Odyssey; Cyn.,* Xenophon, *On Hunting; Hdt.,* Herodotus, *History; Leg.,* Plato, *Laws; Resp.,* Plato, *Republic; Prot.,* Plato, *Protagoras; Phdr.,* Plato, *Phaedrus.* Footnotes have been renumbered to appear in consecutive order.

warriors, as our romantic predecessors like to think; in a sense, they are already knights.

Homeric society succeeded an old civilization whose refinements had not entirely disappeared. The young κοῦροι rendered their superior what can only be called "courtly service." Like the mediaeval squires, they served at table at royal feasts: "The κοῦροι fill the cups to the brim"[1] is a line so aptly descriptive of their role as cup-bearers that we find it repeated or interpolated in four other episodes.[2] And this was a noble service, quite different from that performed by mere servants—κήρυκες.

They served as a retinue: seven young men accompany Ulysses when he brings Briseis to Achilles.[3] They took part in sacrifices, standing by the side of the priest,[4] not only as carvers but also because they "sing the noble paean and dance in honour of the Preserver,"

$$καλὸν \ ἀείδοντες \ παιήονα \ κοῦροι \ ᾿Αχαιῶν$$
$$μέλποντες \ ᾿Εκάεργον.[5]$$

Patroclus came to seek refuge at the court of Phthia, fleeing from Opontus, his fatherland, after accidentally killing someone. His own father, Menoetius, presented him to King Peleus. The latter welcomed him with kindness, and placed him at the side of his son Achilles, to whom he was later to render the noble service of equerry (θεράπων).[6]

Together with the religious ceremonies, the dominant feature of the life of these Homeric knights was sport. The games were sometimes free and spontaneous, mere episodes of daily life (the life of the nobility was already one of elegant leisure) like the feast at the house of Alcinous,[7] which included sports, musical entertainments, dancing by the young Phaeaces, dancing with balls by the sons of Alcinous, the singing of the bard and the playing of the lyre. Achilles, retiring into his hut, found consolation in singing the heroes' exploits to himself, to the accompaniment of the melodious *phorminx*.[8] And also, perhaps, even at this stage, there may have been public debates and wordy jousts.

At other times, again, the games formed part of a solemn display, carefully organized and controlled—we need only think of the song Ψ in the *Iliad,* with its accompanying funeral games in honour of Patroclus. There was boxing (which had been a favourite sport with the Minoans), wrestling, racing, jousting, putting the weight, archery, javelin-throwing, and above

---

[1]*Il.,* I, 463; 470.
[2]*Ibid.,* IX, 175; *Od.,* I, 148;
  III, 339; XXI, 271.
[3]*Il.,* XIX, 238 *seq.*
[4]*Ibid.,* I, 463 *seq.*
[5]*Ibid.,* I, 473-474.
[6]*Ibid.,* XXIII, 90.
[7]*Od.,* VIII, 104 *seq.*
[8]*Il.,* IX, 186 *seq.*

all chariot-racing,[9] which was always the noblest and most highly esteemed sport of all.

Clearly, these knights were no barbaric warriors: their life was a genuine court-life, a life of "courtesy," which involved a great refinement of manners—as witness, for instance, the tact displayed by Achilles as organizer and judge of the games,[10] and the sporting instinct of the champions and spectators—the boxer Epeios lifting his adversary Euryalus to his feet after punching him hard and knocking him out,[11] the Achaeans stopping Diomedes when the life of Ajax was in danger from his blows.[12]

This courtesy still characterized the heroes when they engaged in combat, even in the ritual insults which they hurled at each other as a prelude to action. It appeared in every kind of situation: what refinements of courtesy there are, for instance, in the relations between Telemachus and the suitors, despite the tension between them and the atmosphere of hate.

The atmosphere of refinement which surrounds the later of the two poems, at least—the *Odyssey*—seems to find its natural fulfilment in an attitude of the utmost delicacy towards women. The suitors are infinitely respectful to Penelope. We are told that old Laërtes refused to enjoy the slave girl Euryclea[13] in order not to arouse the jealousy of his wife. The mother of the family is absolute mistress of the house—think of Arete, queen of the Phaeaces; think of Helen at her home in Sparta welcoming Telemachus, guiding the conversation—"entertaining" in the modern sense of the word.

It is a life of courtesy, and also of *savoir-faire* (here we meet the oriental Wisdom again): how to act in polite society, how to react to unforeseen circumstances, how to behave, and above all how to speak—to appreciate the importance of all this one only needs to think of Telemachus at Pylos or Sparta, or Nausicaa faced with the shipwrecked Ulysses.

Such, in brief, is the ideal figure of Homer's "perfect knight." But a man did not become an accomplished κοῦροϛ by the light of nature. This culture, with its rich and complex content, presupposes the appropriate education, of the nature of which we are not left in ignorance. Homer is sufficiently interested in the psychology of his heroes to take care to tell us how they have been brought up, how they have been able to achieve such a flowering of chivalry: the heroic legends contained stories about the education of Achilles which had been handed down from generation to generation—just like our mediaeval epiccycles, which, for example, devoted a whole verse-chronicle to the *Enfances Vivien.*

[9]*Ibid.*, XXIII, 261-897.   [11]*Ibid.*, 694.
[10]*Ibid.*, 257 *seq.*   [12]*Ibid.*, 822.
[13]*Od.*, I, 433.

CHIRON AND PHOENIX

The typical educator is Chiron, "the wise centaur."[14] A large number of legends appear to have gathered around his name. He not only brought up Achilles but many other heroes as well—Asclepius, the son of Apollo,[15] Actaeon, Cephalus, Jason, Melanion, Nestor. Xenophon[16] gives a list of twenty-one names. Here we need only mention Achilles: Chiron was the counsellor and friend of Peleus (it was to Chiron that Peleus owed, amongst other things, the fact that he had been successful in his suit for the hand of Thetis), and it was therefore only natural that the king should entrust his son to his care.

There is a great deal of literature and many monuments showing Chiron teaching Achilles the knightly sports and exercises—hunting, horsemanship, javelin-throwing—courtly arts such as playing the lyre, and even surgery and pharmacopoea[17] (for his kingdom included the valleys of Pelion, rich in medicinal herbs)—a curious touch of encyclopaedic knowledge with a truly oriental flavour: it reminds one of the picture of Solomon's wide culture, painted by the Alexandrian author of the Book of Wisdom.[18] And there is no doubt that in both cases we have an idealized picture: the Homeric hero must know everything, but it must be remembered that he is a hero: it would be naïve to imagine that the average knight of old was a magic healer.

This last "fact" about Achilles and Chiron is the only one mentioned explicitly by Homer, but one episode in the *Iliad*[19] introduces us to another of Achilles' masters who was not so mythical as Chiron and who therefore helps us to gain a more realistic idea of what this knightly education may have been. I refer to the Phoenix episode. To aid Ulysses and Ajax in their difficult mission to Achilles, Nestor wisely arranges for this fine old man to accompany them, believing that he will know how to touch the heart of his old pupil—and indeed Achilles greets his "dear old father," as he calls him —ἄττα γεραιε[20]—most affectionately.

To obtain a hearing, Phoenix finds it advisable to tell Achilles his whole life history, whence follows a long discourse[21] which, with the old man's wandering eloquence, is most illuminating for our present purpose. According to this account, Phoenix fled from his father's wrath because they were at odds over a beautiful girl they held captive, and came to seek refuge at the court of Peleus, who made him lord over the Dolopian marchland.[22]

[14] *Il.*, XI, 832.
[15] *Ibid.*, IV, 219.
[16] Cyn., I.
[17] *Il.*, XI, 831-832; cf. IV, 219.
[18] Wisdom, vii, 17-20.
[19] *Il.*, IX, 434 *seq.*
[20] *Ibid.*, 607.
[21] *Ibid.*, 434-605.
[22] *Ibid.*, 480 *seq.*

Peleus grew so fond of his vassal that he entrusted him with his son's education (again, a truly "mediaeval" touch) and handed him over while he was
still a small child. We see Phoenix take Achilles on his knees, cut up his
food and feed him. "Just think of all the times you wet the front of my tunic
when you spluttered your wine out all over me! Children are such trouble!"[23]

"I made you what you are," declares the old tutor, proudly.[24] For his
role had not ended with Achilles' early childhood: he had been enjoined to
look after him on his departure for the Trojan war, and to give the inexperienced youth all the help he needed. Nothing is more remarkable than the
twofold mission with which Peleus charged him on this occasion. "You
were only a lad; you knew nothing of warfare, which spares no one, nor of
councils, in which men learn to shine. And so your father sent me with
you: I was to teach you how to give good counsel and how to perform great
deeds" ($\mu\acute{u}\theta\omega\nu$ $\tau\epsilon$ $\dot{\rho}\eta\tau\tilde{\eta}$'$\rho$ $\acute{\epsilon}\mu\epsilon\nu\alpha\iota$, $\pi\rho\eta\kappa\tau\tilde{\eta}\rho\acute{\alpha}$ $\tau\epsilon$ $\epsilon\rho\gamma\omega\nu$).[25] In these words are
summed up the two ideals of the perfect knight: he is to be both orator and
warrior, capable of serving his lord in the law courts as well as in war. In
the *Odyssey*, again, we find Athena instructing Telemachus under the
guidance of Mentes[26] or of Mentor.[27]

And so at the very beginning of Greek civilization we see a clearly defined
type of education—that which the young nobleman received through the
precept and the practice of an older man to whom he had been entrusted
for his training.

SURVIVALS OF THE KNIGHTLY EDUCATION

For many centuries, indeed we might say almost to the end of its history,
the education of antiquity was to retain many of the features which it received from its knightly and aristocratic origin. I am not referring to the
fact that the most democratic societies of ancient times must seem aristocratic to us moderns because of the part played in them by slavery; I mean
something more intrinsic. Even when these societies wanted to be democratic, and thought they were so (as did fourth-century Athens with its
demagogic cultural policy —$\theta\epsilon\omega\rho\iota\kappa\acute{o}\nu$— of bringing art within the reach of
the people, etc.), they lived in a tradition which was noble in origin; and
though their culture might indeed be shared in an egalitarian way, it none
the less preserved the marks of its origin. It is not difficult to see here a
parallel with the development of French and modern Western civilization,
which has progressively extended to all social classes—and perhaps vul-

[23] *Il.*, 488-491.   [25] *Ibid.*, 442.
[24] *Ibid.*, 485.   [26] *Od.*, I, 80 *seq.*
[27] *Ibid.*, II, 267 *seq.*

garized—a culture whose origin and inspiration were indubitably aristo-cratic. French culture achieved its own proper form at the court and in the salons of the seventeenth century—every French child makes his first con-tact with poetry and literature through the *Fables* of La Fontaine, which were dedicated either to the Dauphin or (the twelfth book) to the Duke of Burgundy!

For this reason it is necessary to examine the content of Homeric educa-tion, and its ultimate fate, a little more closely. In it, as in all education worthy of the name, we can distinguish two aspects, one technical and the other ethical (the distinction is to be found as far back as Plato).[28] On the technical side, the child was prepared for, and gradually initiated into, a particular way of life. On the ethical side we find more than a set of moral rules: a certain ideal of existence is presented, an ideal type of Man—a war-rior education may aim at producing either efficient barbarians or a re-fined type of "knight."

We have already dealt with the technical side—training in the use of arms, in sport and knightly games, in the art of music (singing and dancing and playing the lyre) and oratory; in good manners, in the ways of the world, and in wisdom. All these technical accomplishments are to be found in the later, classical, education, though only after an evolution whereby the more intellectual elements developed at the expense of the warrior ele-ment. Hardly anywhere save in Sparta did the latter remain primary, though it survived even in the peace-loving city of Athens as a liking for sport, and in that city's distinctively masculine style of life.

It becomes necessary to analyse this knightly ethic, the Homeric ideal of the hero, still further, and see how it survives into the classical period.

HOMER, THE EDUCATOR OF GREECE

At first sight its survival seems to be explained by the fact that throughout its history Greek literary education kept Homer as its basic text, the focus of all its studies. This is a fact of considerable importance, and one whose consequences Frenchmen find it difficult to imagine. For though we French have a number of "classics," we do not possess one classic *par excellence,* as the Italians have Dante and the English have their Shakespeare. And Homer dominated Greek education much more absolutely than Shake-speare did the English or Dante the Italians.

As Plato said,[29] Homer was, in the full sense of the word, the educator of Greece, τὴν Ἑλλάδα πεπαίδευκεν. He was this from the very beginning, ἐξ ἀρχῆς, as Xenaphanes of Colophon[30] insisted as far back as the sixth

---

[28]*Leg.*, I, 643a-644a.   [29]*Resp.*, X, 606; cf. *Prot.*, 339a.   [30]Fr. 10.

century: consider the profound influence he had at the end of the eighth century in Boeotia—a still wholly peasant region—on the style of Hesiod, who began his career as a rhapsodist, reciting Homer. And the educator of Greece he remained: in the twelfth century, when in the Byzantine East the Middle Ages were at their height, Eustathius, Archbishop of Thessalonica, compiled a great commentary on Homer, drawing on the whole heritage of Hellenistic philology. There are many testimonies to the fact that every cultivated Greek had a copy of Homer's works at his bedside (as Alexander did during his campaigns); here I need only select one, from Xenophon's *Banquet*,[31] in which a certain Nicoratus says, "My father, wishing me to become an accomplished man [ἀνήρ ἀγαθός] made me learn the whole of Homer, so that even today I can still recite the *Iliad* and the *Odyssey* by heart." Even when this has been said it remains true that the argument can be reversed, or at least works both ways: it was because the knightly ethic remained at the heart of the Greek ideal that Homer, as the outstanding interpreter of this ethic, remained the basic educational text-book. We must in fact reject any purely aesthetic explanation of the long favour he enjoyed. It was not primarily as a literary masterpiece that the epic was studied, but because its content was ethical, a treatise on the ideal. Indeed, as we shall see later, the technical content of Greek education underwent a profound development which reflected far-reaching changes in the civilization as a whole, and it was only Homer's ethics (together with his undying aesthetic value) which could have any lasting importance.

I am not suggesting, of course, that Homer's importance was always clearly and correctly understood throughout all those centuries. It is true that in the Hellenistic age we come across dense pedagogues without any sense of history or any ability to see the great changes in manners and customs that had gradually come about. They were determined to find in Homer all the elements of a religious and moral education that should still be valid in their day: with an ingenuity that at times became comic they attempted to extract from this fundamentally profane epic a veritable catechism. Nor was this catechism to teach only (as in fact it did)[32] a theogony and the golden legend of gods and heroes, but also a whole theodicy, indeed a whole system of apologetics, a summarization of man's duties to the gods—more, a handbook of practical morality, illustrating precept by example, beginning with good manners for children. Nor was even that all: by a kind of allegorical exegesis Homer was used to throw light on philosophy itself.

But all this was mere foolishness: Homer's real educational significance

---

[32]Hdt., II, 53.   [31]III, 5.

lies elsewhere—in the moral climate in which his heroes act; in their style of life. No attentive reader can escape the pervasive influence of this atmosphere for long. From this point of view we rightly speak of "Homeric education," ὁμηρικὴ παιδεία: the education which the young Greek derived from Homer was that which the poet gave his own heroes, the education Achilles received from Peleus and Phoenix, and Telemachus from Athena.

THE HOMERIC ETHIC

The moral ideal was rather complicated. There is first of all the "cunning" type of person, whom we find a little embarrassing—πολύτροπος ἀνήρ, exemplified in the—to us—ambiguous figure of a Levantine adventurer— as Ulysses sometimes appears in the *Odyssey*. Here, as I have already pointed out, the good manners and *savoir-faire* of the Homeric hero meet the practical wisdom of the oriental scribe: the result is the art of knowing how to get out of any awkward situation! Our conscience, refined by centuries of Christianity, sometimes feels a slight uneasiness about this—think how complaisant Athena is, for example, when one of her dear Ulysses' lies turns out to be particularly successful.[33]

Fortunately this is not the most important thing. It is not the Ulysses of the *Return* but the pure and noble figure of Achilles who embodies the moral ideal of the perfect Homeric knight. This ideal can be defined in one phrase: it was an heroic morality of honour. Homer was the source, and in Homer each succeeding generation of antiquity rediscovered the thing that is absolutely fundamental to this whole aristocratic ethic: the love of glory.

Its basis is that fundamental Hellenic pessimism which so impressed the young Nietzsche. The sadness of Achilles! The shortness of life, the haunting fear of death, the small hope of consolation in the life beyond the grave! There was still no great belief in the possibility of a special destiny in the Elysian fields. And most people were destined for the shades—the mockery of the vague and uncertain shades. We know how Achilles himself regards them from his famous words from Hades to Ulysses, who has been impressed by the way in which the common shades respectfully make way for the shade of the hero. "Ah, do not try to gild death for me, Ulysses! I would rather be looking after some poor farmer's oxen than reigning here over the dead—over these wraiths."[34]

To this short life, rendered still more uncertain by the fact that they are warriors, our heroes are passionately devoted—with the kind of earthy attachment, the frank and unreflecting love, that is the typical feature of a

---

[33] *Od.*, XIII, 287 *seq.*   [34] *Ibid.*, XI, 488 *seq.*

certain kind of pagan soul. Nevertheless this life, however precious it may be, is not supreme; and they are ready, with courage and determination, to sacrifice it for something higher. In this respect the Homeric ethic is an ethic of honour.

The ideal value, to which even life itself must be sacrificed, is ἀρετή—an untranslatable expression, which it is ludicrous to call "virtue" unless into that simple word is compressed all that Machiavelli's contemporaries meant by *virtù*. Roughly speaking, ἀρετή is "valour," in the chivalric sense of the word—the quality of the brave man, the hero. "He fell like the hero he was"— ἀνὴρ ἀγαθὸς γενόμενος ἀπέθανε— were words frequently used in honour of a warrior who had achieved his true destiny by giving his life. The Homeric hero lived and died in the effort to embody a certain ideal, a certain quality of existence, summed up in this word ἀρετή.

Now, glory, the renown recognized by those who know, the company of the brave, is the measure, the objective recognition, of valour. Hence the impassioned longing for glory, the longing to be hailed as the greatest, which was the mainspring of this knightly ethic. Homer was the first to represent this consciously; from Homer the men of antiquity received with rapturous applause the idea that life was a kind of sporting competition in which the great thing was to come first—the "agonistic ideal of life," which was first brilliantly described by Jacob Burckhardt and has since become recognized as one of the most significant aspects of the Greek soul. There can be no doubt that the Homeric hero and hence the actual Greek person of flesh and blood was only really happy when he felt and proved himself to be the first in his category, a man apart, superior.

This idea is certainly fundamental to the actual epic, which repeats the same sentiment in the same words, first putting it in the mouth of Hippolochus when he speaks to his son Glaucus, and next in Nestor's mouth when he tells Patroclus what advice Peleus had given his son Achilles. "Always be the best and keep well ahead of the others":

αἰὲν ἀριστεύειν ραὶ ὑπείροχον ἔμμεναι ἄλλων.[35]

It is from this tension of his whole being in pursuit of this one end that Achilles receives his tragic grandeur and nobility. He knows (for Thetis revealed it to him) that once he has vanquished Hector he is to die, but he advances to meet his fate with head proudly erect. He is not concerned with his country of Achaia or with the threatened expedition; his one aim is to avenge Patroclus and avoid disgrace. His one concern is his own honour. In my view this is not, however, any romantic individualism, however

[35]*Il.*, VI, 208 = XI, 784.

personal it may seem. This love of self $-\phi\iota\lambda\alpha\upsilon\tau\acute{\iota}\alpha-$ which Aristotle was to analyse, is not the love of the ego but of the *Self,* the Absolute Beauty, the Perfect Valour, that the hero longs to express in one Great Deed that will utterly astonish the great envious company of his equals.

To dazzle, to be first, the victor, to triumph, to prove one's worth in competition with others, to oust a rival before the judges, to perform the great deed $-\mathring{\alpha}\rho\iota\sigma\tau\epsilon\acute{\iota}\alpha-$ that will make one pre-eminent amongst men—the living, and perhaps even the dead—that is why a hero lives, and why he dies.

An ethic of honour, that can often seem strange to a Christian. It implies the kind of pride $-\mu\epsilon\gamma\alpha\lambda o\psi\upsilon\chi\acute{\iota}\alpha-$ that is not the vice of the same name but the noble desire of one who aspires to be great, or, in the case of the hero, consciousness of a genuine superiority. It implies also rivalry, jealousy, that noble $"E\rho\iota\zeta$ that inspires great deeds, whose praises Hesiod was to sing,[36] and hate, as the acknowledgment of proven superiority. Thus Thucydides makes Pericles say:[37] "Hatred and hostility are always for a time the lot of those who lay claim to rule over others, but to expose oneself to hatred for a noble cause is an excellent thing."

THE IMITATION OF THE HERO

The poet's function is to educate, and education means inculcating this high idea of glory. The aim of poetry is not essentially aesthetic but the immortalization of the hero. The poet, as Plato was to say,[38] "clothes all the great deeds accomplished by the men of old with glory, *and thus educates those who come after.*" I have emphasized the last few words because they seem absolutely fundamental.

To understand Homer's educational influence one only has to read him and see what his method is, what he regards as proper education for his heroes. Their counsellors must set before them the great examples to be found in the old legends and so arouse the agonistic instinct, the competitive spirit. Thus Phoenix recommends conciliation by reminding Achilles of Meleager. "This is what we learn from the old heroes . . . I am reminded of that great achievement — $\tau\acute{o}\delta\epsilon\,\mathring{\epsilon}o\gamma o\nu$ — a very old story. . . ."[39]

Athena again, in her efforts to awaken a desire for heroism in the immature, irresolute Telemachus, reminds him of Orestes' manly decisiveness. "Stop playing about and act your age. Think of the fame of god-like Orestes when he avenged his father and killed cunning Aegisthus."[40] In all, this event is referred to four times.[41]

---

[36] *Op.,* 17 *seq.*
[37] II, 64.
[38] *Phdr.,* 245a.

[39] *Il.,* IX, 524 *seq.*
[40] *Od.,* I, 296 *seq.*
[41] *Ibid.,* I, 30, 40; III, 306.

This is the secret of Homer's education: the heroic example—παράδειγμα. At the end of the Middle Ages there appeared *The Imitation of Christ;* the Hellenic Middle Ages bequeathed through Homer to classical Greece the Imitation of the Hero. It is in this deep sense that Homer was the educator of Greece. Like Phoenix and Nestor and Athena he was always impressing on his hearers' minds idealized models of heroic ἀρετή; and at the same time the everlasting quality of his work gave tangible proof of the reality of the highest of all rewards—glory.

We know from subsequent history how well his lessons were learnt: his heroes haunted the Greek soul. Alexander (and, later, Pyrrhus) imagined himself, dreamed of himself, as a second Achilles; and there were many other Greeks who like him learned from Homer "to spurn a long dull life and choose instead a brief moment of glory"—a moment brief but heroic.

Homer was not the only person the Greeks listened to, of course. Each century added its own classics, and added something to the Hellenic moral ideal. One of the first people to do this was Hesiod, who introduced such valuable ideas as Right, Justice and Truth. Nevertheless Homer supplied the whole foundation of classical education, and despite sporadic attempts to shake off his tyrannical influence, his feudal ethic of the Great Deed remained unbroken through all the centuries of the classical tradition, to fire the hearts of all Greeks.

II. Pindar: Athletic Victory as the Triumph of Natural Nobility

GREEK competitive athletics were originally an aristocratic exercise, and it became customary to commission poets to compose odes in honor of the victors in the various contests. What is celebrated by Pindar in his odes is not just the victories in particular contests; rather, these are occasions for praising the heroic spirit which is an enduring, even eternal, expression of those who are of noble birth. Victory in athletic contests is a consequence of the advantage which has been granted to some by the gods, and it is natural that this advantage be possessed by those of noble birth. The particular virtues of the victors are not to be celebrated as much for their own sake as for the way in which they remind us of the highest standards of nobility. Pindar, in portraying actual men, was calling forth the ideal of nobility which they exemplified.

For Pindar, poetry had an advantage over sculpture, which also set forth an ideal of beauty; however poems, unlike statues, did not remain on stationary pedestals, but could be sung in celebration of mighty deeds and in praise of heroic nobility. The poet carves, in words, a tale of excellence in deed achieved by the noble few; but for the many—who are less than noble—such an achievement is beyond their limits. Those who do not have noble natures may envy the more favored ones; but such is the "measure" set by the gods, that those who are not godlike will meet with failure if they strive for that which is not theirs. Those merits inherited from the gods continue in generations of mortals, even if there are temporary bad fortunes.

Pindar died in 438 B.C., and so lived into the latter half of the fifth century, when the heroism of natural nobility, as he celebrated it, was becoming an outworn virtue. By that time, the Sophists were already becoming influential, and they would become the spokesmen of a self-critical, intellectualistic culture which held forth the possibility that deliberate educational efforts might offset the disadvantages of not having been nobly born.

The problem which was to become particularly controversial when the Sophists' influence was felt—namely, can certain arts and sciences be taught, or must one possess them somehow by gift of nature?—was already settled, in Pindar's mind. He felt that those who have only learned the poet's lore, or who strive to win fame by mere training, will dwell in darkness and act with "ineffectual spirit." But those who have "inborn valor" and who are true poets, know much by gift of nature, and have heroic souls which will never be subdued. The philosopher Plato later said in reasoned discourse what the poet Pindar celebrated in song: that those highest by nature are fewest in number and most fit to rule.

4. Odes

Pindar

OLYMPIAN ODE I

I must crown the victor with the horseman's song, even with the Aeolian strains, and I am persuaded that there is no host of the present time, whom I shall glorify with sounding bouts of song, as one who is at once more familiar with things noble, or is more sovereign in power. A god who hath this care, Hieron, watcheth and broodeth over thy desires; but, if he doth not desert thee too soon, I trust I shall celebrate a still sweeter victory, even with the swift chariot, having found a path that prompteth praises, when I have reached the sunny hill of Cronus.

Howsoever, for myself, the Muse is keeping a shaft most mighty in strength. Some men are great in one thing; others in another: but the crowning summit is for kings. Refrain from peering too far! Heaven grant that thou mayest plant thy feet on high, so long as thou livest, and that I may consort with victors for all my days, and be foremost in the lore of song among Hellenes in every land.

PYTHIAN ODE I

If thou shouldest speak in season due, blending the strands of many themes into a brief compass, less cavil followeth of men. For dull satiety blunteth all the eagerness of expectation; but that which is heard by fellow-citizens lieth heavy on their secret soul, and chiefly when it concerns the merits of others. Nevertheless, since envy is better than pity, hold to thy noble course! Steer thy people with the helm of justice, and forge thy tongue on the anvil of truth! If any word, be it ever so light, falleth by chance, it is borne along as a word of weight, when it falleth from thee. Thou art the faithful steward of an ample store. Thou hast many trusty witnesses to thy deeds of either kind. But do thou abide in a temper that bloometh in beauty, and, if indeed thou delightest in hearing evermore what is sweet to hear, wax not over-weary in thy spending. Rather, like a steersman, suffer thy sail to be set free to catch the breeze. Be not allured, my friend, by cunning gains! When men are dead and gone, it is only the loud acclaim of praise that surviveth mortals and revealeth their manner of life to chroniclers and

Reprinted by permission of the publishers and *The Loeb Classical Library* from Sir John Sandys, translator, *The Odes of Pindar, Including the Principal Fragments.* (Cambridge, Mass.: Harvard University Press, 1956). Olympian Ode I, pp. 13, 15; Pythian Ode I, pp. 165, 167; Pythian Ode III, pp. 193, 195; Isthmian Ode III, p. 457; Nemean Ode XI, p. 433; Olympian Ode II, p. 27; Nemean Ode III, pp. 337, 339; Olympian Ode IX, pp. 105, 107. The notes are not included here.

to bards alike. The kindly generosity of Croesus fadeth not away, while Phalaris, ruthless in spirit, who burned his victims in his brazen bull, is whelmed for ever by a hateful infamy, and no lyres beneath the roof-tree welcome him as a theme to be softly blended with the warbled songs of boys. The first of prizes is good-fortune; the second falleth to fair fame; but, whosoever findeth and winneth both, hath received the highest crown.

PYTHIAN ODE III

But since thou, Hieron, art skilled to learn the true lesson that is taught by the sayings of former time, the immortals, as thou knowest, apportion to man two trials for every boon they grant; and these trials foolish men cannot bear with a good grace, but the noble can, by ever turning the fairer side to the front.

Yet thou art attended by a happy lot, for lo! the lord of his people, if any man, is viewed with favour by Fortune. But a life free from reverses was the fate neither of Peleus, son of Aeacus, nor of god-like Cadmus. Yet we learn that they attained the highest happiness of all mortal men, in that they heard the Muses of the golden snood singing on mount Pelion, and in seven-gated Thebes, what time Cadmus took to wife Harmonia, with those full-orbed eyes; and when Peleus wedded Thetis, the famous daughter of wise Nereus. And the gods banqueted with them, and they saw the royal sons of Cronus seated on their golden thrones, and received marriage-gifts from them; and, by the favour of Zeus, they escaped from their former troubles, and lifted up their hearts again in gladness.

And yet, in time, Cadmus was reft of his portion of bliss by the bitter woes of three of his daughters, although Father Zeus visited the bridal couch of their sister, the white-armed Semele. Aye, and the son of Peleus, the only son whom immortal Thetis bare in Phthia, reft of his life by the bow in battle, awakened the mourning of the Danai, while his body was burning on the pyre.

But, if any mortal hath in mind the course things take in very truth, right it is for one, who hath received favour from the blessed ones, to enjoy his lot. Yet changeful are the breezes of the winds that blow on high. The bliss of man doth not proceed unimpaired for long, whene'er it followeth them in its full weight and measure. Small shall I be, when small is my estate, and great, when it is great. The fortune that, ever and anon, attendeth me, I shall heartily honour, and shall do it service with all my might. But, if God were to give me the gladness of wealth, I hope, in future days, to find high fame. We know of Nestor, and of Lycian Sarpedon, whose names are on the lips of men, thanks to those lays of sounding song, such as wise builders framed for them. Virtue gaineth a long life by means of glorious strains; but they that find it easy to win those strains, are few.

Isthmian Ode III

If any one among men hath had good fortune, by the winning of glorious prizes, or by might of wealth, yet in his heart restraineth insatiate insolence, such a man is worthy to be blended with his townsmen's praises. For, from thee, O Zeus, do mighty merits attend upon mortals; and, when they reverence thee, their good fortune hath a longer life, but with froward hearts it liveth not in prosperity for all time alike.

But, as a guerdon for glorious exploits, it is meet for us to celebrate the hero, and, amid triumph-songs, exalt him with kindly hymns of praise. Even in two contests hath good fortune been shared by Melissus, to turn his heart to sweet good-cheer. For, in the vales of the Isthmus, hath he won garlands, and again, in the hollow dell of the deep-chested lion, did he cause Thebe to be proclaimed by his victory in the chariot-race. And he bringeth no disgrace on the manliness inherited from his fathers. Ye know, I ween, the olden glory of Cleonymus in the chariot-races: and, being on their mother's side akin to the Labdacidae, they walked in the ways of wealth with toilsome training of their teams of four horses. But time with its rolling days bringeth manifold changes; scatheless indeed are none but the sons of the gods.

Nemean Ode XI

Even so is the race of mortal men driven by the breeze of destiny. As for that which cometh from Zeus, there is no clear sign in heaven that waiteth on man; but yet we embark upon bold endeavours, yearning after many exploits; for our limbs are fettered by importunate hope, while the tides of foreknowledge lie far away from our sight. In our quest of gain, it is right to pursue the due measure; but far too keen are the pangs of madness that come from unattainable longings.

Olympian Ode II

Full many a swift arrow have I beneath mine arm, within my quiver, many an arrow that is vocal to the wise; but for the crowd they need interpreters. The true poet is he who knoweth much by gift of nature, but they that have only learnt the lore of song, and are turbulent and intemperate of tongue, like a pair of crows, chatter in vain against the god-like bird of Zeus.

Nemean Ode III

To what foreign foreland, O my fancy, art thou turning aside the course of thy voyage? I bid thee summon the Muse in honour of Aeacus, but the flower of justice still attendeth the precept, "praise the noble." Nor should any man prefer to foster passionate longings for what belongeth to others. Search at home, and thou hast won a fitting theme for praise, to prompt sweet melody. For, among older examples of valour is king Peleus, who rejoiced in having cloven a matchless spear,—who, alone, without a host, overcame Iolcus, and after many a struggle seized as a captive the sea-nymph Thetis.

And Laomedon was laid low by Telamon, whose might is famed afar as comrade of Iolaus, whom erst he followed, to fight the mighty Amazons with their brazen bows; nor did fear, that quelleth men, ever subdue that heroic soul. 'Tis by means of inborn valour that a man hath mighty power, but he who hath learnt all his lore, dwelleth in darkness, breathing changeful purposes, never entering the lists with a firm step, but essaying countless forms of prowess with ineffectual spirit. Whereas Achilles of the golden hair, while lingering in the home of Philyra, and while yet a child, disported himself in mighty deeds, full often brandishing in his hands a javelin with its tiny blade; and fleet as the wind, he was wont to deal slaughter in fight with savage lions, and he would slay wild boars and carry their panting bodies to the Centaur, son of Cronus, at six years of age at first, but afterwards for all his time: while Artemis and bold Athene gazed at him with wonder, as he slew stags without help of hounds or of crafty nets, for he excelled in fleetness of foot.

OLYMPIAN ODE IX

That which cometh of Nature is ever best, but many men have striven to win their fame by means of merit that cometh from mere training; but anything whatsoever, in which God hath no part, is none the worse for being quelled in silence. Yet some roads lead further than others, and it is not all of us that can prosper in a single path of work. Steep are the heights of skill; but, while offering this prize of song, with a ringing shout do thou boldly declare that our hero hath by the blessing of heaven been born with deftness of hand and litheness of limb, and with valour in his glance—our hero, who, at the banquet of the son of Oileus, crowned by his victory the altar of Aias.

PART III

Man: Enlightened,
Tragic, Sophisticated

I. The Fifth-Century Sophists

IN the latter half of the fifth century, the changes in Greek life
which were to culminate in a more enlightened, deliberately self-
conscious discussion of educational problems brought along with
them the first professional teachers—the Sophists. These teachers
raised questions which were to engage Plato, Isocrates, and Aristotle
and influence them in producing their classic writings in philosophy,
rhetoric, and science. For all their influence, the Sophists have been
viewed unfavorably as most of the surviving writings from antiquity
take issue with them; as a result, the Sophists usually were portrayed
the losers in dialectical argument with Plato's Socrates, or as op-
portunists in Isocrates' orations against them, or as holding views
to be refuted by Aristotle. The account of the fifth century Sophists
by Marrou, which follows, provides a historical context which does
greater justice to their achievements than do their critics, who will
be heard from later.

5. The Pedagogical Revolution of the Early Sophists

H. I. Marrou

THE NEW POLITICAL IDEAL

Nevertheless, it was not these specialized circles that produced the great revolution in teaching which was to put Greek education on the road to maturity; this occurred in the latter half of the fifth century and was the work of a group of innovators who have come to be known as the Sophists.

The problem that faced the Sophists, and which they succeeded in solving, was the fairly common one of how to produce capable statesmen. In their time this had become a matter of the utmost urgency. After the collapse of tyranny in the sixth century most of the Greek cities, and democratic Athens in particular, developed an intensely active political life; and exercise of power, the management of affairs, became the essential concern, the noblest, the most highly-prized activity in the eyes of every Greek, the ultimate aim of his ambition. He was still anxious to excel, to be superior and effective; but it was no longer in sport and polite society that his "valour"—his ἀρετή—sought to assert itself: from now on it expressed itself in political action. The Sophists put their talent as teachers at the service of this new ideal of the political ἀρετή:[1] the training of statesmen, the formation of the personality of the city's future leader—such was their programme.

It would be a mistake, however, to connect this undertaking too closely with the progress of democracy, and imagine that the Sophists' system was meant as a substitute, designed to meet the needs of a new class of democratic politicians, for the old hereditary aristocratic type of education. In the first place, Greek democracy went on recruiting its leaders from amongst the oldest aristocratic families for a very long time—think, for example, of the part played by the Alcmeonidae in Athens. Secondly, it is impossible to discern in the Sophists of the fifth century any definite political bias like that of the *Rhetores Latini* in Rome at the time of Marius: they

From *A History of Education in Antiquity* by H. I. Marrou, © 1956 Sheed & Ward Inc., New York. This selection is from Part I, Chapter V, The Pedagogical Revolution of the Early Sophists, pp. 47-57. Marrou's notes are included and his references make use of the following abbreviations: Pl., Plato; *Cra, Cratylus; Grg., Gorgias; Hipp. Ma., Hippias Major; Lach., Laches; Soph., The Sophists;* DL., Diogenes Laertius, *Lives* of the Philosophers; Plut., *Isoc.,* Plutarch, *Life of Isocrates;* Isoc., *Soph.,* Isocrates, *Against the Sophists;* Arist., Aristotle; *Rhet., Rhetoric; Poet., Poetics;* Mem., Xenophon, *Memorabilia; Conv.,* Xenophon, *The Banquet;* Ael., Aelianus of Preneste; Thuc., Thucydides; Eur., Euripides; Enn., *Fr. Sc.,* Ennius, *Scenic Fragments.*

[1]Pl., *Prot.,* 316b; 319a.

had a wealthy clientèle, which generally included some of the newly-rich seeking "polish," like Aristophanes' Strepsiades; but the old aristocracy, far from resenting them, were eager to sit at their feet, as we can see from Plato's *Dialogues*.

The Sophists offered their services to anyone wishing to acquire the accomplishments needed for success in the political arena. Once again I refer the reader to the *Laches:* Lysimachus, the son of Aristides, and Melesias, the son of Thucydides, want their own sons to have the kind of education that will prepare them for political leadership,[2] and naturally, when the Sophists come and offer something more useful than fencing, they are quick to accept it.

Thus the revolution in education that has come to be known as Sophistry seems to have had a technical rather than a political origin: on the basis of a mature culture, these enterprising educators developed a new technique, a form of teaching that was wider in its scope, more ambitious and more effective than any previous system.

THE SOPHISTS AS EDUCATORS

The Sophists were active during the second half of the fifth century. There seems to be something rather artificial in the attempt that is sometimes made to parcel them out over two generations. In point of fact, their careers over-lapped; Plato was able without any sense of anachronism to introduce the most famous of them to Socrates and Alcibiades at the house of the wealthy Callias in a famous scene in the *Protagoras*.[3] There was not much difference in age between the earlier and the later Sophists. The oldest, Protagoras of Abdera, must have been born in about the year 485, and Gorgias of Leontini, and the Athenian Antiphon (of the deme of Rhamnus), who were almost as old, in about 480. The youngest, Prodicus of Ceos and Hippias of Elis, were born some ten years later and appear in Socrates' day—and Socrates, as we know, lived from 470-69 to 399. Diverse in origin and itinerant from the necessities of their profession, they all, nevertheless, spent some time in Athens; and with them Athens became the crucible in which Greek culture was refined.

Every historian of philosophy or the exact sciences feels bound to devote a chapter to the Sophists. It is a chapter that is extremely difficult to write and rarely satisfactory.

It is not sufficient to say that we know very little about them. As our original sources we have only a few fragments and meagre doxographical notices—very slender evidence to set against the deceptive power of Plato's satirical portraits and parodies. Plato's treatment of the Sophists was

[2] Pl., *Lach.*, 179cd.   [3] 314e-315e.

always highly ambiguous and it has never been easy to grasp where invention and caricature and calumny begin and where they end. There is the further possibility that his representation of the conflict between Socrates and the Sophists was really a camouflaged form of his own struggle against his contemporaries, people like Antisthenes in particular.

The truth is the Sophists do not properly belong to either philosophy or science. They set in motion a number of ideas, some of them their own, some derived from others—Protagoras got his from Heraclitus, for example, and Gorgias his from the Eleatics or Empedocles—but strictly speaking they were not thinkers or seekers after truth, they were teachers. "The education of men"—παιδεύειν ἀνθρώπους—such, according to Plato,[4] was Protagoras' own definition of his art.

And indeed that was the only thing they had in common: their ideas were too heterogeneous, too vague and fleeting for them to belong to any school, in the philosophical sense. The only thing they had in common was their profession; and they deserve our respect as the great forerunners, as the first teachers of advanced education, appearing at a time when Greece had known nothing but sports-trainers, foremen, and, in the academic field, humble school-masters. In spite of the sarcasm thrown at them by the Socratics with their conservative prejudices,[5] I shall continue to respect them because, primarily, they were professional men for whom teaching was an occupation whose commercial success bore witness to its intrinsic value and its social utility.[6]

THE TEACHER'S PROFESSION

It is therefore a matter of some interest to study in detail the way in which they carried on their profession. They did not open any schools—in the institutional sense of that word. Their method, not unlike that of early times, might be described as collective tutoring. They gathered round them the youths entrusted to their care and undertook their entire training. This is generally reckoned to have taken three or four years, and it was agreed to by contract: the sum demanded by Protagoras was considerable—ten thousand drachmas,[7] and a drachma (approximately the equivalent of 2/-) was a qualified worker's daily wage. For a long time this was the standard practice, but prices began to fall rapidly and, in the following century, between 393 and 338, Isocrates was only asking a thousand drachmas,[8] and lamenting the fact that "blacklegs" were ready to carry on business at bargain rates of four hundred or even three hundred drachmas.[9]

[4] *Prot.*, 317b.
[5] Pl., *Hipp. Ma.*, 281b; *Cra.*, 384b; cf. *Soph.*, 231d; Xen, *Cyn.*, 13.
[6] Pl., *Hipp. Ma.*, 282bc.
[7] D.L., IX, 52.
[8] [Plut.] *Isoc.*, 837.
[9] Isoc., *Soph.*, 3.

Protagoras was the first to offer to teach for money in this way: there had been no similar system before. The result was that the Sophists did not find any customers waiting for them but had to go out and persuade the public to take advantage of their services: hence arose a whole publicity system. The Sophist went from town to town[10] in search of pupils, taking those he had already managed to catch with him;[11] to make himself known, to demonstrate the excellence of his teaching and to give a sample of his skill, he would give a sample lecture—ἐπίδειξις—either in a town through which he happened to be passing or in some pan-hellenic sanctuary like Olympus, where he could take advantage of the πανήγυρις, the international assembly that gathered there for the games. The ἐπίδειξις might be either a carefully thought-out discourse or a brilliant improvisation on some theme or other, a free debate on any subject chosen by his audience. This gave rise to the public lecture, a literary form which ever since those earliest days has been quite astonishingly popular.

Some of these lectures were open to anybody: Hippias, haranguing the crowd in the Agora, with the money-changers' table[12] quite close by, reminds one of the speakers in Hyde Park; others were for a select audience only, and had to be paid for even at this early stage:[13] indeed, unless we are being misled by the Socratic irony, there seem to have been different categories—publicity talks at an advertised price of one drachma, and technical lectures, at which the master contracted to give an exhaustive treatment of any scientific subject whatever, at fifty drachmas a seat.[14]

Naturally, this publicity was not carried on without some admixture of charlatanism. This is Greece, and long ago. In his efforts to impress his audience, the Sophist was not afraid to claim omniscience[15] and infallibility[16]—adopting a magisterial tone, a grave or an inspired manner, and pronouncing his decisions from a throne high up in the air;[17] sometimes, it seems, even donning the triumphal costume of the rhapsodist with his great purple robe.[18]

But these stage-effects were legitimate enough. The sarcastic criticisms they received from Plato's Socrates cannot outweigh Plato's own testimony to the extraordinary success this publicity achieved and the extent to which young people became infatuated with the Sophists. There is that scene at the beginning of the *Protagoras*,[19] in which young Hippocrates rushed to Socrates' house in the early dawn: Protagoras has just arrived in Athens and the great man must be visited without delay and be prevailed

[10]Pl., *Prot.*, 313d.
[11]*Ibid.*, 315a.
[12]*Hipp. Mi.*, 368b.
[13]*Hipp. Ma.*, 282bc; Arist., *Rh.*, III, 1415b 16.
[14]Pl., *Cra.*, 384b.

[15]*Hipp. Mi.*, 368bd.
[16]*Grg.*, 447c; 448a.
[17]*Prot.*, 315c.
[18]Ael., *N.H.*, XII, 32.
[19]310a.

upon to accept him as an eventual disciple. This high estimation, which can also be traced in the profound influence that the great Sophists had on the best minds of their day—on men like Thucydides and Euripides and others —was not simply due to fashion and successful publicity-stunts: it was justified by the actual effects of their teaching.

THE ART OF POLITICS

We must now consider the content of this teaching. Its aim was to arm the strong character, to prepare him for political strife so that he would succeed in imposing his will on the city. This was apparently Protagoras' intention in particular: he wanted his pupils to be made into good citizens who could not only rule their own homes properly but also conduct affairs of state with the utmost efficiency. His aim was to teach them "the art of politics"— πολιτικὴ τέχνη.[20]

It was a purely practical aim: the "wisdom" and "valour" which Protagoras and his colleagues provided for their disciples were utilitarian and pragmatic, and they were judged by their concrete effectiveness. There was no time to waste in speculating, like the old physicists of Ionia, on the nature of the world and the nature of the gods: "I do not know whether they exist or not," said Protagoras,[21] "it is a difficult question, and life is too short." The important thing was life, and in life, especially political life, knowledge of the truth was less important than the ability to make any particular audience, *hic et nunc,* admit the probability of any proposition whatsoever.

Consequently this education developed in the direction of a relativistic humanism: this seems to be expressed in one of the few genuine fragments that have come down to us from Protagoras—the famous formula, "Man is the measure of all things."[22] A great deal of mischief has been done by trying to give this a metaphysical significance, turning its author into the fountain-head of phenomenalist empiricism, a forerunner of modern subjectivism. Similarly, on the strength of the few echoes that have come down to us from the *Treatise on Not-Being* by Gorgias,[23] it has been suggested that Gorgias was a philosophical nihilist. This is a gross exaggeration of the meaning of the passages concerned, which were intended to be taken at their face-value: neither Protagoras nor Gorgias had any intention of creating a system; both were simply concerned to formulate a number of practical rules. They never taught their pupils any truths about being or man, but merely how to be always, and in any kind of circumstances, right.

[20] 319a.
[21] Fr. 4 (Diels).
[22] Fr. 1.
[23] Fr. 1-5 (Diels).

DIALECTICS

Protagoras is said[24] to have been the first person to teach that it is possible to argue for or against any proposition whatsoever. His whole system of teaching was based on antilogy. Of his *Discourses in Refutation* we now possess only the famous first phrase quoted above,[25] but we find echoes of them in the *Double Reasons—Δισσοί λόγοι—*a dull catalogue of mutually conflicting opinions compiled in about the year 400 by one of his disciples.

This, then, is the first aspect of the Sophists' education: how to learn to win any kind of argument. Protagoras borrowed his polemical method and his rigorous dialectic from Zeno of Elea, but at the same time he emptied them of their profound and serious content and kept only the bare skeleton, from which, by a process of systematization, he formulated the principles of eristics, a debating-method that was supposed to confound any kind of opponent by taking points he had himself conceded and using them as a starting-point for further argument.

In their different ways, Aristophanes' *Clouds* and Thucydides' *History* furnish remarkable evidence of the prodigious effect that this system of education, which was so brazen in its cynical pragmatism and so astonishing in its practical effectiveness, had on the people of the time. Its historical importance cannot be over-estimated: the tradition inaugurated by Protagoras explains the predominantly dialectical tone that was henceforth to dominate, for better or for worse, the whole Greek philosophy, science and culture. The sometimes excessive use that the men of antiquity made of disputation as a means of discovery or proof, their facile over-confidence in it, their virtuosity at it—all this was part of the Sophist heritage.

They were not content simply to take this intellectual instrument ready-made from the Eleatics: they did a great deal to perfect it, to refine dialectical processes and explain their logical structure. Naturally, such an advance had its ups and downs: not all the weapons in the armoury of sophistry were made of the finest steel, and, since the end justified the means, they looked upon anything that seemed effective as good. Their eristic, being no more than the art of practical debate, tended to put convincing rational argument on the same level as tactical tricks that are sometimes little better than low cunning (we are, after all, in the country of Ulysses). Genuine reasoning gave way to audacious paradoxes, which their naive hearers, still new to the game, could not distinguish from Zeno's arguments, which though equally paradoxical had genuine logic behind them. It was not until Aristotle came along that they learned to distinguish between false "sophistries" and valid inferences. Nevertheless, though this kind of sort-

[24]D.L., IX, 51.   [25]Fr. 1.

ing-out had to be done later, the *Topics* and the *Refutations of the Sophists* in the *Organon* are simply a classification, a restatement, of a great mass of material, much of which goes back to Protagoras and his followers.

RHETORIC

Besides the art of persuasion the Sophists taught the equally important art of speech, and in this too practical effectiveness was their sole concern. In modern times the spoken word has given way to the all-powerful written word, and this remains true even today, despite the great strides made by the radio and the gramophone. But in ancient Greece, and especially in its political life, the spoken word reigned supreme.

This was in a way recognized officially by the practice that was instituted in Athens well before 431 [26] of delivering a prepared speech at the funeral of soldiers fallen in battle. But public speaking was not merely decorative: the democracy of antiquity knew only the direct method of government, and consequently it had most respect for the kind of politician who was able to impose his own point of view in the citizens' assembly, or in the various councils, as a result of his powers of speech. Eloquence was no less important in the law-courts: there was a great deal of litigation in Athens, both private and public—political trials, court enquiries into morality and the rendering of accounts, etc.—and here again the successful person was the one who could get the better of his opponent in front of a jury or panel of judges.[27] As Plato's Sophist, Polos of Agrigentum,[28] declares, skilful orators, like tyrants, can have anyone they dislike condemned to death, or to confiscation of their property, or to exile.

In this field too, the Sophists discovered that it was possible to develop and teach a particular technique for passing on the best lessons of experience in a condensed and perfect form: this was Rhetoric.

The master of rhetoric was Gorgias of Leontini, who is historically as important as Protagoras. Rhetoric indeed arose, not in Elis, nor even in Greece, but in Sicily. Aristotle attributed its rise to the sudden spate of proceedings for the recovery of goods that developed after the expulsion of the tyrants of the Theron dynasty at Agrigentum (471), and those of the Hieron dynasty at Syracuse (463), and the ensuing annulment of the confiscations which they had decreed. This helped to encourage eloquence in both politics and law, and Sicily's example is supposed to have prompted the Greeks to apply themselves with all their penetrating logic to this problem of effective speaking. Beginning with empirical facts, they gradually formulated general rules which when codified into a body of doctrine

---

[26] Thuc., II, 34.   [27] Pl., *Hipp. Ma.*, 304ab.   [28] *Grg.*, 466c.

could serve as a basis for a systematic training in the art of public speaking. The first teachers of rhetoric—Corax and his pupil Tisias—appeared in fact in Syracuse, probably not later than 460; but the original founder is generally considered to be Empedocles of Agrigentum,[29] who taught Gorgias.

With Gorgias, rhetoric appeared fully-fledged, with its own method and principles and set forms, all worked out in minutest detail. The whole of antiquity lived on this achievement: even in the final decadence writers were still embellishing their meretricious art with the three "Gorgiac figures" which the great Sophist had formulated: antithesis, balance of clauses (ἰσόκωλα) and final assonance (ὁμοιοτέλευτον).

We shall have occasion later to study this technique in detail. Once fixed, it never developed much further, except to become more precise and systematized. Here it will be sufficient to give a brief description of how rhetoric was taught from the time of Gorgias onwards. It was divided into two parts, theory and practice. First of all the Sophist instructed his pupil in the rules of the art: this was his τέχνη (Tisias, if not Corax, had already produced this kind of theoretical treatise, and a few fragments of the similar work by Gorgias remain). In all essentials—as for example in the ground-plan of the judicial speech—the main outlines of classical theory seem to have been fixed by the time of the Sophists, although of course they had not then achieved the degree of detail that is to be found in treatises of Hellenistic and Roman times. In the fifth century the teaching of rhetoric was not so precise: the rules were very general and students soon got on to practical exercises.

The master prepared a model and gave it to his pupils to copy. Like the ἐπίδειξις, the sample lecture, the speech might have a poetical or a moral or a political subject. Gorgias transposed into his florid prose the mythological "panegyrics" that had been so beloved by lyric poets like Simonides and Pindar—the panegyric of Helen,[30] the apologia for Palamedes.[31] Xenophon has left us an account of a speech by Prodicus on the subject of Heracles at the cross-roads of vice and virtue;[32] Plato in the *Protagoras*[33] shows us Protagoras improvising on the myth of Prometheus and Epimetheus and again on the subject of justice; and in another dialogue,[34] through the mouth of Hippias, we hear Nestor imparting instruction to Neoptolemus. There are also references to eulogy of the city of Elis[35] by Gorgias. Sometimes a fantastic or paradoxical subject was used as an ex-

[29]Arist., *ap*. D.L., VIII, 57.   [32]*Mem.*, II, I, 21-34.
[30]Fr. II.   [33]320c-322a.
[31]Fr. IIa.   [34]*Hipp. Ma.*, 286ab.
        [35]Fr. 10.

cuse for pure virtuosity, and the result was a eulogy of peacocks or mice. Other teachers preferred a more directly utilitarian approach: Antiphon for instance was only concerned with the eloquence of the lawcourts: his *Tetralogies* give examples of all four speeches necessary in any given case— accusation, defence, reply and rejoinder. The cases were imaginary, but Antiphon also seems to have published real pleadings, which he composed as a logographer, so that they could be studied by his pupils.

These sample speeches were not only delivered to an audience; they were also put into writing so that the pupils could study them at their leisure.[36] Later they would be told to use them as models in compositions of their own, and in this way begin their apprenticeship in the art of rhetoric.

But an effective speech needs more than a mastery of form; it needs content—the ideas and arguments demanded by the subject; and so there was a whole branch of rhetoric devoted to *invention*—where and how to discover ideas. Here again the Sophists' analytical attitude enabled them to formulate a whole mass of ingenious rules, and they developed a complete method for extracting every possible topic from any given case—a method in which rhetoric joins hands with eristic and makes full use of its discoveries.

The Sophists had not been blind to the fact that many of their developments could be applied to different circumstances. Hence arose a number of standard passages, on, for instance, how to flatter judges, how to criticize evidence obtained by torture, and so on (in this way Antiphon composed a collection of *Exordiums* suitable for every occasion). Even more pat to the purpose were general reflections on topics of universal concern—justice and injustice, nature and convention. By skilful manipulation any subject could be reduced to the simple ideas that the Sophists' pupils knew all about in advance—the famous "commonplaces"—κοινοὶ τόποι—whose existence and fecundity the Sophists were the first to discover. And so they engaged on a systematic exploration and exploitation of these great themes: it was from them that ancient education, and consequently the whole of classical literature—Greek and Roman—derived their permanent taste for "general ideas," for those great moral themes of eternal import which, for good and for ill, form one of their most characteristic features, and which, despite the wearisome monotony and banality to which they so frequently led, were also responsible for their profound human value.

GENERAL CULTURE

But a grotesquely inadequate picture of the Sophists' education would be given by an exclusive insistence on these general and formal aspects of

[36] *Phdr.*, 228de.

rhetoric and eristic. The perfect Sophist—like Plato's Gorgias[37] and Hippias[38]—had to be able to speak and hold his own on any subject whatsoever: this meant that his competence had to be universal, his knowledge had to extend over every kind of specialized study. The Greeks had a word for it: he must have a "polymathy."

The Sophists varied in their attitude towards this aspect of culture, as I have suggested. Some seem to have had nothing but contempt for the arts and crafts and to have enjoyed using purely theoretical arguments against anyone who claimed to know anything about them;[39] whereas others proclaimed a universal curiosity and aspired—or seemed to aspire—towards every kind of knowledge. Hippias of Elis[40] is an outstanding example of this: Plato shows him boasting to the crowd of onlookers at Olympia that everything he was wearing was the work of his own hands: he had made the ring on his finger, engraved the signet, made his own massage-kit, woven his own cloak and tunic, embroidered his rich girdle in Persian fashion. . . . Modern scholars are divided about the real extent of this "polymathy," as to whether it was just a sham or genuine knowledge.

It is known from other sources that Hippias taught a system of mnemonics,[41] and some think that all this imposing learning meant no more in practice than providing the orator with the minimum amount of knowledge necessary to enable him to pose as an expert without ever getting caught out. This judgment seems rather harsh. Polymathy and mnemonics are two different things: the latter was retained in classical rhetoric as one of its five parts, and it had a purely practical purpose—to help the orator to learn his piece by heart. As for the former—we can of course have no idea how much technical knowledge Hippias possessed about the mechanical arts, or how much genuine interest Prodicus had in medicine;[42] but at least there is no doubt that Hippias was highly competent in all branches of science.

Plato vouches for this in mathematics;[43] and goes on to show Hippias[44] —unlike the more limited and utilitarian Protagoras—insisting that the young men in his charge should restrict themselves to a solid study of the four sciences that had been developed since the time of Pythagoras—and which were later to form the mediaeval Quadrivium—arithmetic, geometry, astronomy and acoustics. This is a fact worth emphasizing: the important point is not whether or not the Sophists contributed to the progress of mathematics—for Hippias was not alone in his interest: An-

[37] Grg., 447c; 448a.
[38] Hipp. Mi., 364a; 368bd.
[39] Pl., Soph., 232d; 233b.
[40] Hipp. Mi., 368bc.
[41] Ibid., 368d.; Xen., Conv., 4, 62.
[42] Fr. 4.
[43] Prot., 315c; Hipp. Ma., 285b;
    Hipp. Mi., 366c-368a.
[44] Prot., 318e.

tiphon worked on the squaring of the circle[45] — but the fact that they were the first to recognize the great educational value of these sciences and the first to incorporate them into a standard teaching-system. They set an example that was never to be forgotten.

Hippias showed the same lively interest in a variety of erudite studies: his own works included geographical tables (names of peoples),[46] "archaeological" tables (mythology, biography, genealogy),[47] and above all historical tables such as his catalogue of Olympic winners[48] — the first of a whole series of similar investigations and the beginning of scientific chronology in Greek history, of scientific history in the modern sense of the word. Finally, there was his more purely literary erudition, though here he was not alone — a reader of the *Protagoras*[49] might consider Prodicus the specialist in this field, with his passion for synonyms and his remarkable exegesis of Simonides — but in fact all the Sophists engaged in literature with the same enthusiasm.

This last fact had such important consequences that it is worth while inquiring how it came about. We often find that when they start discussing literature the argument soon degenerates into a quibble about some tiny point of language or thought — for example, we find Protagoras remarking that Homer uses the imperative mood where the optative would be expected,[50] and that Simonides contradicts himself from one verse to the next[51] — and so one is inclined to wonder whether the Sophists studied the poets simply to show off their brilliance in argument. For apart from the field of general ideas, which was soon exhausted, poetry supplied the only material in contemporary culture that could be treated in this way.

But even if this was their attitude in the beginning, it was not long before the Sophists deepened their method of approach and turned the criticism of poetry into a special kind of mental exercise, a way of studying the relationships between thought and language: in their hands the study of poetry, as Plato makes Protagoras say,[52] became "the most important part of the whole of education." Here too they were pioneers, for, as we shall see, classical education was to enter wholeheartedly along the way which they had opened up, the way taken by every literary culture since. When we see Hippias comparing the characters of Achilles and Ulysses,[53] we seem to be attending one of our own literature classes and hearing one of those endless comparisons between Corneille and Racine which French children have been making ever since the time of Mme de Sévigné and Vauvenargues.

---

[45] Fr. 13. [49] 337a *seq.*; 358a *seq.*

[46] Fr. 2. [50] Arist., *Poet.*, 1456b 15.

[47] Fr. 4; 6. [51] Pl., *Prot.*, 339c.

[48] Fr. 3. [52] *Prot.*, 338d.

[53] *Hipp. Mi.*, 364c *seq.*

Thus, even though many of the early questions raised about literature were simply an excuse for dialectical fireworks, they soon led the Sophists and their pupils to study the structure and the laws of language seriously: Protagoras composed a treatise "On Correctness of Diction"—'Ορθοέπεια,[54] Prodicus studied etymology, synonymy and precision of language;[55] Hippias wrote about sound and syllabic quantities, rhythm and metre.[56] In this way the Sophists laid the foundations of the second pillar of literary education, the science of grammar.

THE HUMANISM OF THE SOPHISTS

This rapid review will have given some idea of the many innovations which the Sophists introduced into Greek education. They opened up a number of different avenues, of which some were explored more than others, and of which none was explored right to the end. They were pioneers who discovered and set in motion a whole series of new educational tendencies, and though they did not advance far in any one direction themselves, from their time onwards the general direction was fixed, to be followed later. Their fundamental utilitarianism would in any case have prevented them from penetrating to the depths.

But we must not be too ready to blame them for this, for their distrust of over-specialization was one of the noblest and most lasting characteristics of the Greek genius: its sense of reasonable limits, of human nature—in a word, its humanism. The child and the adolescent should study, "not to become experts but to educate themselves"—οὐκ ἐπὶ τέχνη, ἀλλ' ἐπὶ παιδεία.[57] The Sophists' best pupils, Thucydides and Euripides, agree with Gorgias that philosophy is a good thing, but within limits, only to the extent that it helps to form the mind and leads to a proper education.[58]

This was a bold solution of a difficult problem, for there is a fundamental antinomy between scientific research and education. If a young mind is made a slave to science and treated merely as an instrument in furthering scientific progress, its education suffers, becomes narrow and short-sighted. But if on the other hand too much emphasis is laid on the open mind, on a purely humanistic culture, there is a danger of superficiality and unreality. This problem has still not been settled: it was certainly not settled in the fifth century B.C. when against the solution offered by the Sophists there arose the stubborn opposition of Socrates.

.   .   .

[54] Pl., *Phdr.*, 267c.   [56] *Hipp. Mi.*, 368d.
[55] *Cra., 384b.*   [57] Pl., *Prot.*, 312b.
[58] *Grg.*, 485a; Thuc., II, 40, I; Eur. *ap.* Enn., *Fr. Sc.* 376.

II. Aeschylus and Sophocles: The Tragedy and Nobility of Man

THE relentlessness of fate, man wearing "the harness of Necessity," is expressed in Aeschylus' *Agamemnon*. Agamemnon the King, by sacrificing his daughter to avoid failure in a war expedition, is destined to bring disaster to himself. This disaster will come to pass, whatever Agamemnon may do. As the chorus puts it, "Time may show,/ But cannot alter, what shall be."

Man's pride in fulfilling his destiny by acting according to the eternal laws of nature's gods, whatever man-made laws may decree, is acted out by one of the stage's most unforgettable characters, Antigone, in a drama by Sophocles first produced in 440 B.C. Antigone's king, Creon—the ruler who oversteps nature's bounds with an unnatural decree—is no less tragic, as he finds himself caught in a web of unhappy consequences of his own unjust actions. In the passages from *Antigone* Sophocles expresses his sense of wonder of man, man's necessity for natural piety, and the foolishness of his fearing any fellow man, even one proclaimed a ruler of men.

6. Agamemnon

Aeschylus

CHORUS: Ten years have passed since the strong sons of Atreus,
    Menelaus and Agamemnon, both alike
    Honoured by Zeus with throned and sceptred power,
    Gathered and manned a thousand Argive ships,
    And with the youth of Hellas under arms
    Sailed from these ports to settle scores with Priam.

Reprinted by permission from Aeschylus, *The Oresteian Trilogy*, translated by Philip Vellacott (Baltimore: Penguin Books, 1967). *Agamemnon*, pp. 43-51. The play *Agamemnon* opens in Argos as the message is received that Troy has fallen to the Greeks. The Chorus of Twelve Elders of Argos tells something of the events of the past ten years, since Agamemnon, king of Argos, had set out to do battle with Troy. Clytemnestra is Agamemnon's unfaithful wife.

Then loud their warlike anger cried,
As eagles cry, that wild with grief,
On some steep, lonely mountain-side
Above their robbed nest wheel and sail,
Oaring the airy waves, and wail
Their wasted toil, their watchful pride;
Till some celestial deity,
Zeus, Pan, Apollo, hears on high
Their scream of wordless misery;
And pitying their forlorn estate
(Since air is Heaven's protectorate)
Sends a swift Fury to pursue
Marauding guilt with vengeance due.

So against Paris's guilty boast
Zeus, witness between guest and host,
Sends Atreus' sons for stern redress
Of his and Helen's wantonness.
Now Greece and Troy both pay their equal debt
Of aching limbs and wounds and sweat,
While knees sink low in gory dust,
And spears are shivered at first thrust.
Things are—as they are now; their end
Shall follow Fate's decree, which none can bend.
In vain shall Priam's altars burn,
His rich libations vainly flow
To gods above and powers below:
No gift, no sacrificial flame
Can soothe or turn
The wrath of Heaven from its relentless aim.

We were too old to take our share
With those who joined the army then.
We lean on sticks—in strength not men
But children; so they left us here.
In weakness youth and age are one:
The sap sleeps in the unripe bone
As in the withered. The green stalk
Grows without thorns: so, in the grey
And brittle years, old men must walk
Three-footed, weak as babes, and stray
Like dreams lost in the light of day.

Daughter of Tyndareos, Queen Clytemnestra,
What have you heard? What has happened? Why have you ordered
Sacrifice through the city? Is there news?
Altars of all the gods who guard our State,
Gods of the sky, powers of the lower earth,
Altars of town and country, blaze with offerings;
On every hand heaven-leaping flames implore
Anger to melt in gentleness—a glare
Enriched with holy ointment, balm so rare
As issues only from a royal store!

Why are these things? Be gracious, Queen:
Tell what you can, or what you may;
Be healer of this haunting fear
Which now like an enemy creeps near,
And now again, when hope has seen
These altars bright with promise, slinks away—
Tell us, that hope may lift the load
Which galls our souls by night and day,
Sick with the evil which has been,
The evil which our hearts forebode.

(Clytemnestra remains silent, her back turned to the Chorus.
They continue, addressing the audience.)

I am the man to speak, if you would hear
The whole tale from its hopeful starting-place—
That portent, which amazed our marching youth.
It was ten years ago—but I was there.
The poet's grace, the singer's fire,
Grow with his years; and I can still speak truth
With the clear ring the gods inspire;—
How those twin monarchs of our warlike race,
Two leaders one in purpose, were sped forth—
Their vengeful spears in thousands pointing North
To Troy—by four wings' furious beat:
Two kings of birds, that seemed to bode
Great fortune to the kings of the great fleet.
Close to the palace, on spear-side of the road,
One tawny-feathered, one white in the tail,
Perched in full view, they ravenously tear
The body of a pregnant hare

Big with her burden, now a living prey
In the last darkness of their unborn day.
Cry Sorrow, sorrow—yet let good prevail!

The army's learned Seer saw this, and knew
The devourers of the hare
For that relentless pair—
Different in nature, as the birds in hue—
The sons of Atreus; and in council of war
Thus prophesied: 'Your army, it is true,
In time shall make King Priam's town their prey;
Those flocks and herds Troy's priests shall slay
With prayers for safety of her wall
Perish in vain—Troy's violent doom shall swallow all.
Only, see to it, you who go
To bridle Trojan pride, that no
Anger of gods benight your day
And strike before your hulls are under way.
For virgin Artemis, whom all revere,
Hates with a deadly hate
The swift-winged hounds of Zeus who swooped to assail
Their helpless victim wild with fear
Before her ripe hour came;
Who dared to violate
(So warning spoke the priest)
The awe that parenthood must claim,
As for some rite performed in Heaven's name;
Yes, Artemis abominates the eagles' feast!'
Cry Sorrow, sorrow—yet let good prevail!

Still spoke on the prophet's tongue:
'Lovely child of Zeus, I pray,
You who love the tender whelp
Of the ravening lion, and care
For the fresh-wild sucking young
Of fox and rat and hind and hare;
If ever by your heavenly help
Hope of good was brought to flower,
Bless the sign we saw today!
Cancel all its presaged ill,
All its promised good fulfil!
Next my anxious prayers entreat

Lord Apollo's healing power,
That his Sister may not plan
Winds to chain the Hellene fleet;
That her grievance may not crave
Blood to drench another grave
From a different sacrifice
Hallowed by no festal joy —
Blood that builds a tower of hate,
Mad blood raging to destroy
Its self-source, a ruthless Fate
Warring with the flesh of man;
Bloodshed bringing in its train
Kindred blood that flows again,
Anger still unreconciled
Poisoning a house's life
With darkness, treachery and strife,
Wreaking vengeance for a murdered child.'

So Calchas, from that parting prodigy
Auguring the royal house's destiny,
Pronounced his warning of a fatal curse,
With hope of better mingling fear of worse.
Let us too, echoing his uncertain tale,
Cry Sorrow, sorrow — yet let good prevail!

Let good prevail!
So be it! Yet, what is good? And who
Is God? How name him, and speak true?
If he accept the name that men
Give him, Zeus I name him then.
I, still perplexed in mind,
For long have searched and weighed
Every hope of comfort or of aid:
Still I can find
No creed to lift this heaviness,
This fear that haunts without excuse —
No name inviting faith, no wistful guess,
Save only — Zeus.

The first of gods is gone,
Old Ouranos, once blown
With violence and pride;

His name shall not be known,
Nor that his dynasty once lived, and died.
His strong successor, Cronos, had his hour,
Then went his way, thrice thrown
By a yet stronger power.
Now Zeus is lord; and he
Who loyally acclaims his victory
Shall by heart's instinct find the universal key:

Zeus, whose will has marked for man
The sole way where wisdom lies;
Ordered one eternal plan:
Man must suffer to be wise.
Head-winds heavy with past ill
Stray his course and cloud his heart:
Sorrow takes the blind soul's part—
Man grows wise against his will.
For powers who rule from thrones above
By ruthlessness commend their love.

So was it then. Agamemnon, mortified,
Dared not, would not, admit to error; thought
Of his great Hellene fleet, and in his pride
Spread sail to the ill wind he should have fought.
Meanwhile his armed men moped along the shores,
And cursed the wind, and ate his dwindling stores;
Stared at white Chalkis' roofs day after day
Across the swell that churned in Aulis Bay.
And still from Strymon came that Northern blast,
While hulks and ropes grew rotten, moorings parted,
Deserters slunk away,
All ground their teeth, bored, helpless, hungry, thwarted.
The days of waiting doubled. More days passed.
The flower of warlike Hellas withered fast.
Then Calchas spoke again. The wind, he said,
Was sent by Artemis; and he revealed
Her remedy—a thought to crush like lead
The hearts of Atreus' sons, who wept, as weep they must,
And speechless ground their sceptres in the dust.

The elder king then spoke: 'What can I say?
Disaster follows if I disobey;

Surely yet worse disaster if I yield
And slaughter my own child, my home's delight,
In her young innocence, and stain my hand
With blasphemous unnatural cruelty,
Bathed in the blood I fathered! Either way,
Ruin! Disband the fleet, sail home, and earn
The deserter's badge—abandon my command,
Betray the alliance—now? The wind must turn,
There must be sacrifice, a maid must bleed—
Their chafing rage demands it—they are right!
May good prevail, and justify my deed!'

Then he put on
The harness of Necessity.
The doubtful tempest of his soul
Veered, and his prayer was turned to blasphemy,
His offering to impiety.
Hence that repentance late and long
Which, since his madness passed, pays toll
For that one reckless wrong.
Shameless self-willed infatuation
Emboldens men to dare damnation,
And starts the wheels of doom which roll
Relentless to their piteous goal.

So Agamemnon, rather than retreat,
Endured to offer up his daughter's life
To help a war fought for a faithless wife
And pay the ransom for a storm-bound fleet.

Heedless of her tears,
Her cries of 'Father!' and her maiden years,
Her judges valued more
Their glory and their war.
A prayer was said. Her father gave the word.
Limp in her flowing dress
The priest's attendants held her high
Above the altar, as men hold a kid.
Her father spoke again, to bid
One bring a gag, and press
Her sweet mouth tightly with a cord,
Lest Atreus' house be cursed by some ill-omened cry.

Rough hands tear at her girdle, cast
Her saffron silks to earth. Her eyes
Search for her slaughterers; and each,
Seeing her beauty, that surpassed
A painter's vision, yet denies
The pity her dumb looks beseech,
Struggling for voice; for often in old days,
When brave men feasted in her father's hall,
With simple skill and pious praise
Linked to the flute's pure tone
Her virgin voice would melt the hearts of all,
Honouring the third libation near her father's throne.

The rest I did not see,
Nor do I speak of it . . .
      But this I know:
What Calchas prophesies will be fulfilled.
The scale of Justice falls in equity:
The killer will be killed.

But now, farewell foreboding! Time may show,
But cannot alter, what shall be.
What help, then, to bewail
Troubles before they fall?
Events will take their way
Even as the prophet's words foreshadowed all.
For what is next at hand,
Let good prevail!
That is the prayer we pray—
We, who alone now stand
In Agamemnon's place, to guard this Argive land.

7. Antigone

Sophocles

SECOND ODE

STROPHE 1

> CHORUS: Wonders are many, yet of all
>   *(glyconics)* Things is Man the most wonderful.
>   He can sail on the stormy sea
>   Though the tempest rage, and the loud
>   Waves roar around, as he makes his
>   Path amid the towering surge.
>
>   *(dactyls)* Earth inexhaustible, ageless, he wearies, as
>   Backwards and forwards, from season to season, his
>   Ox-team drives along the ploughshare.

ANTISTROPHE 1

>   He can entrap the cheerful birds,
>   Setting a snare, and all the wild
>   Beasts of the earth he has learned to catch, and
>   Fish that teem in the deep sea, with
>   Nets knotted of stout cords; of
>   Such inventiveness is man.
>   Through his inventions he becomes lord
>   Even of the beasts of the mountain: the long-haired
>   Horse he subdues to the yoke on his neck, and the
>   Hill-bred bull, of strength untiring.

STROPHE 2

>   And speech he has learned, and thought
>   So swift, and the temper of mind
>   To dwell within cities, and not to lie bare

From *Sophocles: Three Tragedies* translated by H. D. F. Kitto. © 1962 by Oxford University Press. Reprinted by permission. Antigone: Second Ode, pp. 13-14, 17; Third Ode, pp. 21-27. In the Second Ode, the chorus praises man and sings of his natural piety; Antigone tells King Creon why she disobeyed his decree. In the Third Ode, the chorus sings of the almighty powers of Zeus, and of the rhythm of success and disaster in man's lot; Haemon, Creon's son, who loves the very Antigone who had defied Creon, now defies his own father— the King, says Haemon, has overstepped his mortal bounds by doing an injustice to the very gods whom Antigone has obeyed.

Amid the keen, biting frosts
Or cower beneath pelting rain;
Full of resource against all that comes to him
Is Man. Against Death alone
He is left with no defence.
But painful sickness he can cure
   By his own skill.

ANTISTROPHE 2

Surpassing belief, the device and
Cunning that Man has attained,
And it bringeth him now to evil, now to good.
If he observe Law, and tread
The righteous path God ordained,
Honoured is he; dishonoured, the man whose reckless heart
Shall make him join hands with sin:
May I not think like him,
Nor may such an impious man
   Dwell in my house.

       .   .   .

CREON: And so you dared to disobey the law?
ANTIGONE: It was not Zeus who published this decree,
   Nor have the Powers who rule among the dead
   Imposed such laws as this upon mankind;
   Nor could I think that a decree of yours—
   A man—could override the laws of Heaven
   Unwritten and unchanging. Not of today
   Or yesterday is their authority;
   They are eternal; no man saw their birth.
   Was I to stand before the gods' tribunal
   For disobeying *them,* because I feared
   A man? I knew that I should have to die,
   Even without your edict; if I die
   Before my time, why then, I count it gain;
   To one who lives as I do, ringed about
   With countless miseries, why, death is welcome.
   For me to meet this doom is little grief;
   But when my mother's son lay dead, had I
   Neglected him and left him there unburied,
   That would have caused me grief; this causes none.
   And if you think it folly, then perhaps
   I am accused of folly by the fool.

       .   .   .

THIRD ODE

STROPHE 1

CHORUS: Thrice happy are they who have never known disaster!
Once a house is shaken of Heaven, disaster
Never leaves it, from generation to generation.
'Tis even as the swelling sea,
When the roaring wind from Thrace
Drives blustering over the water and makes it black:
It bears up from below
A thick, dark cloud of mud,
And groaning cliffs repel the smack of wind and angry breakers.

ANTISTROPHE 1

I see, in the house of our kings, how ancient sorrows
Rise again; disaster is linked with disaster.
Woe again must each generation inherit. Some god
Besets them, nor will give release.
On the last of royal blood
There gleamed a shimmering light in the house of Oedipus.
But Death comes once again
With blood-stained axe, and hews
The sapling down; and Frenzy lends her aid, and vengeful Madness.

STROPHE 2

Thy power, Zeus, is almighty! No
Mortal insolence can oppose Thee!
Sleep, which conquers all else, cannot overcome Thee,
Nor can the never-wearied
Years, but throughout
Time Thou are strong and ageless,
In thy own Olympus
Ruling in radiant splendour.
For today, and in all past time,
And through all time to come,
This is the law: that in Man's
Life every success brings with it some disaster.

ANTISTROPHE 2

Hope springs high, and to many a man
Hope brings comfort and consolation;

Yet she is to some nothing but fond illusion:
Swiftly they come to ruin,
As when a man
Treads unawares on hot fire.
   For it was a wise man
First made that ancient saying:
To the man whom God will ruin
One day shall evil seem
Good, in his twisted judgment
He comes in a short time to fell disaster.

CHORUS-LEADER: See, here comes Haemon, last-born of your children,
   Grieving, it may be, for Antigone.

CREON: Soon we shall know, better than seers can tell us.

(Enter Haemon)

My son:
You have not come in rage against your father
Because your bride must die? Or are you still
My loyal son, whatever I may do?

HAEMON: Father, I am your son; may your wise judgment
Rule me, and may I always follow it.
No marriage shall be thought a greater prize
For me to win than your good government.

CREON: So may you ever be resolved, my son,
In all things to be guided by your father.
It is for this men pray that they may have
Obedient children, that they may requite
Their father's enemy with enmity
And honour whom their father loves to honour.
One who begets unprofitable children
Makes trouble for himself, and gives his foes
Nothing but laughter. Therefore do not let
Your pleasure in a woman overcome
Your judgement, knowing this, that if you have
An evil wife to share your house, you'll find
Cold comfort in your bed. What other wound
Can cut so deep as treachery at home?
So, think this girl your enemy; spit on her,
And let her find her husband down in Hell!
She is the only one that I have found
In all the city disobedient.

I will not make myself a liar. I
Have caught her; I will kill her. Let her sing
Her hymns to Sacred Kinship! If I breed
Rebellion in the house, then it is certain
There'll be no lack of rebels out of doors.
No man can rule a city uprightly
Who is not just in ruling his own household.
Never will I approve of one who breaks
And violates the law, or would dictate
To those who rule. Lawful authority
Must be obeyed in all things, great or small,
Just and unjust alike; and such a man
Would win my confidence both in command
And as a subject; standing at my side
In the storm of battle he would hold his ground,
Not leave me unprotected. But there is
No greater curse than disobedience.
This brings destruction on a city, this
Drives men from hearth and home, this brings about
A sudden panic in the battle-front.
Where all goes well, obedience is the cause.
So we must vindicate the law; we must not be
Defeated by a woman. Better far
Be overthrown, if need be, by a man
Than to be called the victim of a woman.

CHORUS-LEADER: Unless the years have stolen away our wits,
    All you say is said most prudently.

HAEMON: Father, it is the gods who give us wisdom;
    No gift of theirs more precious. I cannot say
    That you are wrong, nor would I ever learn
    That impudence, although perhaps another
    Might fairly say it. But it falls to me,
    Being your son, to note what others say,
    Or do, or censure in you, for your glance
    Intimidates the common citizen;
    He will not say, before your face, what might
    Displease you; I can listen freely, how
    The city mourns this girl. 'No other woman,'
    So they are saying, 'so undeservedly
    Has been condemned for such a glorious deed.
    When her own brother had been slain in battle
    She would not let his body lie unburied

To be devoured by dogs or birds of prey.
Is not this worthy of a crown of gold?' —
Such is the muttering that spreads everywhere.
     Father, no greater treasure can I have
Than your prosperity; no son can find
A greater prize than his own father's fame,
No father than his son's. Therefore let not
This single thought possess you: only what
You say is right, and nothing else. The man
Who thinks that he alone is wise, that he
Is best in speech or counsel, such a man
Brought to the proof is found but emptiness.
There's no disgrace, even if one is wise,
In learning more, and knowing when to yield.
See how the trees that grow beside a torrent
Preserve their branches, if they bend; the others,
Those that resist, are torn out, root and branch.
So too the captain of a ship; let him
Refuse to shorten sail, despite the storm —
He'll end his voyage bottom uppermost.
No, let your anger cool, and be persuaded.
If one who is still young can speak with sense,
Then I would say that he does best who has
Most understanding; second best, the man
Who profits from the wisdom of another.
CHORUS-LEADER: My lord, he has not spoken foolishly;
     You each can learn some wisdom from the other.
CREON: What? men of our age go to school again
     And take a lesson from a very boy?
HAEMON: If it is worth the taking. I am young,
     But think what should be done, not of my age.
CREON: What should be done! To honour disobedience!
HAEMON: I would not have you honour criminals.
CREON: And is this girl then not a criminal?
HAEMON: The city with a single voice denies it.
CREON: Must I give orders then by their permission?
HAEMON: If youth is folly, this is childishness.
CREON: Am I to rule for them, not for myself?
HAEMON: That is not government, but tyranny.
CREON: The king is lord and master of his city.
HAEMON: Then you had better rule a desert island!
CREON: This man, it seems, is the ally of the woman.

HAEMON: If you're the woman, yes! I fight for you.
CREON: Villain! Do you oppose your father's will?
HAEMON: Only because you are opposing Justice.
CREON: When I regard my own prerogative?
HAEMON: Opposing God's, you disregard your own.
CREON: Scoundrel, so to surrender to a woman!
HAEMON: But not to anything that brings me shame.
CREON: Your every word is in defence of her.
HAEMON: And me, and you — and of the gods below.
CREON: You shall not marry her this side the grave!
HAEMON: So, she must die — and will not die alone.
CREON: What? Threaten me? Are you so insolent?
HAEMON: It is no threat, if I reply to folly.
CREON: The fool would teach me sense! You'll pay for it.
HAEMON: I'd call you mad, if you were not my father.
CREON: I'll hear no chatter from a woman's plaything.
HAEMON: Would you have all the talk, and hear no answer?
CREON: So?
    I swear to God, you shall not bandy words
    With me and not repent it! Bring her out,
    That loathsome creature! I will have her killed
    At once, before her bridegroom's very eyes.
HAEMON: How can you think it? I will not see that,
    Nor shall you ever see my face again.
    Those friends of yours who can must tolerate
    Your raging madness; I will not endure it.

.   .   .

III. Euripides: Men "as they are, not as they should be"

SOPHOCLES is supposed to have made the remark that he portrayed men as they ought to be, while Euripides showed them as they actually are. Euripides' characters live out stories in which they act less like the heroic Antigone and more like everyday individuals who are weak, even pathetic, in their scheming, their disappointments, their suffering, and their opportunism. Largely missing from Euripides is the notion that men work out eternal, tragic themes of justice and necessity.

While one finds Aeschylus and Sophocles elevating the actions of human beings to express larger-than-human dimensions of heroism, Euripides' men and women are all too human. In the passage from *Hecuba,* Odysseus uses every device to justify his own expedient political motives, yet does so in the name of "solemn public commitment." Dishonor in the name of honor, cowardice in the name of courage, political expediency in the name of a great soldier who has died for his country: these are the traits portrayed by Odysseus.

Yet when Euripides portrays heroism, it is almost too pure to be believable; the noble heroism of pride expressed by Polyxena seems too innocent to have any real meaning in the overwhelming tragedy of the situation. As the beaten and bitter Hecuba replies to Polyxena's prideful speech: "I am proud of you, my child, so very proud, but anguish sticks in this nobility."

8. Hecuba

Euripides

CHORUS: We come to you in haste,
    Hecuba.
    —   We left the tents . . .
— where the lot assigned us.
— Slaves, torn from home
    when Troy was burnt and sacked
    by the conquering Greeks!
— We bring you painful news.
— We cannot lighten your load.
— We bring you worse to bear.

From Euripides, edited by David Grene and Richard Lattimore, *Euripides III: Hecuba, Andromache, The Trojan Women, Ion.* Copyright 1958, The University of Chicago Press. *Hecuba,* translated by William Arrowsmith, pp. 12-25. The play *Hecuba* is set in the Greek camp where, after the fall of Troy, the Trojan women are held captive. The chorus of Trojan women addresses Hecuba, widow of Priam, king of Troy, as this passage begins.

—Just now, in full assembly,
  the Greek decree came down.
—They voted your daughter must die . . .
—to be slaughtered alive
—on the tomb of Achilles!
—The sails had been unfurled,
  and the fleet stood out to sea,
  when from his tomb Achilles rose,
  armor blazing, and held them back,
  crying:
  "Ho, Argives, where do you sail,
  leaving my grave unhonored?"
—Waves of argument broke loose,
  dividing Greek from Greek.
  If one man spoke for death,
  another spoke against it.
—On your behalf spoke Agamemnon,
  lover of your daughter,
  poor, mad Cassandra.
—Then the two sons of Theseus,
  twin shoots of Athens, rose and spoke,
  but both with one intent—
  to crown Achilles' grave
  with living blood, asking
  if Cassandra's love meant more
  than the courage of Achilles.
—And so the struggle swayed,
  equally poised—
—   Until *he* spoke—
  that hypocrite with honeyed tongue,
  that demagogue Odysseus.
  And in the end he won,
  asking what one slave was worth
  when laid in the balance
  with the honor of Achilles.
—He wouldn't have the dead
  descending down to Hades
  telling tales of Greek
  ingratitude to Greeks
  who fell for Hellas
  on the foreign field of Troy.
—And he is coming here

to tear your daughter from your breast
and wrench her from your arms.
— Go to the temples!
—   Go to the shrines
— Fall at Agamemnon's knees!
— Call on heaven's gods!
— Invoke the gods below!
— Unless your prayers prevent her death,
unless your pleas can keep her safe,
then you shall see your child,
face downward on the earth
and the stain in the black earth spread
    as the red blood drops
from the gleaming golden chain
that lies broken at her throat.

HECUBA: O grief!
                    What can I say?
What are the words for loss?
O bitterness of age,
slavery not to be borne,
unendurable pain!
To whom can I turn?
Childless and homeless,
my husband murdered,
my city stained with fire. . . .
Where can I go?
What god in heaven,
what power below
will help me now?
O women of Troy,
heralds of evil,
bringers of loss,
this news you bring is my sentence of death.
Why should I live? How live in the light
when its goodness is gone,
when all I have is grief?
Bear me up,
poor stumbling feet,
and take me to the tent.

*(She stumbles painfully to Agamemnon's tent and then
cries out in terror to Polyxena within.)*

O my child!
          Polyxena,
step from the tent!
Come and hear the news
your wretched mother brings,
this news of horror
that touches your life!

(Enter from the tent Polyxena, a beautiful young girl.)

POLYXENA: That terror in your voice!
   That cry of fear
   flushing me forth
   like a bird in terror!
HECUBA: O my child! My baby. . . .
POLYXENA: Again that cry! Why?
HECUBA: I am afraid for you—
POLYXENA: Tell me the truth, Mother.
   No, I am afraid. Something
   in your face frightens me.
HECUBA: O my child! My child—
POLYXENA: You *must* tell me, Mother.
HECUBA: A dreadful rumor came.
   Some Greek decree
   that touches your life—
POLYXENA: Touches my life how?
   For god's sake, Mother,
   speak!
HECUBA:—The Greeks,
   in full assembly,
   have decreed your death,
   a living sacrifice
   upon Achilles' tomb.
POLYXENA: O my poor mother!
   How I pity you,
   this broken-hearted life
   of pain!
          What god
   could make you suffer so,
   impose such pain,
   such grief in one poor life?
   Alive, at least

I might have shared
your slavery with you,
my unhappy youth
with your embittered age.
But now I die,
and you must see my death: —
butchered like a lamb
squalling with fright,
and the throat held taut
for the gashing knife,
and the gaping hole
where the breath of life
goes out,
        and sinks
downward into dark
with the unconsolable dead.
It is *you* I pity,
Mother.
        For *you* I cry.
Not for myself,
           not for this life
whose suffering is such
I do not care to live,
but call it happiness to die.
CORYPHAEUS: Look, Hecuba. Odysseus is coming here
himself. There must be news.

(Enter Odysseus, attended by several soldiers.)

ODYSSEUS: By now, Hecuba,
I think you know what decision the army has taken
and how we voted.
        But let me review the facts.
By majority vote the Greeks have decreed as follows:
your daughter, Polyxena, must die as a victim
and prize of honor for the grave of Achilles.
The army has delegated me to act as escort.
Achilles' son will supervise the rite
and officiate as priest.
        There matters rest.
You understand your position? You must not attempt
to hold your daughter here by force, nor,

I might add, presume to match your strength with mine.
Remember your weakness and accept this tragic loss
as best you can.
      Nothing you do or say
can change the facts. Under the circumstances,
the logical course is resignation.

HECUBA: O gods,
is there no end to this ordeal of suffering,
this struggle with despair?
      Why do I live?
I should have died, died long ago.
But Zeus preserved me, saved me, kept me alive
to suffer, each time to suffer worse
than all the grief that went before.
        Odysseus,
if a slave may put her question to the free—
without intent to hurt or give offense—
then let me ask you one brief question now
and hear your answer.

ODYSSEUS: Ask me your question.
I can spare you the time.

HECUBA: Do you remember once
how you came to Troy, a spy, in beggar's disguise,
smeared with filth, in rags, and tears of blood
were streaming down your beard?

ODYSSEUS: I remember
the incident. It left its mark on me.

HECUBA: But Helen penetrated your disguise
and told me who you were? Told *me* alone?

ODYSSEUS: I stood, I remember, in danger of death.

HECUBA: And how humble you were? How you fell at my knees
and begged for life?

ODYSSEUS: And my hand almost froze on your dress.

HECUBA: And you were at my mercy, *my* slave then.
Do you remember what you said?

ODYSSEYS: Said?
Anything I could. Anything to live.

HECUBA: And I let you have your life? I set you free?

ODYSSEUS: Because of what you did, I live today.

HECUBA: Then can you say your treatment now of me
is not contemptible? To take from me

what you confess you took, and in return
do everything you can to do me wrong
and ruin me?
                    O gods, spare me the sight
of this thankless breed, these politicians
who cringe for favors from a screaming mob
and do not care what harm they do their friends,
providing they can please a crowd!
                                    Tell me,
on what feeble grounds can you justify
your vote of death?
                    Political necessity?
But how? And do your politics require
the shedding of human blood upon a grave,
where custom calls for cattle?
                                Or is it vengeance
that Achilles' ghost demands, death for his death,
and exacts of her? But what has she to do
with his revenge? Who ever hurt him less
than this poor girl? If death is what he wants,
let Helen die. He went to Troy for *her;*
for *her* he died.
                    Or is it merely looks
that you require, some surpassing beauty in a girl
whose dying loveliness might appease the hurt
of this fastidious ghost? Then do not look
for loveliness from us. Look to Helen,
loveliest of lovely women on this earth
by far—lovely Helen, who did him harm
far more than we.
                    So much by way of answer
to the justice of your case.
                            Now, Odysseus,
I present my claim for your consideration,
my just demand for payment of your debt
of life.
            You admit yourself you took my hand;
you knelt at my feet and begged for life.
                                    But see—

(Hecuba kneels at the feet of Odysseus and takes his hand.)

now I touch you back as you touched me.
I kneel before you on the ground and beg
for mercy back:
>   *Let her stay with me.*
Let her live.
>   Surely there are dead enough
without her death. And everything I lost
lives on in her. This one life
redeems the rest. She is my comfort, my Troy,
my staff, my nurse; she guides me on my way.
She is all I have.
>   And you have power,
Odysseus, greatness and power. But clutch them gently,
use them kindly, for power gives no purchase
to the hand, it will not hold, soon perishes,
and greatness goes.
>   I know. I too was great
but I am nothing now. One day
cut down my greatness and my pride.
>   But I implore you,
Odysseus, be merciful, take pity on me!
Go to the Greeks. Argue, coax them, convince them
that what they do is wrong. Accuse them of murder!
Tell them we are helpless, we are women,
the same women whom they tore from sanctuary
at the altars. But they pitied us, they spared us then.
Plead with them.
>   Read them your law of murder. Tell them how
it applies to slave and free without distinction.
But go.
>   Even if your arguments were weak,
if you faltered or forgot your words, it would not matter.
Of themselves that power, that prestige you have
would guarantee success, swelling in your words,
and borrowing from what you are a resonance and force
denied to less important men.

CORYPHAEUS: Surely
no man could be so callous or so hard of heart
he could hear this mother's heartbroken cry
and not be touched.

ODYSSEUS: Allow me to observe, Hecuba,
that in your hysterics you twist the facts.

First,
I am not, as you fondly suppose, your enemy,
and my advice, believe me, was sincerely and kindly meant.
I readily admit, moreover, the extent of my debt—
everything I am today I owe to you.
And in return I stand ready and willing
to honor my debt by saving your life. Indeed,
I have never suggested otherwise.
                         But note:
I said *your* life, not your daughter's life,
a very different matter altogether.
I gave my word that when we captured Troy
your daughter should be given to our best soldier
as a prize upon request. That was my promise,
a solemn public commitment which I intend to keep.
Besides, there is a principle at stake
and one, moreover, in whose neglect or breach
governments have fallen and cities come to grief,
because their bravest, their most exceptional men,
received no greater honor than the common run.
And Achilles deserves our honor far more than most,
a great man and a great soldier who died greatly
for his country.
                Tell me, what conduct could be worse
than to give your friend a lifetime of honor and respect
but neglect him when he dies?
                         And what then,
if war should come again and we enlist our citizens
to serve? Would we fight or would we look to our lives,
seeing that dead men get no honor?
                                No:
for my lifetime give me nothing more than what I need;
I ask no more. But as regards my grave,
I hope for honor, since honor in the grave
has eternity to run.
                You speak of pity,
but I can talk of pity too. Pity *us,*
pity our old people, those old men and women
no less miserable than yours, the wives and mothers
of all those brave young men who found a grave
in the dust of Troy.
                Endure; bear your losses,

and if you think me wrong to honor courage
in a man, then call me callous.
                                But what of you,
you foreigners who refuse your dead their rights
and break your faith with friends? And then you wonder
that Hellas should prosper while your countries suffer
the fates they deserve!
CORYPHAEUS: This is what it means
to be a slave: to be abused and bear it,
compelled by violence to suffer wrong.
HECUBA: O my child,
all my prayers are lost, thrown away
on the empty air!
                  So try your powers now.
Implore him, use every skill that pity has,
every voice. Be like the nightingale,
touch him, move him! Fall at his knees,
beg him for life!
                Even he has children too
and may pity them in you.
POLYXENA: I see your hand,
Odysseus, hidden in the folds of your robes and your face
averted, lest I try to touch your hand or beard
and beg for life.
             Have no fear. You are safe
from me.
        I shall not call on Zeus who helps
the helpless.
          I shall not beg for life.
                   No:
I go with you because I must, but most
because I wish to die. If I refuse,
I prove myself a coward, in love with life.
But why should I live?
             I had a father once,
king of Phrygia. And so I started life,
a princess of the blood, nourished on lovely hopes
to be a bride for kings. And suitors came
competing for the honor of my hand, while over the girls
and women of Troy, I stood acknowledged mistress,
courted and envied by all, all but a goddess,
though bound by death.

And now I am a slave.
It is that name of slave, so ugly, so strange,
that makes me want to die. Or should I live
to be knocked down to a bidder, sold to a master
for cash? Sister of Hector, sister of princes,
doing the work of a drudge, kneading the bread
and scrubbing the floors, compelled to drag out
endless weary days? And the bride of kings,
forced by some low slave from god knows where
to share his filthy bed?
                              Never.
With eyes still free, I now renounce the light
and dedicate myself to death.
                              Odysseus,
lead me off. For I see nothing in this life
to give me hope, and nothing here at all
worth living for.
                  As for you, Mother,
do nothing, say nothing now to hinder me.
Help me instead; help me to die, now,
before I live disgraced.
                         I am a novice
to this life of shame, whose yoke I might endure,
but with such pain that I prefer to die
than go on living.

CORYPHAEUS: Nobility of birth
    is a stamp and seal, conspicuous and sharp.
    But true nobility allied to birth
    is a greatness and a glory.

HECUBA: I am proud of you,
    my child, so very proud, but anguish sticks
    in this nobility.

                    .   .   .

IV. Thucydides' Pericles: The Noble and the Tragic in History

THUCYDIDES began his *History of the Peloponnesian War* during the first year of the war (431 B.C.) and intended to carry it to the war's end (which came in 404 B.C.), but he died leaving the work unfinished. His *History* shows us that the creation of noble characters to portray tragic and eternal themes was not confined to tragic poetry. Thucydides had orators say what he thought was called for in each situation; furthermore, he hoped that his *History,* which he wrote in the belief that it would last forever, would be useful in understanding not just the particular events of his time but also those events as they would be repeated in the future. Thus, he would have said, history treats eternal themes; that is, if a particular written history is accurate, it will illustrate eternal characteristics of human nature. In a sense, then, man's tragic nature may be found in the actuality of historical events as well as in the imagination of poets.

Pericles' funeral oration in praise of the first Athenians to die in the war provided Thucydides with an opportunity to recount the great spiritual achievement of Athens, or rather, the achievement which *is* Athens. The glorification of the city and its war dead was a celebration of a way of life, an occasion which Thucydides took to point out the actual intimate relationship between the heroic dead, the heroic living, and their heroic city. Athens was praised as having approached as close as possible to an ideal political situation where the laws are nature's laws and the men are truly nature's men. Here men had come closest to living in a way that did not exceed nature's bounds. And, if this state of affairs was to come to pass again at some future time, Thucydides' history would have immortalized for eternity a particular union of man-with-state that is man's most noble earthly achievement.

9. History of the Peloponnesian War

Thucydides

... I do not think that one will be far wrong in accepting the conclusions I have reached from the evidence which I have put forward. It is better evidence than that of the poets, who exaggerate the importance of their themes, or of the prose chroniclers, who are less interested in telling the truth than in catching the attention of their public, whose authorities cannot be checked, and whose subject-matter, owing to the passage of time, is mostly lost in the unreliable streams of mythology. We may claim instead to have used only the plainest evidence and to have reached conclusions which are reasonably accurate, considering that we have been dealing with ancient history. As for this present war, even though people are apt to think that the war in which they are fighting is the greatest of all wars and, when it is over, to relapse again into their admiration of the past, nevertheless, if one looks at the facts themselves, one will see that this was the greatest war of all.

In this history I have made use of set speeches some of which were delivered just before and others during the war. I have found it difficult to remember the precise words used in the speeches which I listened to myself and my various informants have experienced the same difficulty; so my method has been, while keeping as closely as possible to the general sense of the words that were actually used, to make the speakers say what, in my opinion, was called for by each situation.

And with regard to my factual reporting of the events of the war I have made it a principle not to write down the first story that came my way, and not even to be guided by my own general impressions; either I was present myself at the events which I have described or else I heard of them from eye-witnesses whose reports I have checked with as much thoroughness as possible. Not that even so the truth was easy to discover: different eye-witnesses give different accounts of the same events, speaking out of partiality for one side or the other or else from imperfect memories. And it may well be that my history will seem less easy to read because of the absence in it of a romantic element. It will be enough for me, however, if these words of mine are judged useful by those who want to understand clearly the events which happened in the past and which (human nature being

Reprinted by permission from Penguin Books and The Bodley Head from Thucydides, *History of the Peloponnesian War* translated by Rex Warner (Baltimore: Penguin Books, 1954). In this passage in Book One, Chapter 1, pp. 24-25, Thucydides writes of the method and purpose of his history.

what it is) will, at some time or other and in much the same ways, be re-peated in the future. My work is not a piece of writing designed to meet the taste of an immediate public, but was done to last forever.

.   .   .

... Now, at the burial of those who were the first to fall in the war Pericles, the son of Xanthippus, was chosen to make the speech. When the moment arrived, he came forward from the tomb and, standing on a high platform, so that he might be heard by as many people as possible in the crowd, he spoke as follows:

"Many of those who have spoken here in the past have praised the in-stitution of this speech at the close of our ceremony. It seemed to them a mark of honour to our soldiers who have fallen in war that a speech should be made over them. I do not agree. These men have shown themselves valiant in action, and it would be enough, I think, for their glories to be proclaimed in action, as you have just seen it done at this funeral organized by the state. Our belief in the courage and manliness of so many should not be hazarded on the goodness or badness of one man's speech. Then it is not easy to speak with a proper sense of balance, when a man's listeners find it difficult to believe in the truth of what one is saying. The man who knows the facts and loves the dead may well think that an oration tells less than what he knows and what he would like to hear: others who do not know so much may feel envy for the dead, and think the orator over-praises them, when he speaks of exploits that are beyond their own capacities. Praise of other people is tolerable only up to a certain point, the point where one still believes that one could do oneself some of the things one is hearing about. Once you get beyond this point, you will find people becom-ing jealous and incredulous. However, the fact is that this institution was set up and approved by our forefathers, and it is my duty to follow the tradition and do my best to meet the wishes and the expectations of every one of you.

"I shall begin by speaking about our ancestors, since it is only right and proper on such an occasion to pay them the honour of recalling what they did. In this land of ours there have always been the same people living from generation to generation up till now, and they, by their courage and their virtues, have handed it on to us, a free country. They certainly deserve our praise. Even more so do our fathers deserve it. For to the inheritance they

Reprinted by permission from Penguin Books and The Bodley Head from Thucydides, *History of the Peloponnesian War* translated by Rex Warner (Baltimore: Penguin Books, 1954). In this passage in Book Two, Chapter 4, pp. 116-123, Thucydides puts in the mouth of Pericles a funeral speech in praise of the first Athenians to fall in the war.

had received they added all the empire we have now, and it was not without blood and toil that they handed it down to us of the present generation. And then we ourselves, assembled here to-day, who are mostly in the prime of life, have in most directions, added to the power of our empire and have organized our State in such a way that it is perfectly well able to look after itself both in peace and in war.

"I have no wish to make a long speech on subjects familiar to you all: so I shall say nothing about the warlike deeds by which we acquired our power or the battles in which we or our fathers gallantly resisted our enemies, Greek or foreign. What I want to do is, in the first place, to discuss the spirit in which we faced our trials and also our constitution and the way of life which has made us great. After that I shall speak in praise of the dead, believing that this kind of speech is not inappropriate to the present occasion, and that this whole assembly, of citizens and foreigners, may listen to it with advantage.

"Let me say that our system of government does not copy the institutions of our neighbours. It is more the case of our being a model to others, than of our imitating anyone else. Our constitution is called a democracy because power is in the hands not of a minority but of the whole people. When it is a question of settling private disputes, everyone is equal before the law; when it is a question of putting one person before another in positions of public responsibility, what counts is not membership of a particular class, but the actual ability which the man possesses. No one, so long as he has it in him to be of service to the state, is kept in political obscurity because of poverty. And, just as our political life is free and open, so is our day-to-day life in our relations with each other. We do not get into a state with our next-door neighbour if he enjoys himself in his own way, nor do we give him the kind of black looks which, though they do no real harm, still do hurt people's feelings. We are free and tolerant in our private lives; but in public affairs we keep to the law. This is because it commands our deep respect.

"We give our obedience to those whom we put in positions of authority, and we obey the laws themselves, especially those which are for the protection of the oppressed, and those unwritten laws which it is an acknowledged shame to break.

"And here is another point. When our work is over, we are in a position to enjoy all kinds of recreation for our spirits. There are various kinds of contests and sacrifices regularly throughout the year; in our own homes we find a beauty and a good taste which delight us every day and which drive away our cares. Then the greatness of our city brings it about that all the good things from all over the world flow in to us, so that to us it seems just as natural to enjoy foreign goods as our own local products.

"Then there is a great difference between us and our opponents, in our attitude towards military security. Here are some examples: Our city is open to the world, and we have no periodical deportations in order to prevent people observing or finding out secrets which might be of military advantage to the enemy. This is because we rely, not on secret weapons, but on our own real courage and loyalty. There is a difference, too, in our educational systems. The Spartans, from their earliest boyhood, are submitted to the most laborious training in courage; we pass our lives without all these restrictions, and yet are just as ready to face the same dangers as they are. Here is a proof of this: When the Spartans invade our land, they do not come by themselves, but bring all their allies with them; whereas we, when we launch an attack abroad, do the job by ourselves, and, though fighting on foreign soil, do not often fail to defeat opponents who are fighting for their own hearths and homes. As a matter of fact none of our enemies has ever yet been confronted with our total strength, because we have to divide our attention between our navy and the many missions on which our troops are sent on land. Yet, if our enemies engage a detachment of our forces and defeat it, they give themselves credit for having thrown back our entire army; or, if they lose, they claim that they were beaten by us in full strength. There are certain advantages, I think, in our way of meeting danger voluntarily, with an easy mind, instead of with a laborious training, with natural rather than with state-induced courage. We do not have to spend our time practising to meet sufferings which are still in the future; and when they are actually upon us we show ourselves just as brave as these others who are always in strict training. This is one point in which, I think, our city deserves to be admired. There are also others:

"Our love of what is beautiful does not lead to extravagance; our love of the things of the mind does not make us soft. We regard wealth as something to be properly used, rather than as something to boast about. As for poverty, no one need be ashamed to admit it: the real shame is in not taking practical measures to escape from it. Here each individual is interested not only in his own affairs but in the affairs of the state as well: even those who are mostly occupied with their own business are extremely well-informed on general politics—this is a peculiarity of ours: we do not say that a man who takes no interest in politics is a man who minds his own business; we say that he has no business here at all. We Athenians, in our own persons, take our decisions on policy or submit them to proper discussions: for we do not think that there is an incompatibility between words and deeds; the worst thing is to rush into action before the consequences have been properly debated. And this is another point where we differ from other people. We are capable at the same time of taking risks and of estimating them beforehand. Others are brave out of ignorance; and, when they stop to think, they begin to fear. But the man who can most truly be accounted brave is he who best knows the meaning of what is sweet in life and of what is terrible, and then goes out undeterred to meet what is to come.

"Again, in questions of general good feeling there is a great contrast between us and most other people. We make friends by doing good to others, not by receiving good from them. This makes our friendship all the more reliable, since we want to keep alive the gratitude of those who are in our debt by showing continued goodwill to them: whereas the feelings of one who owes us something lack the same enthusiasm, since he knows that, when he repays our kindness, it will be more like paying back a debt than giving something spontaneously. We are unique in this. When we do kindnesses to others, we do not do them out of any calculations of profit or loss: we do them without afterthought, relying on our free liberality. Taking everything together then, I declare that our city is an education to Greece, and I declare that in my opinion each single one of our citizens, in all the manifold aspects of life, is able to show himself the rightful lord and owner of his own person, and do this, moreover, with exceptional grace and exceptional versatility. And to show that this is no empty boasting for the present occasion, but real tangible fact, you have only to consider the power which our city possesses and which has been won by those very qualities which I have mentioned. Athens, alone of the states we know, comes to her testing time in a greatness that surpasses what was imagined of her. In her case, and in her case alone, no invading enemy is ashamed at being defeated, and no subject can complain of being governed by people unfit for their responsibilities. Mighty indeed are the marks and monuments of our empire which we have left. Future ages will wonder at us, as the present age wonders at us now. We do not need the praises of a Homer, or of anyone else whose words may delight us for the moment, but whose estimation of facts will fall short of what is really true. For our adventurous spirit has forced an entry into every sea and into every land; and everywhere we have left behind us everlasting memorials of good done to our friends or suffering inflicted on our enemies.

"This, then, is the kind of city for which these men, who could not bear the thought of losing her, nobly fought and nobly died. It is only natural that every one of us who survive them should be willing to undergo hardships in her service. And it was for this reason that I have spoken at such length about our city, because I wanted to make it clear that for us there is more at stake than there is for others who lack our advantages; also I wanted my words of praise for the dead to be set in the bright light of evidence. And now the most important of these words has been spoken. I have sung the praises of our city; but it was the courage and gallantry of these men, and of people like them, which made her splendid. Nor would you find it true in the case of many of the Greeks, as it is true of them, that no words can do more than justice to their deeds.

"To me it seems that the consummation which has overtaken these men shows us the meaning of manliness in its first revelation and in its final proof. Some of them, no doubt, had their faults; but what we ought to remember first is their gallant conduct against the enemy in defence of their native land. They have blotted out evil with good, and done more service to the common wealth than they ever did harm in their private lives. No one of these men weakened because he wanted to go on enjoying his wealth: no one put off the awful day in the hope that he might live to escape his poverty and grow rich. More to be desired than such things, they chose to check the enemy's pride. This, to them, was a risk most glorious, and they accepted it, willing to strike down the enemy and relinquish everything else. As for success or failure, they left that in the doubtful hands of Hope, and when the reality of battle was before their faces, they put their trust in their own selves. In the fighting, they thought it more honourable to stand their ground and suffer death than to give in and save their lives. So they fled from the reproaches of men, abiding with life and limb the brunt of battle; and, in a small moment of time, the climax of their lives, a culmination of glory, not of fear, were swept away from us.

"So and such they were, these men—worthy of their city. We who remain behind may hope to be spared their fate, but must resolve to keep the same daring spirit against the foe. It is not simply a question of estimating the advantages in theory. I could tell you a long story (and you know it as well as I do) about what is to be gained by beating the enemy back. What I would prefer is that you should fix your eyes every day on the greatness of Athens as she really is, and should fall in love with her. When you realize her greatness, then reflect that what made her great was men with a spirit of adventure, men who knew their duty, men who were ashamed to fall below a certain standard. If they ever failed in an enterprise, they made up their minds that at any rate the city should not find their courage lacking to her, and they gave to her the best contribution that they could. They gave her their lives, to her and to all of us, and for their own selves they won praises that never grow old, the most splendid of sepulchres—not the sepulchre in which their bodies are laid, but where their glory remains eternal in men's minds, always there on the right occasion to stir others to speech or to action. For famous men have the whole earth as their memorial: it is not only the inscriptions on their graves in their own country that mark them out; no, in foreign lands also, not in any visible form but in people's hearts, their memory abides and grows. It is for you to try to be like them. Make up your minds that happiness depends on being free, and freedom depends on being courageous. Let there be no relaxation in face of the perils of the war. The people who have most excuse for despising death are not the wretched and unfortunate, who have no hope of doing well for themselves, but those who run the risk of a complete reversal in their lives, and who would feel the difference most intensely, if things went wrong for them. Any intelligent man would find a humiliation caused by his own slackness more painful to bear than death, when death comes to him unperceived, in battle, and in the confidence of his patriotism.

"For these reasons I shall not commiserate with those parents of the dead, who are present here. Instead I shall try to comfort them. They are well aware that they have grown up in a world where there are many changes and chances. But this is good fortune—for men to end their lives with honour, as these have done, and for you honourably to lament them: their life was set to a measure where death and happiness went hand in hand. I know that it is difficult to convince you of this. When you see other people happy you will often be reminded of what used to make you happy too. One does not feel sad at not having some good thing which is outside one's experience: real grief is felt at the loss of something which one is used to. All the same, those of you who are of the right age must bear up and take comfort in the thought of having more children. In your own homes these new children will prevent you from brooding over those who are no more, and they will be a help to the city, too, both in filling the empty places, and in assuring her security. For it is impossible for a man to put forward fair and honest views about our affairs if he has not, like everyone else, children whose lives may be at stake. As for those of you who are now too old to have children, I would ask you to count as gain the greater part of your life, in which you have been happy, and remember that what remains is not long, and let your hearts be lifted up at the thought of the fair fame of the dead. One's sense of honour is the only thing that does not grow old, and the last pleasure, when one is worn out with age, is not, as the poet said, making money, but having the respect of one's fellow men.

"As for those of you here who are sons of brothers of the dead, I can see a hard struggle in front of you. Everyone always speaks well of the dead, and, even if you rise to the greatest heights of heroism, it will be a hard thing for you to get the reputation of having come near, let alone equalled, their standard. When one is alive, one is always liable to the jealousy of one's competitors, but when one is out of the way, the honour one receives is sincere and unchallenged.

"Perhaps I should say a word or two on the duties of women to those among you who are now widowed. I can say all I have to say in a short word of advice. Your great glory is not to be inferior to what God has made you, and the greatest glory of a woman is to be least talked about by men, whether they are praising you or criticizing you. I have now, as the law demanded, said what I had to say. For the time being our offerings to the dead have been made, and for the future their children will be supported at the public expense by the city, until they come of age. This is the crown and prize which she offers, both to the dead and to their children, for the ordeals which they have faced. Where the rewards of valour are the greatest, there you will find also the best and bravest spirits among the people. And now, when you have mourned for your dear ones, you must depart."

V. Aristophanes: Comic and Critic

THE late fifth century "age of enlightenment" included much criticism of old ideals, old literature, and old education by the Sophists. While Thucydides (who had been instructed in philosophy by Anaxagoras and in oratory by Antiphon) combined the new learning with the old ideals by treating the past so that its events were found to be illustrative of enduring and eternal themes, others who were influenced by the Sophists were more immediate and relativistic in their treatment of the human condition. In *The Clouds,* presented in 423 B.C., Aristophanes staged an *agon* (contest) between Philosophy, representing the values of the traditional education which had been poetic, athletic, and the preserve of the noble born, and Sophistry, representing the values of the "new" education which was intellectualistic, argumentative, and available to whoever was able to pay for it, whatever his origin. The Socrates caricatured by Aristophanes as leader of the Sophists was, of course, very different from the Socrates immortalized in Plato's dialogues, where Socrates opposed the Sophists instead of leading them.

The drama of Euripides (who, like Thucydides and Pericles, had been a student of Anaxagoras and was a friend of Socrates) dealt with everyday matters, showing man "as he is, not as he should be," rather than as a larger-than-life heroic figure. To those who retained an affection for the virtues expressed in the traditional drama represented by Aeschylus and Sophocles Euripides appeared to be dragging man's nobility into the mire of mundane affairs. In *The Frogs* (presented in 405 B.C.), Aristophanes again staged a contest, this time between Euripides and Aeschylus, the latter representing the traditional themes of tragic poetry.

The conflict thus dramatized by Aristophanes was to continue in Greek culture and reappear in somewhat different forms in the work of Plato, Isocrates, and Aristotle. While the Sophists did not destroy the aristocratic ideal, they questioned its vitality and its usefulness in such fundamental ways that Plato and the others who followed them were forced to ground the aristocratic ideal on an intellectual base. Nature as seen by Homer and Pindar would no longer suffice; some training, whatever form it might take, was needed to actualize nature. Marrou wrote, "With the Sophists Greek education finally forsook its knightly origins." We can amplify Vico's account of the relation between poetry and philosophy by saying that with the Sophists philosophic wisdom became a fundamental part of Greek culture; after them poetic wisdom alone was inadequate to make one an educated man. And this is so even if the Sophists themselves were not philosophers.

10. The Clouds

Aristophanes

STREPSIADES: Now don't you worry,
Sokrates. The boy's a born philosopher. Yes, sir,
when he was just a mite of a shaver, *so* high,
he used to make the cleverest things you ever saw.
Why, there were dollhouses, sailboats, little pushcarts
from scraps of leather, and the sweetest little frogs
carved from fruit peel. He's a scholar, all right.
So tutor him in your two logics — traditional Philosophical Logic

Reprinted by permission from Aristophanes, *The Clouds,* translated by William Arrow-smith, pp. 66-80. Copyright © 1962, The University of Michigan Press. (Translator's notes and sketches are not included here.) Earlier in *The Clouds,* Sokrates is portrayed as the leader of a Sophistic school called the Thinkery. The passage included here opens with Strepsiades' request that Pheidippides be instructed in two logics—the traditional "philosophic" logic, and the modern "Sophistic" logic. So Sokrates stages a contest between the two, in order that Strepsiades may see something of what his son will be in for if he studies in the Thinkery.

and that flashy modern sophistic logic they call Immoral
because it's so wonderfully wicked. In any case,
if he can't master both logics, I insist that he learn
the Immoral Kind of argument.
SOKRATES: Philosophy and Sophistry
will instruct your son in person. And now, gentlemen,
if you'll excuse me, I must leave.
STREPSIADES   But remember, Sokrates:
I want him able to make an utter mockery of the truth.

*(Exit Sokrates. After his departure the doors of the Thinkery are thrown
open and Philosophy and Sophistry are rolled forward in great gilded cages.
From the shoulders down, both are human; from the neck up they are
fighting-cocks. Philosophy [or the Traditional Logic] is a large, muscular
rooster, powerful but not heavy, expressing in his movements that inward
harmony and grace and dignity which the Old Education was meant to
produce; his plumage is so simple and dignified as to seem almost dingy.
Sophistry, by contrast, is comparatively slight, with sloping shoulders, an
emaciated pallor, an enormous tongue and a disproportionately large
phallus. His body is graceless but extremely quick-moving; his every motion
expresses defiant belligerence, and his plumage is brilliant to the point of
flashiness. The debate itself should be conducted at top speed with much
scratching and spurring. As the Attendants open the cages, the fighters
step out and circle each other warily, jockeying for position.)*

PHILOSOPHY: Front and center, you Feathered Impertinence.
Take your little bow before the audience.
You like to swagger.
SOPHISTRY: Why, you Pompous Lump,
with all my heart. The bigger the crowd,
the better I'll rebut you.
PHILOSOPHY: *You*'ll rebut *me?*
Who are *you,* runt?
SOPHISTRY: A Logic.
PHILOSOPHY: *You,*
A Logic? Why, you cheap, stunted Loquacity!
You pipsqueak Palaver!
SOPHISTRY: I may be called
Mere Sophistry, but I'll chop you down to size. I'll *refute* you.
PHILOSOPHY: Refute *me? How?*
SOPHISTRY: With unconventionality. With ultramodernity.
With unorthodox ideas.

PHILOSOPHY: For whose present vogue
  we are indebted to this audience of imbeciles
  and asses.
SOPHISTRY: *Asses?* These sophisticated gentlemen?
  These wits?
PHILOSOPHY: I'll *invalidate* you.
SOPHISTRY: Invalidate *me?*
  How, fossil?
PHILOSOPHY: My arguments are Truth and Justice.
SOPHISTRY: Then I'll disarm you and defeat you, friend.
  Your Justice doesn't exist.
PHILOSOPHY: *What?* No Justice?
  Preposterous!
SOPHISTRY: Then show it to me. Where is it?
PHILOSOPHY: *Where* is Justice? Why, in the Lap of the Gods.
SOPHISTRY: In the Lap of the Gods? Then would you explain
  how Zeus escaped punishment after he imprisoned
  his father? The inconsistency is glaring.
PHILOSOPHY: Aaaagh.
  What nauseating twaddle. It turns my stomach.
SOPHISTRY: Why, you Decrepitude! You Doddering Dotard!
PHILOSOPHY: Why,
  you Precocious Pederast! You Palpable Pervert!
SOPHISTRY: Pelt me with roses!
PHILOSOPHY: You Toadstool! O Cesspool!
SOPHISTRY: Wreath my hair with lilies!
PHILOSOPHY: Why, you Parricide!
SOPHISTRY: Shower me with gold! Look, don't you see
  I welcome your abuse?
PHILOSOPHY: *Welcome* it, monster?
  In my day we would have cringed with shame.
SOPHISTRY: Whereas *now* we're flattered. Times change.
  The vices of your age are stylish today.
PHILOSOPHY: Repulsive Whippersnapper!
SOPHISTRY: Disgusting Fogy!
PHILOSOPHY: Because of *you* the schools of Athens
  stand deserted; one whole generation
  chaffers in the streets, gaping and idle.
  Mark my words: someday this city
  shall learn what you have made her men:
  effeminates and fools.
SOPHISTRY: Ugh, you're squalid!

PHILOSOPHY: Whereas you've become a Dandy and a Fop!
   But I remember your beggared beginnings,
   playing as Telephos, grubby and shifty,
   tricked out in Euripidean rags and tatters
   and cramming your wallet with moldy leavings
   from Pandaletos' loaf.
SOPHISTRY: What a prodigy of wisdom
   was there!
PHILOSOPHY: And what a prodigy of madness here —
   your madness, and madder still than you,
   this maddened city which lets you live —
   you, corrupter and destroyer of her youth!
SOPHISTRY *(Throwing a wing about Pheidippides)*:
   Why, you Hoary Fossil! This is one student
   you'll never teach!
PHILOSOPHY *(Pulling Pheidippides back)*:
                    Teach him I *shall* —
   unless he's prepared to devote his career
   exclusively to drivel.
SOPHISTRY: Bah, rave to yourself.
   —Come here, boy.
PHILOSOPHY: You touch him at your peril.
KORYPHAIOS *(Intervening)*:
   Gentleman, forego your wrangling and abuse,
   and each present his arguments in turn.
   Describe how *you* taught the men of the past,
   and *you*, Sir, your New Education,
PHILOSOPHY: I second
   your proposal.
SOPHISTRY: As do I.
KORYPHAIOS: Excellent.
   Who will speak first?
SOPHISTRY: Let him begin.
   I yield the floor. But when he's done,
   I'll smother him beneath so huge
   a driving hail of Modern Thought
   and Latest Views, he cannot speak —
   or if he does, my hornet words
   and waspish wit will sting him so,
   he'll never speak again.
CHORUS: —At last!
                    —The Great Debate begins!

             — Between these two
contending, clever speakers,
               — matched so fairly,
                    — who
will win, is anybody's guess.
             — Both are subtle,
— both facile, both witty,
             — both masters of rebuttal
— and abuse.
       — The stake? Wisdom.
              — Wisdom is the prize.
— For her they fight.
          — For her their rival hackles rise.
— So listen well.
       — Upon their skill, the destinies of Language,
Intellect, and Educated Athens hang.
KORYPHAIOS *(To Philosophy):*
Come, Sir, I summon you — you who conferred your crown of virtue
upon the Older Generation — to take the stand. Be bold; rise
and with clarion tongue tell us what you represent.
PHILOSOPHY: Gentlemen,
I propose to speak of the Old Education, as it flourished once
beneath my tutelage, when Homespun Honesty, Plainspeaking, and
     Truth
were still honored and practiced, and throughout the schools of Athens
the regime of the three D's — DISCIPLINE, DECORUM, and
     DUTY —
enjoyed unchallenged supremacy.
                   Our curriculum was Music and
     Gymnastic,
enforced by that rigorous discipline summed up in the old adage:
BOYS SHOULD BE SEEN BUT NOT HEARD. This was our
     cardinal rule,
and when the students, mustered by groups according to region,
were marched in squads to school, discipline and absolute silence
prevailed.
          Ah, they were hardy, manly youngsters. Why,
even on winter mornings when the snow, like powdered chaff,
came sifting down, their only protection against the bitter weather
was a thin and scanty tunic. In the classes, posture was stressed
and the decencies firmly enforced: the students stood in rows,
rigidly at attention, while the master rehearsed them by rote,

over and over. The music itself was traditional and standard—
such familiar anthems and hymns as those, for instance, beginning
A Voice from Afar or *Hail, O Pallas, Destroyer!*—and the old modes
were strictly preserved in all their austere and simple beauty.
Clowning in class was sternly forbidden, and those who improvised
or indulged in those fantastic flourishes and trills so much in vogue
with the degenerate, effeminate school of Phrynis, were promptly
    thrashed
for subverting the Muses.

                                In the gymnasium too decorum was
    demanded.
The boys were seated together, stripped to the skin, on the bare ground,
keeping their legs thrust forward, shyly screening their nakedness
from the gaze of the curious. Why, so modest were students then,
that when they rose, they carefully smoothed out the ground beneath
    them,
lest even a pair of naked buttocks leaving its trace in the sand
should draw the eyes of desire. Anointing with oil was forbidden
below the line of the navel, and consequently their genitals kept
their boyish bloom intact and the quincelike freshness of youth.
Toward their lovers their conduct was manly: you didn't see *them*
mincing or strutting, or prostituting themselves with girlish voices
or coy, provocative glances.

                                At table courtesy and good manners
were compulsory. Not a boy of that generation would have dreamed
of taking so much as a radish or the merest pinch of parsley
before his elders had been served. Rich foods were prohibited,
raucous laughter or crossing their legs forbidden. . . .

SOPHISTRY: Ugh,
what musty, antiquated rubbish. It reeks of golden grasshoppers,
all gewgaws and decaying institutions!

PHILOSOPHY: Nonetheless, these were the
    precepts
on which I bred a generation of heroes, the men who fought
at Marathon.

                        (To Sophistry)

        And what do *you* teach?
                                Modesty?
                                        No, vanity and
    softness,
and the naked beauty of the body muffled in swirling clothes,

gross and unmanly. Why, at Panathenaia now it sickens me
to see the boys dancing, ashamed of their own bodies, effetely
forgetting their duty to the goddess while they screen their nakedness
behind their shields.
    Bah.

(To Pheidippides)

    No, young man, by your courage
I challenge you. Turn your back upon his blandishments of vice,
the rotten law courts and the cheap, corrupting softness of the baths.
Choose instead the Old, the Philosophical Education. Follow me
and from my lips acquire the virtues of a man: —
         A sense of shame,
that decency and innocence of mind that shrinks from doing wrong.
To feel the true man's blaze of anger when his honor is provoked.
Deference toward one's elders; respect for one's father and mother.
To preserve intact, unsullied by disgrace or stained with wrong,
that image of Manliness and Modesty by which alone you live.
Purity: — to avoid the brothels and the low, salacious leer
of prostituted love — which, being bought, corrupts your manhood
and destroys your name. Toward your father scrupulous obedience;
to honor his declining years who spent his prime in rearing you.
Not to call him Dotard or Fogy —
SOPHISTRY: Boy, if you follow his advice,
you'll finish by looking like one of Hippokrates' sissified sons.
They'll call *you* Mollycoddle Milksop.
PHILOSOPHY: Rubbish. I promise you,
not contentious disputations and the cheap, courtroom cant
of this flabby, subpoena-serving, shyster-jargoned de-generation,
but true athletic prowess, the vigor of contending manhood
in prime perfection of physique, muscular and hard, glowing
with health.
    Ah, I can see you now, as through an idyl moving —
you with some companion of your age, modest and manly like you,
strolling by Akademe perhaps, or there among the olives,
sprinting side by side together, crowned with white reed,
breathing with every breath the ecstasy of Spring returning,
the sudden fragrance of the season's leisure, the smell of woodbine
and the catkins flung by the poplar, while touching overhead,
the leaves of the linden and plane rustle, in love, together.
So follow me, young man, and win perfection of physique. To wit —

(Demonstrating each attribute individually.)

BUILD, Stupendous.
COMPLEXION, Splendid.
SHOULDERS, Gigantic.
TONGUE, Petite.
BUTTOCKS, Brawny.
PECKER, Discreet.
But follow my opponent here, and your reward shall be, as follows:
BUILD, Effeminate.
COMPLEXION, Ghastly.
SHOULDERS, Hunched.
TONGUE, Enormous.
BUTTOCKS, Flabby.
PECKER, Preposterous!
(but thereby insuring you an enormous and devoted political follow-
ing.)
What is worse, you shall learn to make a mockery of all morality,
systematically confounding good with evil and evil with good,
so plumped and pursy with villainy, sodomy, disgrace, and perversion,
you resemble ANTIMACHOS himself.
                              Depravity can skin no lower.
CHORUS: — Bravo!
              — What brilliance!
                          — What finesse!
                                      — This is wisdom
at its noble best!
              — Such Modesty,
                          — such Decorum
in every lovely word distilled!
                          — Ah, lucky they
— whose happy lives were lived
                          — beneath your dispensation,
— by all the ancient virtues blessed!

                  (To Sophistry.)

                          — So, sir,
— despite your vaunted subtlety and wit,
                              — take care:
— Your rival's speech has scored.
                          — Some crushing *tour de force,*

—some master stroke,
                              —is needed now.
                                        —The stage is yours.
KORYPHAIOS: Unless your strategy is shrewdly planned and your attack
    ferocious,
then your cause is lost. We'll laugh you out of court.
SOPHISTRY: At last!
A few minutes more and I would have exploded from sheer impatience
to refute him and demolish his case.
                                   Now then, I freely admit
that among men of learning I am—somewhat pejoratively—dubbed
the Sophistic, or Immoral, Logic. And why? Because I first
devised a Method for the Subversion of Established Social Beliefs
and the Undermining of Morality. Moreover, this little invention of
    mine,
this knack of taking what might appear to be the worse argument
and nonetheless winning my case, has, I might add, proved to be
an *extremely* lucrative source of income.
                                   But observe, gentlemen,
how I refute his vaunted Education.

(To Philosophy)

                                   Now then, in your curriculum
hot baths are sternly prohibited. But what grounds can you possibly
    adduce
for this condemnation of hot baths?
PHILOSOPHY: What grounds can I adduce? Why,
    they're thoroughly vicious. They make a man flabby and effeminate.
SOPHISTRY: You can stop right there, friend. I have you completely at
    my mercy.
    Answer me this: which of the sons of Zeus was the most heroic?
    Who suffered most? Performed the greatest labors?
PHILOSOPHY: In my opinion,
    the greatest hero who ever lived was Herakles.
SOPHISTRY: Very well then.
    But when we speak of the famous Baths of Herakles, are we speaking
    of hot baths or cold baths? Necessarily, sir, of hot baths.
    Whence it clearly follows, by your own logic, that Herakles was
    both flabby and effeminate.
PHILOSOPHY: *Q.E.D.! This* is the rubbish I mean!
    This is the logical claptrap so much in fashion with the young!

This is what fills the baths and empties the gymnasiums!

SOPHISTRY: Very well,
   if you like, consider our national passion for politics and debating,
   pastimes which you condemn and I approve. But surely, friend,
   if politics were quite so vicious as you pretend, old Homer —
   our mentor on moral questions — would never have portrayed Nestor
   and those other wise old men as politicians, would he? Surely
   he would not.
                        Or take the question of education in oratory —
   in my opinion desirable, in yours the reverse. As for Moderation and
      Decorum,
   the very notions are absurd. In fact, two more preposterous
   or pernicious prejudices, I find it hard to imagine. For example,
   can you cite me *one* instance of that profit which a man enjoys
   by exercising moderation? Refute me if you can.

PHILOSOPHY: Why, instances
      abound
   Er . . . Peleus, for example. His virtue won him a sword.

SOPHISTRY: *A sword,*
   you say? What a charming little profit for the poor sucker!
   Look at our Hyberbolos: nothing virtuous about *him*, god knows,
   and yet, what with peddling lamps — plus a knack for swindling —
   he piled up a huge profit. All cold cash. No swords for him.
   No sir, Hyperbolos and swords just don't mix.

PHILOSOPHY: Furthermore,
   Peleus' chastity earned him the goddess Thetis for his wife.

SOPHISTRY: Precisely,
   and what did she do? Promptly ditched him for being cold,
   no passion for that all-night scrimmage between the sheets
   that lusty women love.
                        Bah, you're obsolete.

                   (To Pheidippides.)

                                              — Young man,
   I advise you to ponder this life of Virtue with scrupulous care,
   all that it implies, and all the pleasures of which its daily practice
   must inevitably deprive you. Specifically, I might mention these:
   Sex. Gambling. Gluttony. Guzzling. Carousing. Etcet.
   And what on earth's the point of living, if you leach your life
   of all its little joys?
                        Very well then, consider your natural needs.

Suppose, as a scholar of Virtue, you commit some minor peccadillo,
a little adultery, say, or seduction, and suddenly find yourself
caught in the act. What happens? You're ruined, you can't defend
    yourself
(since, of course, you haven't been taught). But follow me, my boy,
and obey your nature to the full; romp, play, and laugh
without a scruple in the world. Then if caught *in flagrante,*
you simply inform the poor cuckold that you're utterly innocent
and refer him to Zeus as your moral sanction. After all, didn't he,
a great and powerful god, succumb to the love of women?
Then how in the world can you, a man, an ordinary mortal,
be expected to surpass the greatest of gods in moral self-control?
Clearly, you can't be.

PHILOSOPHY: And suppose your pupil, by taking your advice,
is promptly convicted of adultery and sentenced to be publicly reamed
up the rectum with a radish? How, Sir, would you save him from *that?*

SOPHISTRY: Why, what's the disgrace in being reamed with a radish?

PHILOSOPHY: Sir, I can conceive of nothing fouler than being buggered
by a radish.

SOPHISTRY: And what would you have to say, my friend,
if I defeat you on this point too?

PHILOSOPHY: What *could* I say?
I could never speak again for shame.

SOPHISTRY: Very well then.
What sort of men are our lawyers?

PHILOSOPHY: Why, they're all Buggers.

SOPHISTRY: Right!
What are our tragic poets then?

PHILOSOPHY: Why, they're Buggers too.

SOPHISTRY: Right!
And what of our politicians, Sir?

PHILOSOPHY: Why, Buggers to a man.

SOPHISTRY: Right!
You see how stupidly you spoke?
And now look at our audience.
What about them?

PHILOSOPHY: I'm looking hard.

SOPHISTRY: And what do you see?

PHILOSOPHY: By heaven,
I see an enormous crowd of people,
and almost all of them Buggers.

(Pointing to individuals in the audience.)

See there? That man's a Bugger,
and that long-haired fop's a Bugger too.
SOPHISTRY: Then how do we stand, my friend?
PHILOSOPHY: I've been beaten by the Buggers.

(Flinging his cloak to the audience.)

O Buggers, catch my cloak
and welcome me among the Buggers!

*(With a wild shriek Philosophy disappears into
his cage and is wheeled away into the Thinkery, just
as Sokrates comes out.)*

·   ·   ·

11. The Frogs

Aristophanes

EURIPIDES: I won't give up the chair, so stop trying to tell me to.
I tell you, I'm a better poet than he is.
DIONYSOS: You heard him, Aeschylus. Don't you have anything to say?
EURIPIDES: He's always started with the line of scornful silence.
He used to do it in his plays, to mystify us.
DIONYSOS: Now take care, Aeschylus. Don't be overconfident.
EURIPIDES: I know this man. I've studied him for a long time.
His verse is fiercely made, all full of sound and fury,
language unbridled uncontrolled ungated-in
untalkable-around, bundles of blast and boast.

Reprinted by permission from Aristophanes, *The Frogs,* translated by Richard Lattimore, pp. 55-69. Copyright © 1962, The University of Michigan Press. (Translator's notes and sketches are not included here.) According to a story told earlier in the drama, there was a custom that the one who won top rating for his work in literature was allowed to sit in a chair next to Pluto until someone superseded him. Aeschylus held the Chair of Tragedy, and Euripides, emboldened by popular praise of his work, challenged him for it. The public, so the story goes, wanted a contest to determine which one was really better than the other. In the passage included here, Aristophanes gives us such a contest, with Dionysos serving as "moderator."

AESCHYLUS: Is that so, child of the goddess of the cabbage patch?
   You, you jabber-compiler, you dead-beat poet,
   you rag-stitcher-together, you say this to me?
   Say it again. You'll be sorry.
DIONYSOS: Now, Aechylus, stop it.
   Don't in your passion boil your mortal coils in oil.
AESCHYLUS: I won't stop, until I've demonstrated in detail
   what kind of one-legged poet this is who talks so big.
DIONYSOS: Black rams, black rams, boys, run and bring us black rams,
      quick.
   Sacrifice to the hurricane. It's on the way.
AESCHYLUS: Why, you compiler of Cretan solo-arias,
   you fouled our art by staging indecent marriages.
DIONYSOS: Most honorable Aeschylus, please stop right there.
   And as for you, my poor Euripides, if you
   have any sense, you'll take yourself out of the storm's way
   before the hail breaks on your head in lines of wrath
   and knocks it open, and your — *Telephos* oozes out —
   your brains, you know. Now, gently, gently, Aeschylus,
   criticize, don't yell. It's not becoming for two poets
   and gentlemen to squabble like two baker's wives.
   You're crackling like an oak log that's been set ablaze.
EURIPIDES: I'm ready for him. Don't try to make me back down.
   I'll bite before I'm bitten, if that's what he wants,
   with lines, with music, the gut-strings of tragedy,
   with my best plays, with *Peleus* and with *Aiolos,*
   with *Melegros,* best of all, with *Telephos.*
DIONYSOS: All right, Aeschylus, tell us what you want to do.
AESCHYLUS: I would have preferred not to have the match down here.
   It isn't fair. We don't start even.
DIONYSOS: What do you mean?
AESCHYLUS: I mean my poetry didn't die with me, but his
   did die with him; so he'll have it here to quote. Still,
   if this is your decision, then we'll have to do it.
DIONYSOS: All right, bring on the incense and the fire, while I
   in the presence of these great intelligences pray
   that I may judge this match most literarily.
   You, chorus, meanwhile, sing an anthem to the Muses.
CHORUS: Daughters of Zeus, nine maidens immaculate,
   Muses, patronesses of subtly spoken acute brains
   of men, forgers of idiom, when to the contest they hasten, with care —
   sharpened wrestling-hooks and holds for their disputations,

come, O Muses, to watch and bestow
potency on these mouths of magnificence,
figures and jigsaw patterns of words.
Now the great test of artistic ability goes into action.

DIONYSOS: Both of you two pray also, before you speak your lines.

AESCHYLUS *(Putting incense on the fire):*
Demeter, mistress, nurse of my intelligence,
grant me that I be worthy of thy mysteries.

DIONYSOS: Now you put your incense on, too.

EURIPIDES: Excuse me, please.
Quite other are the gods to whom I sacrifice.

DIONYSOS: You mean, you have private gods? New currency?

EURIPIDES: Yes,
I have.

DIONYSOS: Go ahead, then sacrifice to your private gods.

EURIPIDES: Bright upper air, my foodage! Socket of the tongue!
Oh, comprehension, sensitory nostrils, oh
grant I be critical in all my arguments.

CHORUS: We're all eager to listen
to the two great wits debating
and stating
the luminous course of their wissen-
schaft. Speech bitter and wild,
tough hearts, nothing mild.
Neither is dull.
From one we'll get witty designs
polished and filed.
The other can pull
up trees by the roots for his use,
goes wild, cuts loose
stampedes of lines.

DIONYSOS: Get on with it, get on with it, and put your finest wit in all
you say, and be concrete, and be exact; and, be original.

EURIPIDES: I'll make my self-analysis a later ceremony
after having demonstrated that my rival is a phony.
His audience was a lot of louts and Phrynichus was all they knew.
He gypped and cheated them with ease, and here's one thing he used
to do.
He'd start with one veiled bundled muffled character plunked down
in place,
Achilleus, like, or Niobe, but nobody could see its face.
It looked like drama, sure, but not one syllable would it mutter.

DIONYSOS: By Jove, they didn't, and that's a fact.

EURIPIDES: The chorus then
would utter
four huge concatenations of verse. The characters just sat there mum.

DIONYSOS: You know, I liked them quiet like that. I'd rather have
them deaf and dumb
than yak yak yak the way they do.

EURIPIDES: That's because you're an idiot
too.

DIONYSOS: Oh, by all means, and to be sure, and what was Aeschylus
trying to do?

EURIPIDES: Phony effects. The audience sat and watched the panorama
breathlessly. *"When will Niobe speak?"* And that was half the drama.

DIONYSOS: It's the old shell game. I've been had. Aeschylus, why this
agitation?
You're looking cross and at a loss.

EURIPIDES: He doesn't like investigation.
Then after a lot of stuff like this, and now the play was half-way
through,
the character would grunt and moo a dozen cow-sized lines or two,
with beetling brows and hairy crests like voodoo goblins all got up,
incomprehensible, of course.

AESCHYLUS: You're killing me.
                                      Will you shut up?

EURIPIDES: Not one word you could understand . . .

DIONYSOS: No, Aeschylus, don't grind
your teeth . . .

EURIPIDES: . . . but battles of Skamandros, barbicans with ditches
underneath,
and hooknosed eagles bronze-enwrought on shields, verse armed
like infantry,
not altogether easy to make out the sense.

DIONYSOS: You're telling me?
Many a night I've lain awake and puzzled on a single word.
A fulvid roosterhorse is please exactly just what kind of bird?

AESCHYLUS: It was a symbol painted on the galleys, you illiterate block.

DIONYSOS: I thought it was Eryxis, our Philoxenos's fighting-cock.

EURIPIDES: Well, should a rooster—vulgah bird!—get into tragedy at all?

AESCHYLUS: Tell me of *your* creations, you free-thinker, if you have the
gall.

EURIPIDES: No roosterhorses, bullmoosegoats, nor any of the millions
of monsters that the Medes and Persians paint on their pavilions.

When I took over our craft from you, I instantly became aware
that she was gassy from being stuffed with heavy text and noisy air,
so I eased her aches and reduced the swelling and took away the
 weights and heats
with neat conceits and tripping feets, with parsnips, radishes, and
 beets.
I gave her mashed and predigested baby-food strained from my books,
then fed her on solo-arias.
DIONYSOS: Kephisophon had you in his hooks.
EURIPIDES: My openings were never confused or pitched at random.
 They were not
difficult. My first character would give the background of the plot at
 once.
DIONYSOS: That's better than giving away your personal background,
 eh, what, what?
EURIPIDES: Then, from the opening lines, no person ever was left with
 nothing to do.
They all stepped up to speak their piece, the mistress spoke, the slave
 spoke too,
the master spoke, the daughter spoke, and grandma spoke.
AESCHYLUS: And tell me
 why
you shouldn't be hanged for daring that.
EURIPIDES: No, cross my heart and hope
 to die,
I made the drama *democratic.*
DIONYSOS *(To Aeschylus):*
         You'd better let that one pass, old
 sport;
you never were such a shining light in that particular line of thought.
EURIPIDES: Then I taught natural conversational dialogue.
AESCHYLUS: I'll say you
 did.
And before you ever taught them that, I wish you could have split in
 middle.
EURIPIDES *(Going right on):*
 Taught them delicate tests and verbalized commensuration,
 and squint and fraud and guess and god and loving application,
 and always how to think the worst of everything.
AESCHYLUS: So I believe.
EURIPIDES: I staged the life of everyday, the way we live. I couldn't
 deceive

my audience with the sort of stuff they knew as much about as I.
They would have spotted me right away. I played it straight and
didn't try
to bind a verbal spell and hypnotize and lead them by the nose
with Memnons and with Kyknoses with rings on their fingers and
bells on their toes.
Judge both of us by our influence on followers. Give him Manes,
Phormisios and Megainetos and sundry creeps and zanies,
the big moustachio bugleboys, the pinetreebenders twelve feet high,
but Kleitophon is mine, and so's Theramenes, a clever guy.
DIONYSOS: I'll grant your Theramenes. Falls in a puddle and comes
out dry.
The man is quick and very slick, a true Euripidean.
When Chians are in trouble he's no Chian, he's a Keian.
EURIPIDES: So that's what my plays are about,
and these are my contributions,
and I turn everything inside out
looking for new solutions
to the problems of today,
always critical, giving
suggestions for gracious living,
and they come away from seeing a play
in a questioning mood, with "where are we at?,"
and "who's got my this?," and "who took my that?."
DIONYSOS: So now the Athenian hears a pome
of yours, and watch him come stomping home
to yell at his servants every one:
"where oh where are my pitchers gone? —
where is the maid who hath betrayed
my heads of fish to the garbage trade?
Where are the pots of yesteryear?
Where's the garlic of yesterday?
Who hath ravished my oil away?"
Formerly they sat like hicks
fresh out of the sticks
with their jaws hung down in a witless way.
CHORUS (To Aeschylus):
See you this, glorious
Achilleus? What have you got to say?
Don't let your rage
sweep you away,
or you'll never be victorious.

This cynical sage
hits hard. Mind the controls.
Don't lead with your chin.
Take skysails in.
Scud under bare poles.
Easy now. Keep him full in your sights.
When the wind falls, watch him,
then catch him
dead to rights.

DIONYSOS: O mighty-mouthed inventor of harmonies, grand old bulwark
of balderdash,
frontispiece of Hellenic tragedy, open the faucets and let 'er splash.

AESCHYLUS: The whole business gives me a pain in the middle, my rage
and resentment are heated
at the idea of having to argue with *him*. But so he can't say I'm
defeated,
here, answer me, you. What's the poet's duty, and why is the poet
respected?

EURIPIDES: Because he can write, and because he can think, but mostly
because he's injected
some virtue into the body politic.

AESCHYLUS: What if you've broken your trust,
and corrupted good sound right-thinking people and filled them with
treacherous lust?
If poets do that, what reward should they get?

DIONYSOS: The axe. That's what
we should do with 'em.

AESCHYLUS: Then think of the people *I* gave him, and think of the people
when he got through with 'em.
I left him a lot of heroic six-footers, a grand generation of heroes,
unlike our new crop of street-corner loafers and gangsters and
decadent queer-os.
Mine snorted the spirit of spears and splendor, of white-plumed
helmets and stricken fields,
of warrior heroes in shining armor and greaves and sevenfold-oxhide
shields.

DIONYSOS: And that's a disease that never dies out. The munition-
makers will kill me.

EURIPIDES: Just what did you do to make them so noble? Is that what
you're trying to tell me?

DIONYSOS: Well, answer him, Aeschylus, don't withdraw into injured
dignity. That don't go.

AESCHYLUS: I made them a martial drama.

DIONYSOS: Which?

AESCHYLUS: *Seven Against Thebes,* if you want to know.

Any man in an audience sitting through that would aspire to heroic endeavor.

DIONYSOS: That was a mistake, man. Why did you make the Thebans more warlike than ever

and harder to fight with? By every right it should mean a good beating for you.

AESCHYLUS *(To the audience):*

Well, *you* could have practiced austerity too. It's exactly what *you* wouldn't *do.*

Then I put on my *Persians,* and anyone witnessing that would promptly be smitten

with longing for victory over the enemy. Best play I ever have written.

DIONYSOS: Oh, yes, I loved that, and I thrilled where I sat when I heard old Dareios was dead

and the chorus cried "wahoo" and clapped with their hands. I tell you, it went to my head.

AESCHYLUS: There, there is work for poets who also are MEN. From the earliest times

incitement to virtue and useful knowledge have come from the makers of rhymes.

There was Orpheus first. He preached against murder, and showed us the heavenly way.

Musaeus taught divination and medicine; Hesiod, the day-after-day cultivation of fields, the seasons, and plowings. Then Homer, divinely inspired,

is a source of indoctrination to virtue. Why else is he justly admired than for teaching how heroes armed them for battle?

DIONYSOS: He didn't teach Pantakles, though.

He can't get it right. I watched him last night. He was called to parade, don't you know,

and he put on his helmet and tried to tie on the plume when the helm was on top of his head.

AESCHYLUS: Ah, many have been my heroic disciples; the last of them, Lamachos (recently dead).

The man in the street simply has to catch something from all my heroics and braveries.

My Teucers and lion-hearted Patrokloses lift him right out of his knaveries

and make him thrill to the glory of war and spring to the sound of the
   trumpet.
But I never regaled you with Phaidra the floozie—or Sthenoboia the
   strumpet.
I think I can say that a lovesick woman has never been pictured by me.

EURIPIDES: Aphrodite never did notice you much.

AESCHYLUS: Aphrodite can go climb a tree.
But you'll never have to complain that she didn't bestow her attentions.
   on you.
She got you in person, didn't she?

DIONYSOS: Yes, she did, and your stories came
   true.
The fictitious chickens came home to roost.

EURIPIDES: But tell me, o man without pity:
suppose I did write about Sthenoboia. What harm has she done to
   wives
of respectable men, in shame and confusion, to do away with their
   lives.

EURIPIDES: But isn't my story of Phaidra a story that really has
   happened?

AESCHYLUS: So be it.
It's true. But the poet should cover up scandal, and not let anyone see
   it.
He shouldn't exhibit it out on the stage. For the little boys have their
   teachers
to show them example, but when they grow up we poets must act as
   their preachers,
and what we preach should be useful and good.

EURIPIDES: But you, with your
   massive construction,
huge words and mountainous phrases, is that what you call useful
   instruction?
You ought to make people talk like people.

AESCHYLUS: Your folksy style's for the
   birds.
For magnificent thoughts and magnificent fancies, we must have
   magnificent words.
It's appropriate too for the demigods of heroic times to talk bigger
than we. It goes with their representation as grander in costume and
   figure.
I set them a standard of purity. You've corrupted it.

EURIPIDES: How did I do it?

AESCHYLUS: By showing a royal man in a costume of rags, with his skin
   showing through it.

   You played on emotions.

EURIPIDES: But why should it be so wrong to awaken
   their pity?

AESCHYLUS: The rich men won't contribute for warships. You can't find
   one in the city

   who's willing to give. He appears in his rags, and howls, and complains
   that he's broke.

DIONYSOS: But he always has soft and expensive underwear under the
   beggarman's cloak.

   The liar's so rich and he eats so much that he has to feed some to the
   fishes.

AESCHYLUS: You've taught the young man to be disputatious. Each
   argues as long as he wishes.

   You've emptied the wrestling yards of wrestlers. They all sit around
   on their fannies

   and listen to adolescent debates. The sailormen gossip like grannies

   and question their officers' orders. In my time, all that they knew how
   to do

   was to holler for rations, and sing "yeo-ho," and row, with the rest
   of the crew.

DIONYSOS: And blast in the face of the man behind, that's another
   thing too that they knew how to do.

   And how to steal from the mess at sea, and how to be robbers ashore.

   But now they argue their orders. We just can't send them to sea any
   more.

AESCHYLUS: That's what he's begun. What hasn't he done?

   His nurses go propositioning others.

   His heroines have their babies in church

   or sleep with their brothers

   or go around murmuring: "*Is* life life?"

   So our city is rife

   with the clerk and the jerk,

   the altar-baboon, the political ape,

   and our physical fitness is now a disgrace

   with nobody in shape

   to carry a torch in a race.

.   .   .

PART IV

Plato on the Education of a Philosopher

PLATO (429-347 B.C.), who believed that a just state should be ruled by the "nobly born," also understood well that being so born, while necessary, was not sufficient to make one a ruler. For a ruler must be a wise man; and wise men are made, not born. Indeed, according to the argument developed in Plato's *Republic,* it takes a lifetime of education to attempt to develop the sort of person who might know enough to be a wise man. What it means to know enough to deserve to be called wise—to be a philosopher—is to be found, if at all, in a lifetime of inquiry in which the would-be philosopher seeks what he needs to know in order to know himself and others. The knowledge sought is the highest good, and the search for this is the highest activity possible to man. Thus Plato in his dialogues dramatizes the endeavour to know oneself as the search for the kind of knowledge which would enable one to understand the nature of one's being and one's destiny, while the possibility of such knowledge is held forth as the ultimate end of education. For Plato, then, the shaping of the philosopher is the noblest task which education might undertake.

The Republic is the single most important dialogue for the study of Plato's educational thinking, and it proves rewarding if studied by itself. Yet it is well to point out that the *Republic* itself may be viewed as having a place in the development of a way to approach certain educational questions, such as: What is virtue? How may it be learned? And, particularly important, Plato's pre-*Republic* dialogues are good examples of Socratic dialectic and prepare the reader for the more fully developed conclusions which that dialectic reaches in the *Republic*.

In dialogues written prior to the *Republic*, Plato created situations in which Socrates inquired of various persons the meaning of virtues such as friendship, beauty, and courage. In certain dialogues, particularly *Gorgias* and *Protagoras*, the subject discussed is whether a statesman can be produced by education and, if so, what sort of knowledge would be required of him. Socrates was unable to find anyone who knew the meaning of the various virtues in such a way that an agreed-upon meaning could be reached by the end of the dialogues. Even in discussions with the Sophists Gorgias and Protagoras, who as teachers might be expected to know what they were teaching, the result was the same: Socrates could find no one who knew anything in an absolute sense.

Furthermore, most people did not know that they were ignorant or that they possessed mere opinion instead of actual knowledge. Thus, one purpose of the dialogue was to make people realize that their knowledge claims could not stand up under rigorous Socratic questioning and, as a result of such realization, engage in an inquiry together with others who sought to understand the proper status of each other's knowledge claims. To put it another way, the purpose of the dialogue was not to win at debate (since none of the participants fully knew what he was talking about at first), but to purge one another's souls of false knowledge claims so that each might be prepared not to deceive others, be deceived by others, or deceive himself. Rather, each one was to prepare himself to recognize his own knowledge claims and those of others for what they were in the possibility that, in doing so, true knowledge ultimately could be gained.

In the *Republic* Socrates inquires about the meaning of *justice* and agrees to inquire into its true meaning instead of remaining in a situation in which only various opinions have been set forth and found to be inadequate. Plato used this situation to develop what is fundamentally an educational matter. That is, once it is determined what justice is, the question arises, how might justice be attained? To attain justice would be to produce a just state, and to produce such a state would be to produce just individuals. If a just state is to be led by just individuals, educational questions naturally arise, such as what they need to know, and how they might come to know it.

In the selections from the *Republic* included here, the educational questions are developed in three parts: (1) a brief passage in which an inquiry into the nature of justice is summarized by pointing out the fundamental relationship between justice in the state and justice in the individual; (2) a discussion of the claim that philosophers should be the leaders of a just state, their characteristics, and the objects of their knowledge; and (3) the sort of education which Plato proposes so that genuine philosophers might be developed.

12. The Republic

Plato

"Well, it's been a rough passage, but we've got there all right and are pretty well agreed that there are the same three elements in the individual as in the state."

"True."

"Must it not follow, then, that the individual is wise in the same way and with the same part of himself as the state? And similarly with courage and with all the other virtues?"

"It must."

"And so, my dear Glaucon," I went on, "we shall also say that the in-

Reprinted by permission from Plato, *The Republic*, translated by H. D. P. Lee (Baltimore: Penguin Books, 1955), pp. 194-197. (The translator's notes are not included here.) Socrates is the narrator in *The Republic*. In this passage, he and the young Glaucon are summarizing the findings of a long inquiry into the elements that make up the state and the individual, and the relationship between them.

dividual man is just in the same way that the state is just."

"That must follow too."

"And I suppose we have not forgotten that the state was just when the three elements within it each minded their own business."

"No, I don't think we've forgotten that."

"Then we must remember that each of us will be just, and do his duty, only if each part of him is performing its proper function."

"Yes, we must certainly remember that."

"So the reason ought to rule, having the ability and foresight to act for the whole, and the spirit ought to obey and support it. And this concord between them is effected, as we said, by a combination of intellectual and physical training, which tunes up the reason by intellectual training and tones down the crudeness of natural high spirits by harmony and rhythm."

"Certainly."

"When these two elements have been brought up and trained to their proper function, they must be put in charge of appetite, which forms the greater part of each man's make-up and is naturally insatiable. They must prevent it taking its fill of the so-called physical pleasures, for otherwise it will get too large and strong to mind its own business and will try to subject and control the other elements, which it has no right to do, and so wreck life entirely."

"True."

"At the same time," I went on, "won't these two elements be the best defence that mind and body have against external enemies? One of them will do the thinking, the other will fight under the orders of its superior and provide the courage to carry its decisions into effect."

"Yes, I agree."

"And we call an individual brave, I think, when he has the spirit to obey reason in danger, in spite of pleasure and pain?"

"That is quite right."

"And we call him wise in virtue of that small part of him which is in control and issues the orders, knowing as it does what is best for each of the three elements and for the whole."

"Yes, I agree."

"Then don't we call him self-controlled when all these three elements are in harmonious agreement, when reason and its subordinates are all agreed that reason should rule and there is no dissension?"

"That is exactly what we mean by self-control or discipline in a city or in an individual."

"And a man will be just in virtue of the principle we have referred to so often."

"That must be so."

"Well, then," I said, "is our picture in any way indistinct? Does it look as if justice in the individual were different from what we found it to be in the state?"

"I can't see any difference," he answered.

"If there are still any doubts in anyone's mind," I said, "a few elementary examples should finally convince them."

"What sort of examples?"

"Well, suppose for instance we were asked whether our state or a man of corresponding nature and training would embezzle money. Do you think we should reckon him more likely to do it than other people?"

"He would be the last person to do such a thing."

"And wouldn't it be out of the question for him to commit sacrilege or theft, or to betray his friends or his country?"

"Out of the question."

"And he would never break any promise or agreement, and be most unlikely to commit adultery, dishonour his parents or be irreligious."

"Most unlikely."

"And is not the reason for all this that each element within him is performing its proper function, whether it is giving or obeying orders?"

"Yes, that is the reason."

"Are you now convinced, then, that justice is the quality that produces men and states of this character?"

"Yes, I am quite convinced," he said.

"So our dream has come true, and, as we guessed, we have been lucky enough to run across an elementary type of justice right at the beginning of the foundation of our state."

"Yes, we have."

"In fact the provision that the man naturally fitted to be a shoemaker, or carpenter, or anything else, should stick to his own trade has turned out to be a kind of image of justice—hence its usefulness."

"So it seems."

"Justice, therefore, we may say, is a principle of this kind; but its real concern is not with external actions, but with a man's inward self. The just man will not allow the three elements which make up his inward self to trespass on each other's functions or interfere with each other, but, by keeping all three in tune, like the notes of a scale (high, middle, and low, or whatever they be), will in the truest sense set his house in order, and be his own lord and master and at peace with himself. When he has bound these elements into a single controlled and orderly whole, and so unified himself, he will be ready for action of any kind, whether personal, financial, political or commercial; and whenever he calls any course of action just and fair, he will mean that it contributes to and helps to maintain this disposition of mind, and will call the knowledge which controls such action wisdom. Similarly, by injustice he will mean any action destructive of this disposition, and by ignorance the ideas which control such action."

"That is all absolutely true, Socrates."

"Good," I said. "So we shan't be very far wrong if we claim to have discerned what the just man and the just state are, and in what their justice consists."

"Certainly not."

"Shall we make the claim, then?"

"Yes."

.   .   .

13. The Republic

Plato

"If we are to escape the attack with which you threaten us, we must define these philosophers whom we have claimed should be rulers. When that is clear we shall be able to defend ourselves by showing that there are some who are naturally fitted for philosophy and political leadership, while the rest should follow their lead and let philosophy alone."

"It's time for a definition," he said.

"Then follow my lead," I replied, "and we will see if we can reach a satisfactory explanation somehow or other."

"Lead on."

"Well, I hardly need to remind you," said I, "that if a man can be properly said to love something, it is the whole he loves and not merely parts of it."

"I'm afraid I do need reminding," he replied, "because I don't understand."

"I hardly expected that answer from you, Glaucon," I replied; "anyone as susceptible as you should surely know that those of your temperament are always getting bitten with a passion for some boy in the bloom of youth, who absorbs all their attention and affection. You know how it is. You praise a snub nose by calling it charming, a Roman nose you call commanding, and one between the two just right; a dark complexion is manly,

Reprinted by permission from Plato, *The Republic,* translated by H. D. P. Lee (Baltimore: Penguin Books, 1955), pp. 236-247 and 265-278. (The translator's notes are not included here.) In the first part of this excerpt, Socrates and Glaucon try to establish the claim that philosophers should be the leaders of a just state. In the second part, they consider the characteristics of philosophers, and what the objects of their knowledge are like.

a fair one angelic. And who do you think invented the description 'honey-pale' but some lover making fond excuses for pallor on the cheek of youth? In fact there's no excuse you won't make and nothing you won't say to defend youth at its flower."

"If you insist on attributing all the habits of lovers to me, I'll agree for the sake of argument."

"Oh come," I said, "it's just the same with people who are fond of wine. Haven't you noticed how with them any excuse is good enough for any kind of drink?"

"Yes indeed."

"And I expect you've noticed too how ambitious people, if they can't get command of any army, will take a battalion, and if the more important people don't look up to them, are content if the smaller fry do, so keen are they on having prestige of some sort."

"That's very true."

"Then tell me this—when we say someone has a passion for something or other, don't we mean that he wants everything of that particular kind, and not some things only?"

"Yes."

"And so a philosopher's passion is for wisdom of every kind without distinction?"

"True."

"Then we shan't regard anyone as fond of knowledge or wisdom who is fussy about what he studies, especially if he is young and has not yet got the judgment to know what is good for him and what is not. Just as we don't say that anyone who is fussy about his food has a good appetite or a passion for eating, but call him a poor eater."

"And we shall be quite right."

"But the man who is ready to taste every form of knowledge, is glad to learn and never satisfied—he's the man who deserves to be called a philosopher, isn't he?"

"Your philosophers will be an odd crowd, then," was Glaucon's reply to this. "For theatre-fans and music-lovers are anxious enough to learn, and so fall under your description; but they're an odd crew to class as philosophers, because nothing would induce them to spend time on rational argument. They run round the city and country Dionysia, never missing a festival, as if they were under contract to listen to every performance. Shan't we have to call all those who share their enthusiasm, or are devotees of the minor arts, philosophers?"

"Certainly not, though there is some resemblance."

"Then who are the true philosophers?" he asked.

"Those whose passion is to see the truth."

"That is clearly right; but what does it mean?"

"It would be difficult to explain to everyone; but you, I think, will agree with me on the following point."

"What point?"

"That, since beauty and ugliness are opposites, they are two things, each of the pair being a single thing."

"Yes."

"The same is true of justice and injustice, good and evil, and all formal characteristics; each is a single thing in itself, but each appears as a multiplicity because it is seen in combination with actions and material objects and other characteristics."

"That is true."

"I use this principle to distinguish your theatre-lovers and art-lovers and practical men from the philosophers in the true sense, who are the subject of our discussion."

"And how do you do it?"

"The music-lovers and theatre-lovers are delighted by the beauty of sound and colour and form, and the works of art which make use of them, but their minds are incapable of seeing and delighting in the essential nature of beauty itself."

"That is certainly so," he agreed.

"And those who can reach absolute Beauty and see it as it is in itself are likely to be few."

"Very few indeed."

"Then what about the man who recognizes the existence of beautiful things, but does not believe in absolute Beauty, and is incapable of following anyone who wants to lead him to a knowledge of it? Is he awake, or merely dreaming? Look; by dreaming don't we simply mean the confusion between image and the reality of which it is an image, whether the dreamer be asleep or awake?"

"I should certainly say that a man in that state of mind was dreaming."

"Then what about the man in the opposite state of mind, who believes in absolute Beauty and can see both it and the particular things which share its character, and does not confuse the particular thing and universal character? Do you think he is awake or dreaming?"

"He is very much awake."

"So we might say that, because he knows, his state of mind is one of knowledge; whereas the other man, who believes only, is in a state of belief."

"Certainly."

"And if the man whom we say believes but does not know is annoyed, and objects to our statement, can we soothe him and win him over gently, without letting him know the extent of his disease?"

"We must if we can."

"Let's think what to say to him. Shall we tell him that we don't in the least grudge him any knowledge he has, and are indeed delighted he has it; and then go on to ask him if he will answer this question, Does a man who knows, know something or nothing? You answer for him."

"I shall answer that he knows something."

"Something existent or non-existent?"

"Something existent; how could something that didn't exist be known?"

"Then are we satisfied that, whichever way we look at it, the full existent is fully knowable, and the completely non-existent entirely unknowable?"

"Quite satisfied."

"Good. Then if there were anything whose nature was such that it was both existent and non-existent, would it not lie between the fully existent and completely non-existent?"

"Yes."

"Then since the object of knowledge is existent, and the object of ignorance, necessarily, non-existent, we shall have to see if there is something between knowledge and ignorance to correspond to this intermediate reality."

"Yes."

"Isn't there something we call belief?"

"Of course."

"Is its function the same as that of knowledge or different?"

"Different."

"So belief and knowledge must have different objects corresponding to their different functions."

"They must."

"Then the object of knowledge is what exists, whose reality it is its function to know. — But there's a definition I think I should make before I go on."

"What is it?"

"Let us class together as 'faculties' the powers in us and in other things that enable us to perform our various functions. Thus I call sight and hearing faculties — do you understand the class I mean?"

"Yes, I understand."

"Then let me tell you what I think about them. A faculty has neither colour, nor shape, nor any of the similar qualities which enable me to distinguish other things one from another; I can only identify a faculty by its object and its function, and say that one faculty has one object and function, and another faculty another. What about you? What do you do?"

"The same as you."

"Let us go back, then," I said. "Tell me, do you think knowledge is a faculty? Could you classify it otherwise?"

"No; it is the most powerful of all faculties."

"And should belief be classified as a faculty?"

"Yes; it is the power which enables us to believe."

"But a little while ago you agreed that knowledge and belief were different."

"Yes," he replied, "because no reasonable person would identify the infallible with the fallible."

"Splendid," I said; "we are clearly agreed that opinion and knowledge are different."

"We are."

"Each therefore has a different object and a different function."

"That follows."

"The object of knowledge is what exists and its function to know about reality."

"Yes."

"But the function of belief is to believe, didn't we say?"

"Yes."

"Is its object the same as the object of knowledge? And are the fields of knowledge and belief the same? Or is that impossible?"

"It's impossible on the principles we've agreed. If different faculties have different objects, and belief and knowledge are two separate faculties, as we maintain, then it follows that the fields of knowledge and belief must be different."

"Then if the field of knowledge is what exists, the field of belief must be something other than what exists."

"Yes."

"Is it the non-existent? or is it impossible even to believe what does not exist? Consider. Belief is surely directed to something. Or is it possible to believe and yet believe in nothing?"

"No, that's impossible."

"So a man who believes, believes something."

"Yes."

"But what does not exist can hardly be called something—it is, properly speaking, nothing."

"True."

"Now, we correlated ignorance with the non-existent, knowledge with the existent."

"Quite right."

"So belief must be correlated with neither?"

"Agreed."

"So belief is neither ignorance nor knowledge."

"So it seems."

"Then does it lie beyond them? Is it clearer than knowledge or less clear than ignorance?"

"No."

"Then in that case," I asked, "do you think it is obscurer than knowledge, but clearer than ignorance?"

"Very much so."

"Does it lie between the two?"

"Yes."

"Belief is in fact an intermediate state."

"Certainly."

"Now we said before that if it appeared that there was anything that was both existent and non-existent, this would lie between pure existence and complete non-existence, and would be the object of neither knowledge nor ignorance, but of a faculty to be found between them."

"True."

"And we now see that what we call belief occupies that intermediate position."

"That is so."

"It remains for us to discover something that has the characteristics both of existence and non-existence, and cannot be said to have the characteristics of either without qualification; if we find it we can fairly say that it is the object of belief, thus correlating extremes to extremes and mean to mean. Do you agree?"

"Yes."

"Having established these principles, I shall return to our friend who denies that there is any absolute Beauty or any eternally unchanging Form of Beauty, but believes in the existence of many beautiful things, who loves visible beauty but cannot bear to be told that Beauty is really one, and Justice one, and so on—I shall return to him and ask him, 'Is there any of these many beautiful objects of yours that may not also seem ugly? or of your just and righteous acts that may not appear unjust and unrighteous?'"

"No," replied Glaucon, "they are all bound to seem in a sense both beautiful and ugly; and the same is true of the other characteristics in question."

"And what about things which are double something else? If they are double one thing can't they be equally well regarded as half something else?"

"Yes."

"And things which are large or heavy may equally well, from another point of view, be called small and light."

"Yes; any such thing will in a sense have both characteristics."

"Then can we say that such things *are*, any more than they *are not*, any of the many things we say they are?"

"They are ambiguous like the puzzles you hear at parties," he replied, "or the children's riddle about the eunuch hitting the bat and what he threw at it and what it was sitting on. They are neither one thing nor the other, and one can't think of them either as being or as not being, or as both, or as neither."

"Can you think of anything better to do with them, then, than place them between existence and non-existence? They are not so obscure as to be less real than non-existence, or so luminously clear as to be more real than existence."

"True."

"Our conclusion, therefore, it seems, is that conventional opinions about beauty and similar terms hover somewhere between the realms of non-existence and full existence."

"Yes."

"And we agreed that, if it appeared that there was any such realm of reality, it should be called the object of belief and not of knowledge; the fluctuating intermediate realm being apprehended by the intermediate faculty."

"Yes, we did."

"Those, then, who are able to see visible beauty — or justice or the like — in their many manifestations, but are incapable, even with another's help, of reaching absolute Beauty, may be said to *believe,* but cannot be said to *know* what they believe."

"That follows."

"And what about those who see the eternal, unchanging absolute realities? They surely have knowledge and not opinion."

"That follows too."

"And they set their hearts on the objects of knowledge, while those of the other type are set on the objects of belief—for, as you will remember, we said that their eyes and hearts were fixed on the beauty of sound and colour and so on, and that they could not bear the suggestion that there was such a thing as absolute Beauty."

"Yes, I remember."

"We shan't be far wrong, therefore, to say that they love belief rather than knowledge. Do you think they will be very annoyed with us for saying so?"

"Not if they take my advice," he replied; "they ought not to be annoyed at the truth."

"And those whose hearts are fixed on Reality itself deserve the title of Philosophers."

"Yes, certainly."

"Well, Glaucon," I said, "we can now see, at last, what a philosopher is and what he is not, but we've had to go a long way round to find out."

"I doubt if we could have done it more shortly," he replied.

"I don't think we could. Though I think we could have managed better if it had been the only subject we were discussing, and we hadn't so much else to get through before we can see the difference between a good life and a bad."

"Then where do we go from here?"

"The next question is this. If philosophers have the ability to grasp eternal and immutable truth, and those who are not philosophers are lost in multiplicity and change, which of the two should be in charge of a state?"

"What would be a reasonable line to take?" he asked.

"To say that we will choose as Guardians whichever of them seem able to maintain the laws and customs of society."

"Right."

"And isn't it obvious whether it's better for a blind man or a clear-sighted one to keep an eye on anything?"

"There's not much doubt about that," he agreed.

"But surely 'blind' is just how you would describe men who have no true knowledge of reality, and no clear standard in their mind to refer to, as a painter refers to his model, and which they can study closely before they start laying down rules about what is fair or right or good where they are needed, or maintaining, as Guardians, any rules that already exist."

"Yes, blind is just about what they are."

"Shall we make them Guardians, then? Or shall we prefer the philosophers, who know the truth, and have no less experience, and can rival them in all qualities of character?"

"It would be absurd not to choose the philosophers, if they are not inferior in all these other qualities; for in the vital quality of knowledge they are clearly superior."

"Then oughtn't we to show how knowledge can be combined with these other qualities in the same person?"

"Yes."

"As we said at the beginning of our discussion, the first thing is to find out what their natural character is. When we have agreed about that we shall, I think, be ready to agree that they can have those other qualities as well, and that they are the people to put in charge of society."

"Explain."

"One trait in the philosopher's character we can assume is his love of the knowledge that reveals eternal reality, the realm unaffected by change and decay. He is in love with the whole of that reality, and will not willingly be deprived even of the most insignificant fragment of it—just like the lovers and men of ambition we described earlier on."

"Yes, we can take that for granted."

"Then if the philosopher is to be as we have described him must he not have a further characteristic?"

"What?"

"Truthfulness. He will never willingly tolerate an untruth, but will hate it as much as he loves truth."

"That seems likely enough."

"It's not only likely," I replied, "it is an absolutely necessary characteristic of the lover that he should be devoted to everything closely connected to the object of his affection."

"True."

"And is there anything more closely connected with wisdom than truth?"

"No."

"So it's hardly possible to combine in the same character a love of wisdom and a love of falsehood."

"Quite impossible."

"So the man who has a real love of knowledge will aim at the whole truth from his earliest years."

"Certainly."

"And we know that if man's desires set strongly in one direction, they are correspondingly less strong in other directions, like a stream whose water has been diverted into other channels. So when the current of a man's desires flows towards knowledge and the like, his pleasure will be entirely in things of the mind, and physical pleasures will pass him by—that is if he is a genuine philosopher and not a sham."

"That most certainly follows."

"And he will be self-controlled and not grasping about money. Other people are more likely to worry about the things which make men so eager to get and spend money."

"True."

"And of course, when you are distinguishing the philosophic character, you must see it has no touch of meanness; pettiness of mind is quite incompatible with the attempt to grasp things divine or human as a whole and in their entirety."

"Very true."

"And if a man has greatness of mind and the breadth of vision to contemplate all time and all reality, can he regard human life as a thing of any great consequence?"

"No, he cannot."

"So he won't think death anything to be afraid of."

"No."

"And so mean and cowardly natures can't really have any dealing with philosophy."

"No, they can't."

"And a good man, who is neither mean nor ungenerous nor boastful nor cowardly, can hardly be difficult to get on with or unjust."

"Hardly."

"So when you are looking for the your philosophic character you will look to see whether it has been, from its early days, just and civilized or uncooperative and barbarous."

"Certainly."

"And you will also, I think, want to know whether it learns easily or not. For you can't expect anyone to like anything which he does with pain and trouble and little success."

"No, you can't."

"And can a man avoid being entirely without knowledge if he can't retain anything he's learnt, and has no memory at all? He will labour in vain and in the end be compelled to hate himself and the whole business of learning."

"Inevitably."

"So we can't include forgetfulness as a character that qualified a man for philosophy; we must demand a good memory."

"Yes, certainly."

"Again, a nature that has no refinement or style will tend inevitably to lack a sense of proportion; and a sense of proportion is nearly related to truth."

"Yes, it is."

"So we want, in addition to everything else, a character with a grace and sense of proportion that will automatically lead it on to see the truth about things."

"I agree."

"Do you agree, then, that we have now been through a list of characteristics, which all go together, and which the mind must have if it is to grasp reality fully and completely?"

"Yes, it must certainly have them all."

.   .   .

"Well, then, that part of our job is done—and it's not been easy; we must now go on to the next, and ask about the position and training of these saviours of our society. What are they to learn and at what age are they to learn it?"

"Yes, that's our next question."

"I didn't really gain anything," I said, "by being clever, and putting off the difficulties about the possession of women, the production of children and the establishment of Rulers till later. I knew that my true society would give offence and be difficult to realize; but I have had to describe it all the same. I've dealt with the business about women and children, and now I've got to start again on the Rulers. You will remember that we said they must love their country, and be tested both in pleasure and pain, to ensure that their loyalty remained unshaken by pain or fear or any other misfortune; those who failed the test were to be rejected, but those who emerged unscathed, like gold tried in the fire, were to be established as rulers and given honours and rewards both in life and after death. This is roughly what we said, but we were afraid of stirring up the problems we are now facing, and our argument evaded the issue and tried to get by without being seen, as it were."

"Yes, I remember," he said.

"You know, I hesitated before to say the rash things I've said," I replied; "but now let me be brave and say that our Guardians, in the fullest sense, must be philosophers."

"So be it."

"Think how few of them there are likely to be. The elements in the character which we have insisted they must have don't usually combine into a whole, but are normally found separately."

"What do you mean?"

"Readiness to learn and remember, quickness and keenness of mind and the qualities that go with them, and enterprise and breadth of vision, aren't usually combined with steadiness, discipline, and willingness to lead a quiet life; such keen temperaments are very unstable and quite devoid of steadiness."

"True."

"And again steady, trustworthy, reliable characters, who are unmoved by fear in war, are equally unmoved by instruction. Their immobility amounts indeed to numbness and, faced with anything that demands intellectual effort, they yawn and sink into slumber."

"That's all quite true."

"But we demand a fair share of both sets of qualities from anyone who is to be given the highest form of education and any share of office or authority."

"And rightly."

"So the character we want will be a rare occurrence."

"It will."

"And we must not only test it in the pains and fears and pleasures we have already described, but also try it out in a series of intellectual studies which we omitted before, to see if it has the endurance to pursue the highest forms of knowledge, without flinching as others flinch in physical trials."

"A fair test; but what," he asked, "are these highest forms of knowledge?"

"You remember," I answered, "that we distinguished three elements in the mind, and then went on to deal with justice, self-control, courage and wisdom."

"If I didn't remember that," he said, "I shouldn't have any claim to hear the rest of the argument."

"Then do you remember what we said just before that?"

"What?"

"We said that a really clear view of them could only be got by making a detour for the purpose, though we could get an approximate idea of them on the basis of our earlier argument. You said that was good enough, and so our subsequent description fell short, in my view, of real precision; whether it was precise enough for you, is for you to say."

"I thought you gave us fair measure, and so, I think, did the others."

"In matters like this nothing is fair measure that falls short of the truth in any respect," I replied. "You can't use the imperfect as a standard — though people are sometimes content with it, and don't want to look further."

"Yes, but it's usually because they're too lazy."

"A most undesirable quantity in a Guardian of constitution and laws."

"A fair comment."

"Then he must take the longer way round," I said, "and must work as hard at his intellectual training as his physical; otherwise he will never reach the highest form of knowledge, as he certainly should."

"But is there anything higher than justice and the other qualities we discussed?"

"There is," I said. "And we ought not to be content with a mere sketch even of these qualities, or fail to complete the picture. For it would be absurd, would it not, to devote all our energies to securing the greatest possible precision and clarity in matters of little consequence, and not to demand the highest precision in the most important things of all?"

"Quite absurd," he agreed. "But you can hardly expect to escape cross-questioning about what you mean by the highest form of knowledge and its object."

"I don't expect anything of the kind," I returned; "ask your questions. Though you've heard about it often enough, and either don't understand for the moment, or else are deliberately giving me trouble by your persistence — I suspect it's the latter, because you have certainly often been told that the highest form of knowledge is knowledge of the essential nature of goodness, from which things that are just and so on derive their usefulness and value. You know pretty well that that's what I have to say, and that

I'm going to add that our knowledge of it is inadequate, and that because we are ignorant of it the rest of our knowledge, however perfect, can be of no benefit to us, just as it's no use possessing anything if you can't get any good out of it. Or do you think there's any point in possessing anything if it's no good? Is there any point in having all other forms of knowledge, if you don't know what is right and good?"

"I certainly don't think there is."

"And you know of course that most people think that pleasure is the Good, while the more sophisticated think it is knowledge."

"Yes."

"But those who hold this last view can't tell us what knowledge they mean, but are compelled in the end to say they mean knowledge of the Good."

"Which is quite absurd."

"An absurdity they can't avoid, if, after criticizing us for *not* knowing the Good, they then turn round and talk to us as if we *did* know it; for they say it is 'knowledge of the good' as if we understood what they meant when they use the word 'good'."

"That's perfectly true."

"Then what about those who define Good as pleasure? Is their confusion any less? Aren't they compelled to admit that there are bad pleasures?"

"Of course they are."

"And they thus find themselves admitting that the same things are both good and bad, don't they?"

"Yes."

"So it's obvious that the subject is full of obscurities."

"It is indeed."

"Well, then, isn't it obvious too that when it's a matter of justice or fairness many people prefer the appearance to the reality, and are glad to appear to have these qualities even when they haven't; but that no one is satisfied with something that only *appears* good for him, but wants something that *really* is, and has no use here for appearances?"

"Absolutely true."

"Good, then, is the end of all endeavour, the object on which every heart is set, whose existence it divines, though it finds it difficult to say just what it is; and because it can't grasp it with the same assurance as other things it misses any value those other things have. Can we possibly agree that the best of our citizens, to whom we are going to entrust everything, should be in the dark about so important a subject?"

"It's the last thing we can admit."

"At any rate a man will not be a very useful Guardian of what is right and fair if he does not know in what their goodness consists; and I suspect that until he knows this no one can understand them."

"Your suspicions are well founded."

"So our society will not be properly regulated unless it is in charge of a Guardian who has this knowledge."

"That must be so," he said. "But what about you? Do you think that the Good is knowledge or pleasure? or do you think it's something else?"

"What a man!" I exclaimed. "I knew it! It's been obvious for some time that you wouldn't be satisfied with other people's opinions!"

"But I don't think it's right, Socrates," he protested, "for you to be able to tell us other people's opinions but not your own, when you've given so much time to the subject."

"Yes, but do you think it's right for a man to talk as if he knows what he does not?"

"He has no right to talk as if he knew; but he should be prepared to say what his opinion is, so far as it goes."

"Well," I said, "haven't you noticed that opinion without knowledge is always a poor thing? At the best it is blind—isn't anyone with a true but unthinking opinion like a blind man on the right road?"

"Yes."

"Then do you want a poor, blind, halting display from me, when you can get splendidly clear accounts from other people?"

"Now, for goodness' sake don't give up when you're just at the finish, Socrates," begged Glaucon. "We shall be quite satisfied if you give an account of the Good similar to that you gave of justice and self-control and the rest."

"And so shall I too, my dear chap," I replied, "but I'm afraid it's beyond me, and if I try I shall only make a fool of myself. So please let us give up asking for the present what the Good is in itself; I'm afraid a satisfactory answer is beyond the scope of our present inquiry. But I will tell you, if you like, about something which I imagine to be a child of the Good, and to resemble it very closely—or would you rather I didn't?"

"Tell us about the child and you can owe us your account of the parent," he said.

"It's a debt I wish I could pay you in full, instead of only paying interest on the loan," I replied. "But for the present you must accept my description of the child of the Good as interest. But take care I don't inadvertently cheat you by paying in bad money."

"We'll be as careful as we can," he said. "Go on."

"I must first get your agreement to, and remind you of something we have said earlier in our discussion, and indeed on many other occasions."

"What is it?"

"We distinguish between the many particular things which we call beautiful or good, and absolute beauty and goodness. Similarly with all other collections of things, we say there is corresponding to each set a single, unique Form which we call an 'absolute' reality."

"That is so."

"And we say that the particulars are objects of sight but not of intelligence, while the Forms are the objects of intelligence but not of sight."

"Certainly."

"And with what part of ourselves do we see what we see?"

"With our eyes."

"And we hear with our ears, and so on with the other senses and their objects."

"Of course."

"Then have you noticed," I asked, "how extremely lavish the designer of our senses was when he gave us the faculty of sight and made objects visible?"

"I can't say I have."

"Then look. Do hearing and speech need something else in addition to themselves to enable the ear to hear and the sound to be heard—some third element without which the one cannot hear or the other be heard?"

"No."

"And the same is true of most, indeed all, the other senses. Or can you think of any that needs such an element?"

"No, I can't."

"But haven't you noticed that sight and its objects do need one?"

"How?"

"If your eyes have the power of sight and you try to use them, and if objects have colour, yet you will see nothing and the colours will remain invisible unless a third element is present which is specially constituted for the purpose."

"What is that?" he asked.

"What you call light," I answered.

"True."

"Then the sense of sight and the visibility of objects are connected by something that is by a long way the most valuable of all links—that is, if light is a thing of value."

"Which it most certainly is."

"Which, then, of the heavenly bodies do you regard as responsible for it? Whose light would you say it is that makes our eyes see and objects be seen most perfectly?"

"I should say the same as you or anyone else; you mean the sun, of course."

"Then is the relation of sun and sight such that the sun is identical neither with sight itself nor with the eye in which sight resides, though the eye is the sense-organ most similar to the sun?"

"Yes."

"So the eye's power of sight is a kind of effusion dispensed to it by the sun."

"Yes."

"Then, moreover, though the sun is not itself sight, it is the cause of sight and is seen by the sight it causes."

"That is so."

"Well, this is the child of the Good, of which I spoke," I said. "The Good has begotten it in its own likeness, and it bears the same relation to sight and visibility in the visible world that the Good bears to intelligence and intelligibility in the intelligible world."

"Will you explain that a bit further?" he asked.

"You know that when we turn our eyes to objects whose colours are no longer illuminated by daylight, but only by moonlight or starlight, they see dimly and appear to be almost blind, as if they had no clear vision."

"Yes."

"But when we turn them on things on which the sun is shining, then they see clearly and their power of vision is restored."

"Certainly."

"Apply the analogy to the mind. When the mind's eye rests on objects illuminated by truth and reality, it understands and comprehends them, and functions intelligently; but when it turns to the twilight world of change and decay, it can only form opinions, its vision is confused and its beliefs shifting, and it seems to lack intelligence."

"That is true."

"Then what gives the objects of knowledge their truth and the mind the power of knowing is the Form of the Good. It is the cause of knowledge and truth, and you will be right to think of it as being itself known, and yet as being something other than, and even higher than, knowledge and truth. And just as it was right to think of light and sight as being like the sun, but wrong to think of them as being the sun itself, so here again it is right to think of knowledge and truth as being like the Good, but wrong to think of either of them as being the Good, which must be given a still higher place of honour."

"You are making it something remarkably exalted, if it is the source of knowledge and truth, and yet itself higher than they are. For I suppose you can't mean it to be pleasure?" he asked.

"A monstrous suggestion," I replied. "Let us pursue our analogy further."

"Go on."

"The sun, I think you will agree, not only makes the things we see visible, but causes the processes of generation, growth and nourishment, without itself being such a process."

"True."

"The Good therefore may be said to be the source not only of the intelligibility of the objects of knowledge, but also of their existence and reality; yet it is not itself identical with reality, but is beyond reality, and superior to it in dignity and power."

"It really must be devilish superior," remarked Glaucon with a grin.

"Now, don't blame me," I protested; "it was you who made me say what I thought about it."

"Yes, and please go on. At any rate finish off the analogy with the Sun, if you haven't finished it."

"I've not nearly finished it."

"Then go on and don't leave anything out."

"I'm afraid I must leave a lot out," I said. "But I'll do my best to get in everything I can at the moment."

"Yes, please do."

"You must suppose, then," I went on, "that there are these two powers of which I have spoken, and that one of them is supreme over everything in the intelligible world, the other over everything in the visible world—I won't say in the physical universe or you will think I'm playing with words. At any rate you understand there are these two orders of things, the visible and the intelligible?"

"Yes, I understand."

"Well, take a line divided into two unequal parts, corresponding to the visible and the intelligible worlds, and then divide the two parts again in the same ratio, to represent degrees of clarity and obscurity. In the visible world one section stands for images: by 'images' I mean first shadows, then reflections in water and other close-grained, polished surfaces, and all that sort of thing if you understand me."

"I understand."

"Let the other section stand for the objects which are the originals of the images—animals, plants and manufactured objects of all kinds."

"Very good."

"Would you be prepared to admit that these sections differ in their degree of truth, and that the relation of image to original is the same as that of opinion to knowledge?"

"I would."

"Then consider next how the intelligible part of the line is to be divided. In one section the mind uses the originals of the visible world in their turn as images, and has to base its inquiries on assumptions and proceed from them to its conclusions instead of going back to first principles: in the other it proceeds from assumption back to self-sufficient first principle, making no use of the images employed in the other section, but pursuing its inquiry solely by means of Forms."

"I don't quite understand."

"I will try again; and what I have just said will help you to understand. I think you know that students of geometry and similar forms of reasoning begin by taking for granted odd and even numbers, geometrical figures and the three kinds of angle, and other kindred data in their various subjects; these they regard as known, and treat as basic assumptions which it is quite unnecessary to explain to themselves or anyone else because they are self-evident. Starting from them, they proceed through a series of consistent steps to the propositions which they set out to examine."

"Yes, I know that."

"You know too that they make use of and reason about visible figures, though they are not really thinking about them at all, but about the originals which they resemble; they are arguing not about the square or diagonal which they have drawn but about the absolute square or diagonal, or whatever the figure may be. The figures they draw or model, which again have their shadows and reflections in water, they treat as illustrations only, the real subjects of their investigation being invisible except to the eye of the mind."

"That is quite true."

"This sort of reality I described as intelligible, but said that the mind was forced to use assumptions in investigating it, and because it was unable to ascend from these assumptions to a first principle, used as illustrations objects which in turn have their images on a lower plane, in comparison with which they are themselves thought to have a superior clarity and value."

"I understand," he said. "You are referring to what happens in geometry and kindred sciences."

"Then when I speak of the other section of the intelligible part of the line you will understand that I mean that which reason apprehends directly by the power of pure thought; it treats assumptions not as principles, but as assumptions in the true sense, that is, as starting points and steps in the ascent to the universal, self-sufficient first principle; when it has reached that principle it can again descend, by keeping to the consequences that follow from it, to a final conclusion. The whole procedure involves nothing in the sensible world, but deals throughout with Forms and finishes with Forms."

"I understand," he said; "though not entirely, because what you describe sounds like a long job. But you want to distinguish the section of intelligible reality which is studied by the activity of pure thought, as having greater clarity and certainty than the section studied by the mathematical sciences; in these sciences assumptions serve as principles and their subject-matter must be reasoned about and not directly perceived, and because they proceed *from* assumptions and not *to* first principles they can never finally understand their subject-matter, even though it can be understood with the help of a first principle. And I think that you call the state of mind of geometers and the like Reason but not Intelligence, meaning by Reason something midway between opinion and intelligence."

"You have understood me well enough," I said. "And you may assume that there are, corresponding to the four sections of the line, four states of mind: to the top section Intelligence, to the second Reason, to the third Opinion, and to the fourth Illusion. And you may arrange them in a scale, and assume that they have degrees of clarity corresponding to the degree of truth and reality possessed by their subject-matter.

"I understand," he replied, "and agree with your proposed arrangement."

.   .   .

14. The Republic

Plato

"We may assume then that our guardians need these qualities. But how are they to be brought up and educated? If we try to answer this question, I wonder whether it will help us at all in our main enquiry into the origin of justice and injustice? We do not want to leave out anything relevant, but we don't want to embark on a long digression."

To which Adeimantus replied, "I expect it will help us all right."

"Then, my dear Adeimantus, we must certainly pursue the question," I rejoined, "even though it proves a long business. So let us set about educat-

Reprinted by permission from Plato, *The Republic,* translated by H. D. P. Lee (Baltimore: Penguin Books, 1955), pp. 113-122, 138-144, 300-311. (The translator's notes are not included here.) The sort of education which Plato thinks will enable philosophers to take shape is treated here. First, Socrates and Adeimantus discuss poetry and drama. Then Socrates and Glaucon discuss the place of music in education, and sum up Plato's view of the relationship between character formation and aesthetics. Finally Socrates and Glaucon discuss Dialectic, the highest functioning of intelligence and the last stage in the education of a philosopher; they conclude here by discussing the selection of potential philosophers and the duration of the various stages in their education.

ing our guardians as if we had as much time on our hands as the traditional story-teller."

"Let us by all means."

"What kind of education shall we give them then? We shall find it difficult to improve on the time-honoured distinction between the training we give to the body and the training we give to the mind and character."

"True."

"And we shall begin with the mind and character, shall we not?"

"Of course."

"In this type of education you would include stories, would you not?"

"Yes."

"These are of two kinds, true stories and fiction. Our education must use both, and start with fiction."

"I don't understand you."

"But you know that we begin by telling children stories. These are, in general, fiction, though they contain some truth. And we tell children stories before we start them on physical training."

"That is so."

"That is what I meant by saying that we start to train the mind before the body. And the first step, as you know, is always what matters most, particularly when we are dealing with those who are young and tender. That is the time when they are taking shape and when any impression we choose to make leaves a permanent mark."

"That is certainly true."

"Shall we therefore allow our children to listen to any stories written by anyone, and to form opinions the opposite of those we think they should have when they grow up?"

"We certainly shall not."

"Then it seems that our first business is to supervise the production of stories, and choose only those we think suitable, and reject the rest. We shall persuade mothers and nurses to tell our chosen stories to their children and so mould their minds and characters rather than their bodies. The greater part of the stories current today we shall have to reject."

"Which are you thinking of?"

"We can take some of the major legends as typical. For all are cast in the same mould and have the same effect. Do you agree?"

"Yes: but I'm not sure which you refer to as major."

"The stories in Homer and Hesiod and the poets. For it is the poets who have always made up stories to tell to men."

"Which stories do you mean and what fault do you find in them?"

"The worst fault possible," I replied, "especially if the story is an ugly one."

"And what is that?"

"Misrepresenting gods and heroes, like a portrait painter who fails to catch a likeness."

"That is a fault which certainly deserves censure. But give me more details."

"Well, on the most important of subjects, there is first and foremost the foul story about Ouranos and the things Hesiod says he did, and the revenge Cronos took on him. While the story of what Cronos did, and what he suffered at the hands of his son, is not fit to be repeated as it is to the young and innocent, even if it were true; it would be best to say nothing about it, or if it must be told, tell it to a select few under oath of secrecy, at a rite which required, to restrict it still further, the sacrifice not of a mere pig but of something large and expensive."

"These certainly are awkward stories."

"And they shall not be repeated in our state, Adeimantus," I said. "Nor shall any young audience be told that anyone who commits horrible crimes, or punishes his father unmercifully, is doing nothing out of the ordinary but merely what the first and greatest of the gods have done before."

"I entirely agree," said Adeimantus, "that these stories are unsuitable."

"Nor can we permit stories of wars and plots and battles among the gods; they are quite untrue, and if we want our prospective guardians to believe that quarrelsomeness is one of the worst of evils, we must certainly not let them embroider robes with the story of the Battle of the Giants, or tell them the tales about the many and various quarrels between gods and heroes and their friends and relations. On the contrary, if we are to persuade them that no citizen has ever quarrelled with any other, because it is sinful, our old men and women must tell children stories with this end in view from the first, and we must compel our poets to tell them similar stories when they grow up. But we can permit no stories about Hera being tied up by her son, or Hephaestus being flung out of Heaven by his father for trying to help his mother when she was getting a beating, or any of Homer's Battles of the Gods, whether their intention is allegorical or not. Children cannot distinguish between what is allegory and what isn't, and opinions formed at that age are usually difficult to eradicate or change; it is therefore of the utmost importance that the first stories they hear shall aim at producing the right moral effect."

"Your case is a good one," he agreed, "but if someone wanted details, and asked what stories we were thinking of, what should we say?"

To which I replied, "My dear Adeimantus, you and I are not writing stories but founding a state. And the founders of a state, though they must know the type of story the poet must produce, and reject any that do not conform to that type, need not write them themselves."

"True: but what are the lines on which our poets must work when they deal with the gods?"

"Roughly as follows," I said. "God must surely always be represented as he is, whether the poet is writing epic, lyric, or drama."

"He must."

"And the truth is that God is good, and he must be so described."

"True."

"But nothing good is harmful or can do harm. And what does no harm does no evil. Nor can a thing which does no evil be the cause of any evil."

"That is true."

"And what is good is of service and a cause of well-being."

"Yes."

"So the good cannot be the cause of everything. It can only account for the presence of good and not for evil."

"Most certainly," he agreed.

"Then God, being good, cannot be responsible for everything, as is commonly said, but only for a small part of human life, for the greater part of which he has no responsibility. For we have a far smaller share of good than of evil, and while we can attribute the good to God, we must find something else to account for the evil."

"I think that's very true," he said.

"So we cannot allow Homer or any other poet to make this stupid mistake about the gods, or say that

Zeus has two jars standing on the floor of his palace, full of fates,
good in one and evil in the other;

and that the man to whom Zeus allots a mixture of both has 'varying fortunes sometimes good and sometimes bad,' while the man to whom he allots unmixed evil is 'chased by the gadfly of despair over the face of the earth.' Nor can we allow references to Zeus as 'dispenser of good and evil.' And we cannot approve if it is said that Athene and Zeus prompted the breach of solemn promises by Pandarus, or that the strife of the goddesses and the judgment of Paris was due to Themis and Zeus. Nor again can we let our children hear from Aeschylus that

God implants guilt in man, when he wishes to destroy a house utterly.

No: we must forbid anyone who writes a play about the sufferings of Niobe (the subject of the play from which these last lines are quoted), or the woes of the house of Pelops, or the Trojan war, or any similar topic, to say they are acts of God; or if he does he must give the sort of reason we are now demanding, and say that God's acts were good and just, and that the sufferers were benefited by being punished. What the poet must not be allowed to say is that those who were punished were made wretched through God's action. He may refer to the wicked as wretched because they needed punishment, provided he makes it clear that in punishing them God did them good. But if our state is to be run on the right lines, we must take every possible step to prevent anyone, young or old, either saying or being told, whether in poetry or prose, that God, being good, can cause harm or evil to any man. To say so would be sinful, inexpedient, and inconsistent."

"I should approve of a law for this purpose and you have my vote for it," he said.

"Then of our laws laying down the principles which those who write or speak about the gods must follow, one would be this: *God is the source of good only.*"

"I am quite content with that," he said.

"And what about our second law? Do you think God is a kind of magician who can appear at will in different forms at different times, sometimes turning into them himself and appearing in many different shapes, at other times misleading us into the belief that he has done so? Or is he without deceit and least likely of all things to change his proper form?"

"I don't, at the moment, know what the answer to that is."

"Well, if he does change his proper form, must not the change be due either to himself or to another?"

"It must."

"And is not the best always least liable to change or alteration by an external cause? For instance, the healthiest and strongest animals are least liable to change owing to diet and exercise, or plants owing to sun and wind and the like."

"That is so."

"And characters which have most courage and sense are least liable to be upset and changed by external influences. And similarly any composite object, a piece of furniture or a house or a garment, is least subject to wear if it is well made and in good condition."

"That is true."

"So in general, whether a thing is natural or artificial or both, it is least subject to change from outside if its condition is good."

"So it seems."

"But the state of God and the Divine is perfect; and therefore God is least liable of all things to be changed into other forms."

"That is so."

"Then will God change or alter himself of his own will?"

"If he changes at all," he replied, "that must be how he does."

"Will the change be for the better or for the worse?"

"Any change must be for the worse. For God's goodness is perfect."

"You are absolutely right," I said. "And, that being so, do you think that any man or god would deliberately make himself worse in any respect? If you agree that this is impossible, then it must also be impossible for a god to wish to change himself. Every god is as perfect and as good as possible, and remains in his own form without variation for ever."

"The conclusion is unavoidable."

"So we cannot have any poet saying that the gods 'disguise themselves as strangers from abroad, and wander round our towns in every kind of shape'; we cannot have stories about the transformations of Proteus and Thetis, or poets bringing Hera on the stage disguised as a priestess begging alms for 'the lifegiving children of Inachus river of Argos.' We must stop all stories of this kind, and stop mothers being misled by them and scaring their children by perversions of the myths, and telling tales about a host of fantastic spirits that prowl about at night; they are merely blaspheming the gods and making cowards of their children."

"None of these things should be allowed."

"Then if the gods are themselves unchangeable, will they use their power to deceive us into thinking that they appear in all sorts of disguises?"

"They might, I suppose."

"Come," said I, "can God want to disguise himself and deceive us, either in word or action?"

"I don't know," he replied.

"But," I asked, "don't you know that gods and men all detest true falsehood, if I may so describe it?"

"I don't understand."

"I mean that in things which touch most nearly the most important part of him no man really wants to be deceived, but is terrified of it."

"I still don't understand."

"Because you think I'm talking about something mysterious," I answered. "But all I mean is that no one wants to be deceived in his own mind about things and not to know the truth; that's where men are least ready to put up with falsehood and detest it most."

"Yes, I agree with that."

"But surely when a man is deceived in his own mind about something, we can fairly call his ignorance of the truth 'true falsehood.' For a false statement is merely some kind of representation of a state of mind, an expression consequent on it, and not the original unadulterated falsehood. Don't you agree?"

"Yes."

"So real falsehood is detested by gods and men."

"I agree."

"But what about spoken falsehood? Is it not sometimes and on some occasions useful, and so not utterly detestable? We can use it, for example, as a kind of preventive medicine against our enemies, or when one of our own friends tries to do something wrong from madness or folly. And we can make use of it in the myths we are engaged in discussing; we don't know the truth about the past but we can invent a fiction as like it as may be."

"That's perfectly true."

"In which of these ways is falsehood of use to God? Does he need to make up fictions because he does not know the past?"

"That is absurd."

"So God is not the author of poetic fictions."

"No."

"Does he tell lies because he is afraid of his enemies, then?"

"Certainly not."

"Or because of the folly or madness of any of his friends?"

"God loves neither the foolish or the mad," he replied.

"God has, then, no reason to tell lies; and we conclude that there is no falsehood at all in the realm of the spiritual and divine?"

"Most certainly."

"God is therefore without deceit or falsehood in action or word, he does not change himself, nor deceive others, awake or dreaming, with visions or signs or words."

"I agree entirely with what you say."

"Do you agree then that the second principle to be followed in all that is said or written about the gods is that they shall not be represented as using magic disguises or fraud to deceive us in any way?"

"I agree."

"And so among the many things we admire in Homer we shall not include the dream Zeus sent to Agamemnon. Nor shall we admire Aeschylus when he makes Thetis say that Apollo sang at her wedding in praise of her child

> Promising him long life, from sickness free,
> And every blessing: his triumphant praise
> Rejoiced my heart. Those lips, I thought, divine,
> Flowing with prophecy, must God's promise speak.
> Yet he the speaker, he our wedding guest,
> Phoebus Apollo, prophet, slew my son.

If a poet says this sort of thing about the gods we shall be angry and refuse to let him produce his play; nor shall we allow it to be used to educate our children—that is if our guardians are to grow up godfearing and holy, so far as that is humanly possible."

"I agree entirely with your principles," he said, "and we can treat them as law."

.   .   .

"Then we are left with the varieties of music and song to discuss," I went on; "and I suppose that it's pretty obvious to everyone what requirements we shall have to make about them, if we are to be consistent."

Glaucon laughed. "I'm afraid I'm not included in your 'everyone'," he said; "for at the moment I can't really suggest what we ought to say — though I'm not without my suspicions."

"Well at any rate you can agree easily enough that song consists of three elements, words, mode, and rhythm."

"Yes, I agree to that."

"As far as the words are concerned, then, the same rules will apply as those we laid down for words not set to music, both for their content and form."

"True."

"And surely the mode and rhythm should suit the words."

"Certainly."

"But we agreed to ban dirges and laments, did we not?"

"We did."

"Tell me then—you are a musician—which are the modes suitable for dirges?"

"The Mixed Lydian and the Extreme Lydian."

"Then we can reject them," I said: "even women, if they are respectable, have no use for them, let alone men."

"Quite right."

"But drunkenness, softness, or idleness are also qualities most unsuitable in a Guardian?"

"Of course."

"What, then, are the relaxing modes and the ones we use for drinking songs?"

"The Ionian and certain Lydian modes, commonly described as 'languid'."

"Will they then," I asked, "be of any use for training soldiers?"

"None at all," he replied. "You seem to be left with the Dorian and Phrygian."

"I'm no expert on modes," said I; "but I want one that will represent appropriately the voice and accent of a brave man on military service or any dangerous undertaking, who faces injury, defeat, or death, or any other misfortune with the same steadfast endurance. And I want another mode to represent him in the ordinary voluntary occupations of peace-time: for instance, persuading someone to grant a request, praying to God or instructing or admonishing his neighbour, or again submitting himself to the requests or instruction or persuasion of others, and in all showing no conceit, but moderation and common sense and willingness to accept the out-

come. Give me these two modes, one stern, one pleasant, to express courage
and moderation in good fortune or in bad."

"The two modes you are asking for," he rejoined, "are the two I have
just mentioned."

"And so," I went on, "we shan't need for our music and song instruments of many strings with a wide harmonic range. We shan't keep craftsmen to make instruments of this kind, such as harps and harpsichords."

"I suppose not."

"Then shall we allow flutes and flute-makers in our city? Has not the
flute the widest range of all, being in fact the original which other instruments of wide range imitate?"

"That's plain enough," he said.

"We are left, then, with the lyre and the cithara for use in our city.
Though the shepherds in the country might have some sort of pipe."

"That seems to be the conclusion of our argument."

"We aren't really doing anything revolutionary, you know," I said, "in
preferring Apollo and his instruments to Marsyas and his."

"No, I quite agree," he replied.

"And what is more," I pointed out, "we are insensibly getting rid of the
luxury from which we said our state suffered."

"Quite right too," he replied.

"Well, let us continue the process," said I. "After mode we should presumably deal next with rhythm. We shan't want very elaborate or varied
combinations, but merely need to find which rhythms suit a life of courage
and discipline. We shall then adapt the metre and tune to the appropriate
words, and not the words to the metre and tune. But it's your business to
say what these rhythms are, as you did with the modes."

"I'm afraid I really can't do that," he replied. "There are three basic
types of rhythm, from which the various combinations are built up, just
as there are four elements which go to build up the modes. So much I know
and can tell you. But which are suited to represent which kind of life, I
cannot say."

"Well, we'll consult Damon about it," I said, "and ask him what combinations are suitable to express meanness, insolence, madness, and other
evil characteristics, and which rhythms we must keep to express their opposites. I seem to remember hearing him talking about 'march rhythms'
and 'composite rhythms,' 'dactyls,' and 'heroics,' arranging them in various
ways and marking the stresses; he talked also, I think, about 'iambics and
trochees,' and assigned them longs and shorts. And I believe that he praised
or blamed the composition of the foot as well as the rhythm as a whole, or
perhaps it was the combination of the two: I really can't remember. In any
case, as I said, we can refer to Damon. For it would need a lot of argument to settle the details, don't you think?"

"It would indeed."

"But there is one thing we can decide at once, that beauty and ugliness result from good rhythm and bad."

"That is undeniable."

"And good rhythm is the consequence of music that suits good poetry, bad rhythm of the opposite; and the same is true of mode and tune, if, as we said a moment ago, both the rhythm and mode should be suited to the words and not vice versa."

"The words must of course determine the music," he said.

"But what about the style and content of the poetry themselves?" I asked. "Don't they depend on character, just as the other things depend on them?"

"They must."

"Good literature, therefore, and good music and beauty of form generally all depend on goodness of character; I don't mean that lack of awareness of the world which we politely call 'goodness,' but a character of real judgment and principle."

"I quite agree."

"And are not these things which our young men must try to acquire, if they are to perform their function in life properly?"

"They must."

"And they are to be seen in painting and similar arts, in weaving and embroidery, in architecture and furniture, and in living things, animals and plants. For in all of these we find beauty and ugliness. And ugliness of form and disharmony are akin to bad art and bad character, and their opposites are akin to and represent good character and discipline."

"That is perfectly true."

"It is not only to the poets therefore that we must issue orders requiring them to represent good character in their poems or not to write at all; we must issue similar orders to all artists and prevent them portraying bad character, ill-discipline, meanness, or ugliness in painting, sculpture, architecture, or any work of art, and if they are unable to comply they must be forbidden to practise their art. We shall thus prevent our guardians being brought up among representations of what is evil, and so day by day and little by little, by feeding as it were in an unhealthy pasture, insensibly doing themselves grave psychological damage. Our artists and craftsmen must be capable of perceiving the real nature of what is beautiful, and then our young men, living as it were in a good climate, will benefit because all the works of art they see and hear influence them for good, like the breezes from some healthy country, insensibly moulding them into sympathy and conformity with what is rational and right."

"That would indeed be the best way to bring them up."

"And that, my dear Glaucon," I said, "is why this stage of education is crucial. For rhythm and harmony penetrate deeply into the mind and have a most powerful effect on it, and if education is good, bring balance and fairness, if it is bad, the reverse. And moreover the proper training we propose to give will make a man quick to perceive the short-comings of works of art or nature, whose ugliness he will rightly dislike; anything beautiful he will welcome, and will accept and assimilate it for his own good, anything ugly he will rightly condemn and dislike, even when he is still young and cannot understand the reason for so doing, while when reason comes he will recognize and welcome her as a familiar friend because of his education."

"In my view," he said, "that is the purpose of this stage of education."

"Well then," I went on, "when we were learning to read we were not satisfied until we could recognize the letters of the alphabet wherever they occurred; we did not think them beneath our notice in large words or small, but tried to recognize them everywhere on the grounds that we should not have learned to read till we could."

"That is true."

"And we can't recognize reflections of the letters in water or in a mirror till we know the letters themselves. The same process of learning gives us skill to recognize both."

"Yes, it does."

"Then I must surely be right in saying that we shall not be properly educated ourselves, nor will the guardians whom we are training, until we can recognize the qualities of discipline, courage, generosity, greatness of mind, and others akin to them, as well as their opposites, in all their many manifestations. We must be able to perceive both the qualities themselves and representations of them wherever they occur, and must not despise instances great or small, but reckon that the same process of learning gives us skill to recognize both."

"You are most certainly right," he agreed.

"And is not the fairest sight of all," I asked, "for him who has eyes to see it, the combination in the same person of good character and good looks to match them, each bearing the same stamp?"

"It is indeed."

"And such a combination will also be most attractive, will it not?"

"Certainly."

"It is, then, with people of this sort that the educated man will fall in love; where the combination is imperfect he will not be attracted."

"Not if the defect is one of character," he replied; "if it's a physical defect, he will not let it be a bar to his affection."

"I know," I said; "you've got, or once had, a boy friend like that. And I agree with you. But tell me: does excessive pleasure go with self-control and moderation?"

"Certainly not; excessive pleasure breaks down one's control just as much as excessive pain."

"Does it go with other kinds of goodness?"

"No."

"Then does it go with excess and indiscipline?"

"Certainly."

"And is there any greater or keener pleasure than that of sex?"

"No: nor any more frenzied."

"But to love rightly is to love what is beautiful and good with discipline and intelligence."

"I entirely agree."

"Then can true love have any contact with frenzy or excess of any kind?"

"It can have none."

"It can therefore have no contact with this sexual pleasure, and lovers whose love is true must neither of them indulge in it."

"They certainly must not, Socrates," he replied emphatically.

"And so I suppose that you will lay down laws in the state we are founding which will allow a lover to associate with his boy-friend and kiss him and touch him, if he permits it, as a father does his son, if his motives are good; but require that his association with anyone he's fond of must never give rise to the least suspicion of anything beyond this, otherwise he will be thought a man of no taste or education."

"That is how I should legislate."

"And that, I think," said I, "concludes what we have to say about this stage of education, and a very appropriate conclusion too—for the object of education is to teach us to love beauty."

"I agree."

.   .   .

"Yes," I said, "for it's only if we can pursue all these studies until we see their kinship and common ground, and can work out their relationship, that they contribute to our purpose and are worth the trouble we spend on them."

"So I should imagine. But it means a great deal of work."

"And you don't suppose it's more than a beginning, do you?" I asked. "The subjects we've described are only a prelude to our main theme. For you don't think that people who are good at them are trained philosophers, do you?"

"Heavens, no, with very few exceptions."

"And can they ever acquire the knowledge we regard as essential if they can't argue logically?"

"No, they can't."

"But isn't this just the note which Dialectic must strike? It is an intellectual process, but is paralleled in the visible world, as we said, by the progress of sight from shadows to real creatures, and then to the stars, and finally to the sun itself. So when one tries to reach ultimate realities by the exercise of pure reason, without any aid from the senses, and refuses to give up until the mind has grasped what the Good is, one is at the end of an intellectual progress parallel to the visual progress we described."

"That's perfectly true."

"And isn't this progress what we call 'dialectic'?"

"Yes."

"The prisoners in our cave," I went on, "were released and turned round from the shadows to the images which cast them and to the fire, and then climbed up into the sunlight; there they were unable to look at animals and plants and at the light of the sun, but turned to reflections in water and shadows of things (real things, that is, and not mere images throwing shadows in the light of a fire itself derivative compared with the sun). Well, the whole study of the subjects we have described has the effect of leading the best element in the mind up towards the vision of the highest reality, just as the body's most perceptive organ was led to see the brightest of all things in the material and visible world."

"I quite agree with all you've said myself," said Glaucon; "I think it's very difficult to accept in some ways, but as hard to deny in others. However, as this isn't the only occasion on which we shall hear about it and there will be plenty of opportunities to return to it in the future, let us suppose it is so for the present and go on to deal with the main course as thoroughly as we have dealt with the prelude. Tell us what sort of power Dialectic has, and how many kinds of it there are and how they are pursued; for they seem to lead to our destination, where we shall get some rest at the end of our journey."

"My dear Glaucon," I said, "you won't be able to follow me further, not because of any unwillingness on my part, but because what you'd see would no longer be an image but truth itself, that is, so far as I can see it; I would not like to be sure my vision is true, but I'm quite sure there is something for us to see, aren't you?"

"Of course."

"And you agree that dialectic ability can only be acquired after the course of study we have described, and in no other way?"

"I'm quite sure of that."

"And it can't be denied that it's the only activity which systematically sets about the definition of the essential nature of things. Of other activities some are concerned with human opinions or desires, or with growing or making things and looking after them when they are grown or made; others, geometry and the like, though, as we have said, concerned with reality, can only see it in a kind of dream, and never clearly, so long as they leave their assumptions unquestioned and cannot account for them. For how can any chain of reasoning result in knowledge if it starts from a premise it does not really know and proceeds to a conclusion and through steps which it does not know either?"

"It can't possibly."

"Dialectic, in fact, is the only activity whose method is to challenge its own assumptions so that it may rest firmly on first principles. When the eye of the mind gets really bogged down in a morass of ignorance, dialectic gently pulls it out and leads it up, using the studies we have described to convert and help it. These studies we have often, through force of habit, referred to as branches of *knowledge,* but we really need another term, to indicate a greater degree of clarity than opinion but a lesser degree than knowledge—we called it Reasoning earlier on. But I don't think we shall quarrel about a word, the subject of our inquiry is too important for that."

"It is indeed."

"So we shall be content to use any term that will indicate clearly the faculty we mean."

"Yes."

"Then let us be content with the terms we used earlier on for the four divisions of our line—knowledge, reason, belief, and illusion. The last two we class together as opinion, the first two as intelligence, opinion being concerned with the world of becoming, knowledge with the world of reality. Knowledge stands to opinion as the world of reality does to that of becoming, and intelligence stands to belief and reason to illusion as knowledge stands to opinion. The relation of the realities corresponding to intelligence and opinion and the twofold divisions into which they fall we had better omit if we're not to land ourselves in an argument even longer than we've already had."

"Yes," said Glaucon; "I agree about all that, so far as I can follow you."

"So you agree in calling the ability to give an account of the essential nature of each particular thing Dialectic; and in saying that anyone who is unable to give such an account of things either to himself or to other people has to that extent failed to understand them."

"I can hardly do otherwise."

"Then doesn't the same apply to the Good? If a man can't define the Form of the Good and distinguish it clearly from everything else, and then defend it against all comers, not merely as a matter of opinion but in strict logic, and come through with his argument unshaken, you wouldn't say he knew what Absolute Good was, or indeed any other good. Any notion such a man has is based on opinion rather than knowledge, and he's living in a dream from which he's unlikely to awake this side of the grave, where he will finally sleep forever."

"With all that I agree emphatically."

"Well, then, if you ever really had the job of bringing up and educating these imaginary children of yours, you would not, I imagine, let them reach positions of high responsibility in society without having their ideas put in order?

"No."

"So you will lay it down that their powers of argument must be developed by an appropriate education."

"With your help I will."

"Then we can regard Dialectic as the coping-stone of our educational system, which completes the course of studies and needs no further addition."

"Yes."

"All you have to do now, then," I went on, "is to decide who should study these subjects and how."

"Yes, that's all."

"Do you remember the kind of people we picked when you were choosing our Rulers?"

"Of course I do."

"In most respects we should pick them again—we should prefer the steadiest and bravest and, so far as possible, the best-looking. But we shall also look not only for moral integrity and toughness, but for natural aptitude for this kind of education."

"And how would you define that?"

"Well, my dear chap," I said, "they need intellectual eagerness, and must learn easily. For the mind shirks mental effort more than physical, in which it can share the hard work with the body."

"True."

"They must have good memories, determination and a fondness for hard work. How, otherwise, will they be ready to go through with such an elaborate course of study on top of their physical training?"

"They won't unless they have every natural advantage."

"Which explains what is wrong with philosophy today and why it has a bad reputation; as we said before, it isn't taken seriously enough, and the people who take it up aren't genuine about it as they should be."

"How do you mean?" he asked.

"First of all," I said, "anyone who takes it up must have no inhibitions about hard work. He mustn't be only half inclined to work and half not —for instance, a man who is very fond of hunting and athletics and all kinds of physical exercise, but has no inclination to learn and dislikes intellectual effort of any kind. And there are people just as one-sided in the opposite way."

"That's very true."

"We shall regard as equally crippled for the pursuit of truth a mind which, while it detests deliberate lying, and will not abide it in itself and is indignant to find it in others, cheerfully acquiesces in conventional misrepresentations and feels no indignation when its own ignorance is shown up, but wallows in it like a pig in a sty."

"I entirely agree."

"We must be as careful to distinguish genuine and bogus in dealing with all the virtues — discipline, courage, broadmindedness and the rest. Failure to make the distinction on the part of an individual or a community merely leads to the unwitting employment of people who are unsound and bogus in some way whether as friends or rulers."

"That is very true."

"We must avoid these mistakes," I went on. "If we pick those who are sound in body and mind and then put them through our long course of instruction and training, Justice herself can't blame us and we shall preserve the constitution of our society; if we make any other choice the effect will be precisely the opposite, and we shall plunge philosophy even deeper in ridicule than it is at present."

"Which would be a shameful thing to do."

"It would," I agreed. "But I'm not sure I'm not being slightly ridiculous at the moment myself."

"How?"

"I was forgetting that we are amusing ourselves with an imaginary sketch, and got too worked up. I had in mind as I spoke the unjust criticisms that are made of philosophy, which annoyed me, and my anger at the critics made me speak more seriously than I should."

"Oh, come!" he said, "I didn't think you were too serious."

"Well, I felt I was. However, don't let's forget that when we were making our earlier choice, we chose elderly men; but that won't do now. We must not let Solon persuade us that as one grows old one's capacity for learning increases, any more than one's ability to run; the time for all serious effort is when we are young."

"Undoubtedly."

"Arithmetic and geometry and the other studies leading to Dialectic should be introduced in childhood, though we mustn't exercise any form of compulsion."

"Why?" he asked.

"Because a free man ought not to learn anything under duress. Compulsory physical exercise does no harm to the body, but compulsory learning never sticks in the mind."

"True."

"Then don't use compulsion," I said to him, "but let your children's lessons take the form of play. You will learn more about their natural abilities that way."

"There's something in what you say."

"Do you remember," I reminded him, "that we said that our children ought to be taken on horseback to watch fighting, and, if it was safe, taken close up and given their taste of blood, like your hounds?"

"Yes, I remember."

"Well, we must enrol in a select number those who show themselves most at home in all these exercises and studies and dangers."

"At what age?" he asked.

"As soon as their necessary physical training is over. During that time, whether it be two or three years, they won't be able to do anything else; physical fatigue and sleep are unfavourable to study. And one of the most important tests is to see how they show up in their physical training."

"True."

"After that time, then, at the age of twenty, some of them will be selected for promotion, and will have to bring together the disconnected subjects they studied in childhood and take a comprehensive view of their relationship with each other and with reality."

"That is the only way to make knowledge permanent."

"And also the best test of aptitude for Dialectic, which is the ability to take the comprehensive view."

"I agree."

"You will have to keep all this in view and make a further choice among your selected candidates when they pass the age of thirty. Those who show the required perseverance in their studies, in war, and in their other duties, will be promoted to higher privileges, and their ability to follow truth into the realm of pure reality, without the use of sight or any other sense, tested by means of Dialectic. And here, my friend, you will have to go to work very carefully."

"Why particularly?"

"Haven't you noticed the appalling harm done by Dialectic at present?"

"What harm?"

"It fills people with indiscipline."

"Oh, yes, I've noticed that."

"And does it surprise you?" I asked. "Aren't you sorry for the victims?"

"Why should I be?"

"Well, imagine a child who has been brought up in a large, rich, and powerful family, with many hangers-on; when he grows up he discovers that he is not the child of his so-called parents, but can't discover who his real parents are. Can you imagine how he will feel towards the hangers-on and his supposed parents, first while he still doesn't know they aren't his real parents, and then when he does? Shall I tell you what I should expect?"

"Yes, do."

"Well, I should expect that, so long as he didn't know they weren't his real parents, he would respect his mother and father and supposed relations more than the hangers-on, be more concerned with their needs, and less inclined to do or say anything outrageous to them, or to disobey them in matters of importance."

"Very likely."

"But when he discovered the truth, I should expect him to give up respecting them seriously and devote himself to the hangers-on; their influ- ·ence with him would increase, he'd associate with them openly and live by their standards, and, unless his natural instincts were particularly decent, he'd pay no more attention to his reputed parents and relations."

"That's all very likely. But," he asked, "what bearing has the illustration on philosophic discussions?"

"This. There are certain opinions about what is right and fair in which we are brought up from childhood, and whose authority we respect like that of our parents."

"True."

"And there are certain habits of an opposite kind, which have a deceitful attraction because of the pleasures they offer, but which no one of any decency gives in to, because he respects the authority of tradition."

"True again."

"Yes," I said, "but what happens when he is confronted with the question, What do you mean by "fair"?' When he gives the answer tradition has taught him, he is refuted in argument, and when that has happened many times and on many different grounds, he is driven to think that there's no difference between fair and foul, and so on with all the other moral values, like right and good, that he used to revere. What sort of respect for their authority do you think he'll feel at the end of it all?"

"He's bound to feel quite differently."

"Then when he's lost any respect or feeling for his former beliefs but not yet found the truth, where is he likely to turn? Won't it be to the deceitful attractions of pleasure?"

"Yes, it will."

"And so we see indiscipline supplanting tradition."

"Inevitably."

"Yet all this is a natural consequence of starting on philosophic discussions in this way, and, as I've just said, there's every reason for us to excuse it."

"Yes, and be sorry about it," he agreed.

"Then if you want to avoid being sorry for your thirty-year-olders, you must be very careful how you introduce them to such discussions."

"Very careful."

"And there's one great precaution you can take, which is to stop their getting a taste of them too young. You must have noticed how young men, after their first taste of argument, are always contradicting people just for the fun of it; someone proves them wrong, like puppies who love to pull and tear at anyone within reach."

"They like nothing better," he said.

"So when they've proved a lot of people wrong and been proved wrong often themselves, they soon slip into the belief that nothing they believed before was true; with the result that they discredit themselves and the whole business of philosophy in the eyes of the world."

"That's perfectly true," he said.

"But someone who's a bit older," I went on, "will refuse to have anything to do with this sort of idiocy; he won't contradict just for the fun of the thing but will be more likely to follow the lead of someone whose arguments are aimed at finding the truth. He's a more reasonable person and will get philosophy a better reputation."

"True."

"In fact all we've been saying has been said in the attempt to ensure that only men of steady and disciplined character shall be admitted to philosophic discussions, and not anyone, however unqualified, as happens at present."

"I entirely agree."

"Then suppose twice as long is spent on a continuous and intensive study of philosophy as we proposed should be spent on physical training, will that be enough?"

"Do you mean six years or four?"

"It doesn't matter," said I; "make it five. After that they must be sent down again into the Cave we spoke of, and compelled to hold any military or other office suitable for the young, so that they may have as much practical experience as their fellows. And here again they must be tested to see if they stand up to the temptations of all kinds or give way to them."

"And how long do you allow for this stage?"

"Fifteen years. And when they are fifty, those who have come through all our practical and intellectual tests with success must be brought to their final trial, and made to lift their mind's eye to look at the source of all light, and see the Good itself, which they can take as a pattern for ordering their own life as well as that of society and the individual. For the rest of their lives they will spend most of their time in philosophy, but when their turn comes they will turn to the weary business of politics and do their duty as

Rulers, not for the honour they get by it but as a matter of necessity. And so, when they have brought up successors like themselves, they will depart this life, and the state will set up a public memorial to them and sacrifice to them, if the Pythian Oracle approves, as divinities, or at any rate as saints."

"It's a fine picture you have drawn of our Rulers, Socrates."

"And some of them will be women," I reminded him. "All I have said about men applies equally to women, if they have the necessary qualifications."

"Of course," he agreed, "if they are to share equally in everything with the men, as we described."

"Well, then, do you agree that the society and constitution we have sketched is not merely an idle dream, difficult though its realization may be? The indispensable condition is that political power should be in the hands of one or more true philosophers. They would despise all present honours as mean and worthless, and care most for doing right and any rewards it may bring; and—most important and essential of all—they would, throughout their reorganization of society, serve and forward the interests of justice."

"How would they proceed?"

"They would begin by sending away into the country all citizens over the age of ten; having thus removed the children from the influence of their parents' present way of life, they would bring them up on their own methods and rules, which we have described. This is the best and quickest way to establish our society and constitution, and for it to succeed and bring its benefits to any people among which it is established."

"Yes, that's much the best way; and I think, Socrates," he added, "that you have explained very well how such a society would come into existence, if ever it did."

"Then haven't we said enough about this state of ours and the corresponding type of man? For it's surely obvious what type we shall want."

"Perfectly obvious," he agreed. "And I agree with you that there's no more to be said."

PART V

Isocrates:
Teacher of Statesmen

ISOCRATES (436-338 B.C.), a contemporary of Plato, opened a
school of rhetoric about 392 B.C., a few years before Plato's
Academy was founded. Cicero would later refer to Isocrates' school
as one from which, "as if it had been the Trojan horse," there came
forth nothing but princes.

Isocrates viewed his orations written as part of his work in the
school as literary efforts of the highest order. In a sense, they were
intended to express something so fundamental about life and character that they might come to occupy the place once held by poetry
in the literary and educational life of the Greeks. In one of his orations, the *Antidosis,* Isocrates said that if he succeeded in writing an
oration which truly gave expression to his character, his life, and the
kind of education to which he was devoted, then such an oration
would be a monument more noble than one of bronze. This calls to
mind Pindar's praise of the poet and poetry in an earlier, less enlightened day.

Marrou has pointed out that the most famous Sophists aimed to teach "the art of politics" and that the arts of persuasion and rhetoric constituted the largest part of the Sophists' curriculum for prospective statesmen. Isocrates' place in the development of Greek educational ideals may best be understood if he is recognized as one of the finest of the Sophists. As a teacher of rhetoric, he believed there was more to his work than developing the techniques of speechmaking. Quintilian's later characterization of the true orator as "the good man speaking well" brings to mind Isocrates' conception of what his most successful students might come to be.

Like the philosopher Plato, Isocrates sought to educate a man to wisdom—to know the good thing and do it. But, unlike Plato, Isocrates did not concern himself with seeking the absolute Form of Goodness; with other relativistic Sophists, Isocrates thought that such philosophic efforts were exercises in futility. It was not that he opposed philosophy, but his conception of philosophy was different from that of Plato. Instead of seeking a kind of virtue and wisdom that was thought to be beyond the ken of most ordinary cultured Greeks and would likely remain obscure from their vision, Isocrates claimed that there is a kind of virtue and wisdom that can be recognized by all reasonably intelligent human beings if the proper care is taken with their education. In brief, he thought that the Greeks, and notably the Athenians, had developed a culture of which they could justly be proud and that this could stand as a secure, though not infallible, basis for education and the further development of culture.

Praising Athens for producing the teachers of the world, Isocrates set forth a happy statement which suggests probably better than does any other one passage from his writings the possibility which this teacher of rhetoric envisages for the Athenian cultural achievement: "The name 'Hellenes' suggests no longer a race but an intelligence, and . . . the title 'Hellenes' is applied rather to those who share our culture than to those who share a common blood." Surely this statement places Isocrates among the best of the Sophists, and the educational aim which it implies, while Greek in its origin, is larger than Greek in its prospects for a wider view of mankind.

The selections from his orations included here are presented so as to develop three related themes: (1) the glory and greatness of Athens, which gave philosophy to the world, which it also provided with teachers (Athenians surpassed others both in natural endowments and in cultural achievements), with a plea for recognition of what was best in an older moral education; (2) Isocrates' conception of the art of discourse, of philosophy, and of the sort of wisdom it is possible to achieve; and (3) a plea to orators to address themselves to significant subjects as well as a reminder that the good orator will speak in a manner worthy of his subject.

15. Orations

Isocrates

I reproach men in private life when they succeed in a few things and fail in many, and regard them as falling short of what they ought to be; and, more than that, when men are sprung from noble ancestors and yet are only a little better than those who are distinguished for depravity, and much worse than their fathers, I rebuke them and would counsel them to cease from being what they are. And I am of the same mind also regarding public affairs. For I think that we ought not to be proud or even satisfied should we have shown ourselves more law-regarding than men accursed by the gods and afflicted with madness, but ought much rather to feel aggrieved and resentful should we prove to be worse than our ancestors; for it is their excellence and not the depravity of the Thirty which we should strive to emulate, especially since it behoves Athenians to be the best among mankind.

This is not the first time that I have expressed this sentiment; I have done so many times and before many people. For I know that while other regions produce varieties of fruits and trees and animals, each peculiar to its locality and much better than those of other lands, our own country is able to bear and nurture men who are not only the most gifted in the world in the arts and in the powers of action and of speech, but are also above all others in valour and in virtue.

This conclusion we may justly draw from the ancient struggles which they carried on against the Amazons and the Thracians and all of the Peloponnesians, and also from the wars which they waged against the Persians,

Reprinted by permission of the publishers and *The Loeb Classical Library* from George Norlin, translator, *Isocrates*, Volume II (Cambridge, Mass.: Harvard University Press, 1945). *Areopagiticus*, pp. 151, 153. (The translator's notes are not included here.)

in which, both when they fought alone and when they were aided by the Peloponnesians, whether on land or on the sea, they were victorious over the barbarians and were adjudged the meed of valour; for they could not have achieved these things, had they not far surpassed other men in the endowments of nature.

But let no one think that this eulogy is appropriate to those who compose the present government—far from it; for such words are a tribute to those who show themselves worthy of the valour of their forefathers, but a reproach to those who disgrace their noble origin by their slackness and their cowardice. And this is just what we are doing; for you shall have the truth. For although we were blessed with such a nature at our birth, we have not cherished and preserved it, but have, on the contrary, fallen into folly and confusion and lust after evil ways.

. . .

The Athenians of that day were not watched over by many preceptors during their boyhood only to be allowed to do what they liked when they attained to manhood; on the contrary, they were subjected to greater supervision in the very prime of their vigour than when they were boys. For our forefathers placed such strong emphasis upon sobriety that they put the supervision of decorum in charge of the Council of the Areopagus—a body which was composed exclusively of men who were of noble birth and had exemplified in their lives exceptional virtue and sobriety, and which, therefore, naturally excelled all the other councils of Hellas. And we may judge what this institution was at that time even by what happens at the present day; for even now, when everything connected with the election and the examination of magistrates has fallen into neglect, we shall find that those who in all else that they do are insufferable, yet when they enter the Areopagus hesitate to indulge their true nature, being governed rather by its traditions than by their own evil instincts. So great was the fear which its members inspired in the depraved and such was the memorial of their own virtue and sobriety which they left behind them in the place of their assembly.

Such, then, as I have described, was the nature of the Council which our forefathers charged with the supervision of moral discipline—a council which considered that those who believed that the best citizens are produced in a state where the laws are prescribed with the greatest exactness were blind to the truth; for in that case there would be no reason why all

Reprinted by permission of the publishers and *The Loeb Classical Library* from George Norlin, translator, *Isocrates,* Volume II (Cambridge, Mass.: Harvard University Press). *Areopagiticus,* pp. 127, 129, 131, 133, 135. (The translator's notes are not included here.)

of the Hellenes should not be on the same level, at any rate in so far as it is easy to borrow written codes from each other. But in fact, they thought, virtue is not advanced by written laws but by the habits of everyday life; for the majority of men tend to assimilate the manners and morals amid which they have been reared. Furthermore, they held that where there is a multitude of specific laws, it is a sign that the state is badly governed; for it is in the attempt to build up dikes against the spread of crime that men in such a state feel constrained to multiply the laws. Those who are rightly governed, on the other hand, do not need to fill their porticoes with written statutes, but only to cherish justice in their souls; for it is not by legislation, but by morals, that states are well directed, since men who are badly reared will venture to transgress even laws which are drawn up with minute exactness, whereas those who are well brought up will be willing to respect even a simple code. Therefore, being of this mind, our forefathers did not seek to discover first how they should penalize men who were lawless, but how they should produce citizens who would refrain from any punishable act; for they thought that this was their duty, while it was proper for private enemies alone to be zealous in the avenging of crime.

Now our forefathers exercised care over all the citizens, but most of all over the young. They saw that at this age men are most unruly of temper and filled with a multitude of desires, and that their spirits are most in need of being curbed by devotion to noble pursuits and by congenial labour; for only such occupations can attract and hold men who have been educated liberally and trained in high-minded ways.

However, since it was not possible to direct all into the same occupations, because of differences in their circumstances, they assigned to each one a vocation which was in keeping with his means; for they turned the needier towards farming and trade, knowing that poverty comes about through idleness, and evil-doing through poverty. Accordingly, they believed that by removing the root of evil they would deliver the young from the sins which spring from it. On the other hand, they compelled those who possessed sufficient means to devote themselves to horsemanship, athletics, hunting, and philosophy, observing that by these pursuits some are enabled to achieve excellence, others to abstain from many vices.

But when they had laid down these ordinances they were not negligent regarding what remained to be done, but, dividing the city into districts and the country into townships, they kept watch over the life of every citizen, haling the disorderly before the Council, which now rebuked, now warned, and again punished them according to their deserts. For they understood that there are two ways both of encouraging men to do wrong and of checking them from evil-doing; for where no watch is kept over such matters and the judgments are not strict, there even honest natures grow corrupt; but where, again, it is not easy for wrong-doers either to escape detection or, when detected, to obtain indulgence, there the impulse to do evil disappears. Understanding this, they restrained the people from wrong-doing in both ways—both by punishment and by watchfulness; for so far from failing to detect those who had gone astray, they actually saw in advance which were likely to commit some offence. Therefore the young men did not waste their time in the gambling-dens or with the flute-girls or in the kind of company in which they now spend their days, but remained steadfastly in the pursuits to which they had been assigned, admiring and emulating those who excelled in these. And so strictly did they avoid the market-place that even when they were at times compelled to pass through it, they were seen to do this with great modesty and sobriety of manner. To contradict one's elders or to be impudent to them was then considered more reprehensible than it is nowadays to sin against one's parents; and to eat or drink in a tavern was something which no one, not even an honest slave, would venture to do; for they cultivated the manners of a gentleman, not those of a buffoon; and as for those who had a turn for jesting and playing the clown, whom we today speak of as clever wits, they were then looked upon as sorry fools.

.   .   .

But reflect upon the glory and the greatness of the deeds wrought by our city and our ancestors, review them in your minds and consider what kind of man was he, what was his birth and what the character of his education, who expelled the tyrants, brought the people into their own, and established our democratic state; what sort was he who conquered the barbarians in the battle at Marathon and won for the city the glory which has come to Athens from this victory; what was he who after him liberated the Hellenes and led our forefathers forth to the leadership and power which they achieved, and who, besides, appreciating the natural advantage of the Piraeus, girded the city with walls in despite of the Lacedaemonians; and what manner of man was he who after him filled the Acropolis with gold and silver and made the homes of the Athenians to overflow with prosperity and wealth: for you will find if you review the career of each of these, that it was not those who lived unscrupulously or negligently nor those who did not stand out from the multitude who accomplished these things, but that it was men who were superior and pre-eminent, not only in birth and reputation, but in wisdom and eloquence, who have been the authors of all our blessings.

Reprinted by permission of the publishers and *The Loeb Classical Library* from George Norlin, translator, *Isocrates,* Volume II (Cambridge, Mass.: Harvard University Press, 1945). *Antidosis,* pp. 355, 357. (The translator's notes are not included here.)

You ought to lay this lesson to heart and, while seeing to it in behalf of the mass of the people that they shall obtain their just rights in the trials of their personal disputes and that they shall have their due share of the other privileges which are common to all, you ought, on the other hand, to welcome and honour and cherish those who stand out from the multitude both in ability and in training and those who aspire to such eminence, since you know that leadership in great and noble enterprises, and the power to keep the city safe from danger and to preserve the rule of the people, rests with such men, and not with the sycophants.

.   .   .

. . . Whatever advantage there is in our associating together, this also has been compassed by our city, Athens. Besides, it is possible to find with us as nowhere else the most faithful friendships and to enjoy the most varied social intercourse; and, furthermore, to see contests not alone of speed and strength, but of eloquence and wisdom and of all the other arts—and for these the greatest prizes; since in addition to those which the city herself sets up, she prevails upon the rest of the world also to offer prizes; for the judgments pronounced by us command such great approbation that all mankind accept them gladly. But apart from these considerations, while the assemblages at the other great festivals are brought together only at long intervals and are soon dispersed, our city throughout all time is a festival for those who visit her.

Philosophy, moreover, which has helped to discover and establish all these institutions, which has educated us for public affairs and made us gentle towards each other, which has distinguished between the misfortunes that are due to ignorance and those which spring from necessity, and taught us to guard against the former and to bear the latter nobly—philosophy, I say, was given to the world by our city. And Athens it is that has honoured eloquence, which all men crave and envy in its possessors; for she realized that this is the one endowment of our nature which singles us out from all living creatures, and that by using this advantage we have risen above them in all other respects as well; she saw that in other activities the fortunes of life are so capricious that in them often the wise fail and the foolish succeed, whereas beautiful and artistic speech is never allotted to ordinary men, but is the work of an intelligent mind, and that it is in this respect that those who are accounted wise and ignorant present the strongest contrast; and she knew, furthermore, that whether men have been liberally educated from their earliest years is not to be determined by their

Reprinted by permission of the publishers and *The Loeb Classical Library* from George Norlin, translator, *Isocrates,* Volume I (Cambridge, Mass.: Harvard University Press, 1945). *Panegyricus,* pp. 147, 149. (The translator's notes are not included here.)

courage or their wealth or such advantages, but is made manifest most of all by their speech, and that this has proved itself to be the surest sign of culture in every one of us, and that those who are skilled in speech are not only men of power in their own cities but are also held in honour in other states. And so far has our city distanced the rest of mankind in thought and in speech that her pupils have become the teachers of the rest of the world; and she has brought it about that the name "Hellenes" suggests no longer a race but an intelligence, and that the title "Hellenes" is applied rather to those who share our culture than to those who share a common blood.

.   .   .

16. Orations

Isocrates

In my treatment of the art of discourse, I desire, like the genealogists, to start at the beginning. It is acknowledged that the nature of man is compounded of two parts, the physical and the mental, and no one would deny that of these two the mind comes first and is of greater worth; for it is the function of the mind to decide both on personal and on public questions, and of the body to be servant to the judgments of the mind. Since this is so, certain of our ancestors, long before our time, seeing that many arts had been devised for other things, while none had been prescribed for the body and for the mind, invented and bequeathed to us two disciplines, physical training for the body, of which gymnastics is a part, and, for the mind, philosophy, which I am going to explain. These are twin arts—parallel and complementary—by which their masters prepare the mind to become more intelligent and the body to become more serviceable, not separating sharply the two kinds of education, but using similar methods of instruction, exercise, and other forms of discipline.

For when they take their pupils in hand, the physical trainers instruct their followers in the postures which have been devised for bodily contests, while the teachers of philosophy impart all the forms of discourse in which the mind expresses itself. Then, when they have made them familiar and thoroughly conversant with these lessons, they set them at exercises, ha-

Reprinted by permission of the publishers and *The Loeb Classical Library* from George Norlin, translator, *Isocrates*, Volume II (Cambridge, Mass.: Harvard University Press, 1945). *Antidosis*, pp. 289, 291, 293, 295. (The translator's notes are not included here.)

bituate them to work, and require them to combine in practice the particular things which they have learned, in order that they may grasp them more firmly and bring their theories into closer touch with the occasions for applying them—I say "theories," for no system of knowledge can possibly cover these occasions, since in all cases they elude our science. Yet those who most apply their minds to them and are able to discern the consequences which for the most part grow out of them, will most often meet these occasions in the right way.

Watching over them and training them in this manner, both the teachers of gymnastic and the teachers of discourse are able to advance their pupils to a point where they are better men and where they are stronger in their thinking or in the use of their bodies. However, neither class of teachers is in possession of a science by which they can make capable athletes or capable orators out of whomsoever they please. They can contribute in some degree to these results, but these powers are never found in their perfection save in those who excel by virtue both of talent and of training.

I have given you now some impression of what philosophy is. But I think that you will get a still clearer idea of its powers if I tell you what professions I make to those who want to become my pupils. I say to them that if they are to excel in oratory or in managing affairs or in any line of work, they must, first of all, have a natural aptitude for that which they have elected to do; secondly, they must submit to training and master the knowledge of their particular subject, whatever it may be in each case; and, finally, they must become versed and practised in the use and application of their art; for only on these conditions can they become fully competent and pre-eminent in any line of endeavour. In this process, master and pupil each has his place; no one but the pupil can furnish the necessary capacity; no one but the master, the ability to impart knowledge; while both have a part in the exercises of practical application: for the master must painstakingly direct his pupil, and the latter must rigidly follow the master's instructions.

Now these observations apply to any and all the arts. If anyone, ignoring the other arts, were to ask me which of these factors has the greatest power in the education of an orator I should answer that natural ability is paramount and comes before all else. For given a man with a mind which is capable of finding out and learning the truth and of working hard and remembering what it learns, and also with a voice and a clarity of utterance which are able to captivate the audience, not only by what he says, but by the music of his words, and, finally, with an assurance which is not an expression of bravado, but which, tempered by sobriety, so fortifies the spirit that he is no less at ease in addressing all his fellow-citizens than in reflecting to himself—who does not know that such a man might, without the advantage of an elaborate education and with only a superficial and common training, be an orator such as has never, perhaps, been seen among the Hellenes? Again, we know that men who are less generously endowed by nature but excel in experience and practice, not only improve upon themselves, but surpass others who, though highly gifted, have been too negligent of their talents. It follows, therefore, that either one of these factors may produce an able speaker or an able man of affairs, but both of them combined in the same person might produce a man incomparable among his fellows.

These, then, are my views as to the relative importance of native ability and practice. I cannot, however, make a like claim for education; its powers are not equal nor comparable to theirs. For if one should take lessons in all the principles of oratory and master them with the greatest thoroughness, he might, perhaps, become a more pleasing speaker than most, but let him stand up before the crowd and lack one thing only, namely, assurance, and he would not be able to utter a word.

.   .   .

We ought, therefore, to think of the art of discourse just as we think of the other arts, and not to form opposite judgments about similar things, nor show ourselves intolerant toward that power which, of all the faculties which belong to the nature of man, is the source of most of our blessings. For in the other powers which we possess, as I have already said on a former occasion, we are in no respect superior to other living creatures; nay, we are inferior to many in swiftness and in strength and in other resources; but, because there has been implanted in us the power to persuade each other and to make clear to each other whatever we desire, not only have we escaped the life of wild beasts, but we have come together and founded cities and made laws and invented arts; and, generally speaking, there is no institution devised by man which the power of speech has not helped us to establish. For this it is which has laid down laws concerning things just and unjust, and things honourable and base; and if it were not for these ordinances we should not be able to live with one another. It is by this also that we confute the bad and extol the good. Through this we educate the ignorant and appraise the wise; for the power to speak well is taken as the surest index of a sound understanding, and discourse which is true and lawful and just is the outward image of a good and faithful soul. With this

Reprinted by permission of the publishers and *The Loeb Classical Library* from George Norlin, translator, *Isocrates,* Volume II. (Cambridge, Mass.: Harvard University Press, 1945). *Antidosis,* pp. 327, 329, 331, 333, 335, 337, 339, 341, 343. (The translator's notes are not included here.)

faculty we both contend against others on matters which are open to dispute and seek light for ourselves on things which are unknown; for the same arguments which we use in persuading others when we speak in public, we employ also when we deliberate in our own thoughts; and, while we call eloquent those who are able to speak before a crowd, we regard as sage those who most skilfully debate their problems in their own minds. And, if there is need to speak in brief summary of this power, we shall find that none of the things which are done with intelligence take place without the help of speech, but that in all our actions as well as in all our thoughts speech is our guide, and is most employed by those who have the most wisdom.

I believe that the teachers who are skilled in disputation and those who are occupied with astronomy and geometry and studies of that sort do not injure but, on the contrary, benefit their pupils, not so much as they profess, but more than others give them credit for. Most men see in such studies nothing but empty talk and hair-splitting; for none of these disciplines has any useful application either to private or to public affairs; nay, they are not even remembered for any length of time after they are learned because they do not attend us through life nor do they lend aid in what we do, but are wholly divorced from our necessities. But I am neither of this opinion nor am I far removed from it; rather it seems to me both that those who hold that this training is of no use in practical life are right and that those who speak in praise of it have truth on their side. If there is a contradiction in this statement, it is because these disciplines are different in their nature from the other studies which make up our education; for the other branches avail us only after we have gained a knowledge of them, whereas these studies can be of no benefit to us after we have mastered them unless we have elected to make our living from this source, and only help us while we are in the process of learning. For while we are occupied with the subtlety and exactness of astronomy and geometry and are forced to apply our minds to difficult problems, and are, in addition, being habituated to speak and apply ourselves to what is said and shown to us, and not to let our wits go wool-gathering, we gain the power, after being exercised and sharpened on these disciplines, of grasping and learning more easily and more quickly those subjects which are of more importance and of greater value. I do not, however, think it proper to apply the term "philosophy" to a training which is no help to us in the present either in our speech or in our actions, but rather I would call it a gymnastic of the mind and a preparation for philosophy. It is, to be sure, a study more advanced than that which boys in school pursue, but it is for the most part the same sort of thing; for they also when they have laboured through their lessons in grammar, music, and the other branches, are not a whit advanced in their ability to speak and deliberate on affairs, but they have increased their aptitude for mastering greater and more serious studies. I would, therefore, advise young men to spend some time on these disciplines but not to allow their minds to be dried up by these barren subtleties, nor to be stranded on the speculations of the ancient sophists, who maintain, some of them, that the sum of things is made up of infinite elements; Empedocles that it is made up of four, with strife and love operating among them; Ion, of not more than three; Alcmaeon, of only two; Parmenides and Melissus, of one; and Gorgias, of none at all. For I think that such curiosities of thought are on a par with jugglers' tricks which, though they do not profit anyone, yet attract great crowds of the empty-minded, and I hold that men who want to do some good in the world must banish utterly from their interests all vain speculations and all activities which have no bearing on our lives.

Now I have spoken and advised you enough on these studies for the present. It remains to tell you about "wisdom" and "philosophy." It is true that if one were pleading a case on any other issue it would be out of place to discuss these words (for they are foreign to all litigation), but it is appropriate for me, since I am being tried on such an issue, and since I hold that what some people call philosophy is not entitled to that name, to define and explain to you what philosophy, properly conceived, really is. My view of this question is, as it happens, very simple. For since it is not in the nature of man to attain a science by the possession of which we can know positively what we should do or what we should say, in the next resort I hold that man to be wise who is able by his powers of conjecture to arrive generally at the best course, and I hold that man to be a philosopher who occupies himself with the studies from which he will most quickly gain that kind of insight.

What the studies are which have this power I can tell you, although I hesitate to do so; they are so contrary to popular belief and so very far removed from the opinions of the rest of the world, that I am afraid lest when you first hear them you will fill the whole court-room with your murmurs and your cries. Nevertheless, in spite of my misgivings, I shall attempt to tell you about them; for I blush at the thought that anyone might suspect me of betraying the truth to save my old age and the little of life remaining to me. But, I beg of you, do not, before you have heard me, judge that I could have been so mad as to choose deliberately, when my fate is in your hands, to express to you ideas which are repugnant to your opinions if I had not believed that these ideas follow logically on what I have previously said, and that I could support them with true and convincing proofs.

I consider that the kind of art which can implant honesty and justice in depraved natures has never existed and does not now exist, and that people who profess that power will grow weary and cease from their vain pretensions before such an education is ever found. But I do hold that people can become better and worthier if they conceive an ambition to speak well, if they become possessed of the desire to be able to persuade their hearers, and, finally, if they set their hearts on seizing their advantage—I do not mean "advantage" in the sense given to that word by the empty-minded, but advantage in the true meaning of that term; and that this is so I think I shall presently make clear.

For, in the first place, when anyone elects to speak or write discourses which are worthy of praise and honour, it is not conceivable that he will support causes which are unjust or petty or devoted to private quarrels, and not rather those which are great and honourable, devoted to the welfare of man and our common good; for if he fails to find causes of this character, he will accomplish nothing to the purpose. In the second place, he will select from all the actions of men which bear upon his subject those examples which are the most illustrious and the most edifying; and, habituating himself to contemplate and appraise such examples, he will feel their influence not only in the preparation of a given discourse but in all the actions of his life. It follows, then, that the power to speak well and think right will reward the man who approaches the art of discourse with love of wisdom and love of honour.

Furthermore, mark you, the man who wishes to persuade people will not be negligent as to the matter of character; no, on the contrary, he will apply himself above all to establish a most honourable name among his fellow-citizens; for who does not know that words carry greater conviction when spoken by men of good repute than when spoken by men who live under a cloud, and that the argument which is made by a man's life is of more weight than that which is furnished by words? Therefore, the stronger a man's desire to persuade his hearers, the more zealously will he strive to be honourable and to have the esteem of his fellow-citizens.

And let no one of you suppose that while all other people realize how much the scales of persuasion incline in favour of one who has the approval of his judges, the devotees of philosophy alone are blind to the power of good will. In fact, they appreciate this even more thoroughly than others, and they know, furthermore, that probabilities and proofs and all forms of persuasion support only the points in a case to which they are severally applied, whereas an honourable reputation not only lends greater persuasiveness to the words of the man who possesses it, but adds greater lustre to his deeds, and is, therefore, more zealously to be sought after by men of intelligence than anything else in the world.

I come now to the question of "advantage"—the most difficult of the points I have raised. If any one is under the impression that people who rob others or falsify accounts or do any evil thing get the advantage, he is wrong in his thinking; for none are at a greater disadvantage throughout their lives than such men; none are found in more difficult straits, none live in greater ignominy; and, in a word, none are more miserable than they. No, you ought to believe rather that those are better off now and will receive the advantage in the future at the hands of the gods who are the most righteous and the most faithful in their devotions, and that those receive the better portion at the hands of men who are the most conscientious in their dealings with their associates, whether in their homes or in public life, and are themselves esteemed as the noblest among their fellows.

This is verily the truth, and it is well for us to adopt this way of speaking on the subject, since, as things now are, Athens has in many respects been plunged into such a state of topsy-turvy and confusion that some of our people no longer use words in their proper meaning but wrest them from the most honourable associations and apply them to the basest pursuits. On the one hand, they speak of men who play the buffoon and have a talent for mocking and mimicking as "gifted"—an appellation which should be reserved for men endowed with the highest excellence; while, on the other hand, they think of men who indulge their depraved and criminal instincts and who for small gains acquire a base reputation as "getting the advantage," instead of applying this term to the most righteous and the most upright, that is, to men who take advantage of the good and not the evil things of life. They characterize men who ignore our practical needs and delight in the mental juggling of the ancient sophists as "students of philosophy," but refuse this name to whose who pursue and practise those studies which will enable us to govern wisely both our own households and the commonwealth—which should be the objects of our toil, of our study, and of our every act.

.   .   .

17. Orations

Isocrates

Many times have I wondered at those who first convoked the national assemblies and established the athletic games, amazed that they should have thought the prowess of men's bodies to be deserving of so great boun-

Reprinted by permission of the publishers and *The Loeb Classical Library* from George Norlin, translator, *Isocrates,* Volume I (Cambridge, Mass.: Harvard University Press, 1945). *Panegyricus,* pp. 121, 123, 125, 127. (The translator's notes are not included here.)

ties, while to those who had toiled in private for the public good and trained their own minds so as to be able to help also their fellow-men they apportioned no reward whatsoever, when, in all reason, they ought rather to have made provision for the latter; for if all the athletes should acquire twice the strength which they now possess, the rest of the world would be no better off; but let a single man attain to wisdom, and all men will reap the benefit who are willing to share his insight.

Yet I have not on this account lost heart nor chosen to abate my labours; on the contrary, believing that I shall have a sufficient reward in the approbation which my discourse will itself command, I have come before you to give my counsels on the war against the barbarians and on concord among ourselves. I am, in truth, not unaware that many of those who have claimed to be sophists have rushed upon this theme, but I hope to rise so far superior to them that it will seem as if no word had ever been spoken by my rivals upon this subject; and, at the same time, I have singled out as the highest kind of oratory that which deals with the greatest affairs and, while best displaying the ability of those who speak, brings most profit to those who hear; and this oration is of that character. In the next place, the moment for action has not yet gone by, and so made it now futile to bring up this question; for then, and only then, should we cease to speak, when the conditions have come to an end and there is no longer any need to deliberate about them, or when we see that the discussion of them is so complete that there is left to others no room to improve upon what has been said. But so long as conditions go on as before, and what has been said about them is inadequate, is it not our duty to scan and study this question, the right decision of which will deliver us from our mutual warfare, our present confusion, and our greatest ills?

Furthermore, if it were possible to present the same subject matter in one form and in no other, one might have reason to think it gratuitous to weary one's hearers by speaking again in the same manner as his predecessors; but since oratory is of such a nature that it is possible to discourse on the same subject matter in many different ways—to represent the great as lowly or invest the little with grandeur, to recount the things of old in a new manner or set forth events of recent date in an old fashion—it follows that one must not shun the subjects upon which others have spoken before, but must try to speak better than they. For the deeds of the past are, indeed, an inheritance common to us all; but the ability to make proper use of them at the appropriate time, to conceive the right sentiments about them in each instance, and to set them forth in finished phrase, is the peculiar gift of the wise. And it is my opinion that the study of oratory as well as the other arts would make the greatest advance if we should admire and honour, not those who make the first beginnings in their crafts, but those who are the most finished craftsmen in each, and not those who seek to speak on subjects on which no one has spoken before, but those who know how to speak as no one else could.

Yet there are some who carp at discourses which are beyond the powers of ordinary men and have been elaborated with extreme care, and who have gone so far astray that they judge the most ambitious oratory by the standard of the pleas made in the petty actions of the courts; as if both kinds should be alike and should not be distinguished, the one by plainness of style, the other by display; or as if they themselves saw clearly the happy mean, while the man who knows how to speak elegantly could not speak simply and plainly if he chose. Now these people deceive no one; clearly they praise those who are near their own level. I, for my part, am not concerned with such men, but rather with those who will not tolerate, but will resent, any carelessness of phrase, and will seek to find in my speeches a quality which they will not discover in others. Addressing myself to these, I shall proceed with my theme, after first vaunting a little further my own powers. For I observe that the other orators in their introductions seek to conciliate their hearers and make excuses for the speeches which they are about to deliver, sometimes alleging that their preparation has been on the spur of the moment, sometimes urging that it is difficult to find words to match the greatness of their theme. But as for myself, if I do not speak in a manner worthy of my subject and of my reputation and of the time which I have spent — not merely the hours which have been devoted to my speech but also all the years which I have lived — I bid you show me no indulgence but hold me up to ridicule and scorn; for there is nothing of the sort which I do not deserve to suffer, if indeed, being no better than the others, I make promises so great.

.   .   .

There are some who are much pleased with themselves if, after setting up an absurd and self-contradictory subject, they succeed in discussing it in tolerable fashion; and men have grown old, some asserting that it is impossible to say, or to gainsay, what is false, or to speak on both sides of the same questions, others maintaining that courage and wisdom and justice are identical, and that we possess none of these as natural qualities, but that there is only one sort of knowledge concerned with them all; and still others waste their time in captious disputations that are not only entirely useless, but are sure to make trouble for their disciples.

Reprinted by permission of the publishers and *The Loeb Classical Library* from La Rue Van Hook, translator, *Isocrates,* Volume III. (Cambridge, Mass.: Harvard University Press, 1945). *Helen,* pp. 61, 63, 65, 67. (The translator's notes are not included here.)

For my part, if I observed that this futile affectation had arisen only recently in rhetoric and that these men were priding themselves upon the novelty of their inventions, I should not be surprised at them to such degree; but as it is, who is so backward in learning as not to know that Protagoras and the sophists of his time have left to us compositions of similar character and even far more overwrought than these? For how could one surpass Gorgias, who dared to assert that nothing exists of the things that are, or Zeno, who ventured to prove the same things as possible and again as impossible, or Melissus who, although things in nature are infinite in number, made it his task to find proofs that the whole is one! Nevertheless, although these men so clearly have shown that it is easy to contrive false statements on any subject that may be proposed, they still waste time on this rhetorical method. They ought to give up the use of this claptrap, which pretends to prove things by verbal quibbles, which in fact have long since been refuted, and to pursue the truth, to instruct their pupils in the practical affairs of our government and train to expertness therein, bearing in mind that likely conjecture about useful things is far preferable to exact knowledge of the useless, and that to be a little superior in important things is of greater worth than to be pre-eminent in petty things that are without value for living.

But the truth is that these men care for naught save enriching themselves at the expense of the youth. It is their "philosophy" applied to eristic disputations that effectively produces this result; for these rhetoricians care nothing at all for either private or public affairs, but take most pleasure in those discourses which are of no practical service in any particular. These young men, to be sure, may well be pardoned for holding such views; for in all matters they are and always have been inclined toward what is extraordinary and astounding. But those who profess to give them training are deserving of censure because, while they condemn those who deceive in cases involving private contracts in business and those who are dishonest in what they say, yet they themselves are guilty of more reprehensible conduct; for the former wrong sundry other persons, but the latter inflict most injury upon their own pupils. And they have caused mendacity to increase to such a degree that now certain men, seeing these persons prospering from such practices, have the effrontery to write that the life of beggars and exiles is more enviable than that of the rest of mankind, and they use this as a proof that, if they can speak ably on ignoble subjects, it follows that in dealing with subjects of real worth they would easily find abundance of arguments. The most ridiculous thing of all, in my opinion, is this, that by these arguments they seek to convince us that they possess knowledge of the science of government, when they might be demonstrating it by actual work in their professed subject; for it is fitting that those who lay claim to learning and profess to be wise men should excel laymen and be better than they, not in fields neglected by everybody else, but where all are rivals. But as it is, their conduct resembles that of an athlete who, although pretending to be the best of all athletes, enters a contest in which no one would condescend to meet him. For what sensible man would undertake to praise misfortunes? No, it is obvious that they take refuge in such topics because of weakness. Such compositions follow one set road and this road is neither difficult to find, nor to learn, nor to imitate. On the other hand, discourses that are of general import, those that are trustworthy, and all of similar nature, are devised and expressed through the medium of a variety of forms and occasions of discourse whose opportune use is hard to learn, and their composition is more difficult as it is more arduous to practise dignity than buffoonery and seriousness than levity. The strongest proof is this: no one who has chosen to praise bumble-bees and salt and kindred topics has ever been at a loss for words, yet those who have essayed to speak on subjects recognized as good or noble, or of superior moral worth have all fallen far short of the possibilities which these subjects offer. For it does not belong to the same mentality to do justice to both kinds of subjects; on the contrary, while it is easy by eloquence to overdo the trivial themes, it is difficult to reach the heights of greatness of the others; and while on famous subjects one rarely finds thoughts which no one has previously uttered, yet on trifling and insignificant topics whatever the speaker may chance to say is entirely original.

.   .   .

PART VI

Aristotle on a Science of the Good and of the State

A RISTOTLE (384-322 B.C.), like his teacher Plato, found an intriguing relationship between the good for man and for the state. The nature of the relationship is such that his systematic inquiry into the subject matter bearing on the good *(Nichomachean Ethics)* leads directly into the subject matter bearing on the state *(Politics)*. Indeed, he says near the beginning of the *Ethics* that the end of the state is the good for man, which means that ethics, in a certain sense, is political science. And he writes in the *Politics* that the end of individuals and of states is the same. The three things which make men good and virtuous are nature, habit, and rational principle; to become good and virtuous, one's nature, habit, and rational principles must be in harmony with one another. The way of making them harmonious is clearly an educational question, for while men have certain natural gifts, these are shaped by habit and are given direction by the persuasion of rational principles. In short, goodness and virtue in men and in states are not entirely a matter of chance but are the result of purpose and knowledge.

It is *man* who has purpose, who comes to know whatever gods may do and know, and who determines what constitutes good purposes and knowledge. Aristotle opened his *Metaphysics* with the words, "All men by nature desire to know." His thoroughgoing naturalism—expressed here as the view that it is natural for man to want to know—has been one of Aristotle's most enduring characteristics not only in the sense that it places him squarely within the long-standing Greek tradition that man is continuous with nature and not apart from it but also because his unique contribution to this tradition was to attempt to determine the criteria by which natural things can be determined to be the kinds of things they are and the reasons why they are those kinds of things. In other words, Aristotle was a scientist in theory and in practice—he established the criteria for adequacy of treatment of various subject matters and then attempted to treat the subject matters according to those criteria. This means, as he says in the *Ethics,* that a discussion of an inquiry into a particular subject matter "will be adequate if it has as much clearness as the subject matter admits of"; one should therefore expect different criteria in a political science from those in a mathematical science.

A beautiful illustration of Aristotle's naturalism is found in the *Politics,* where he maintains that a study of the origins of the state leads him to the conclusion that the state is a creation of nature. This means that man is a "political animal" or, put in another way, man has a "social instinct." However it is put, man needs the state to actualize his potentiality. Again, it is "natural" that the end of individuals and of states be the same. And men, not gods, must determine what constitutes the end and what means are to be employed to seek it. Aristotle's inquiry in the *Ethics* and in the *Politics* constitutes the most thoroughgoing effort of the Greek mind up to his time to make a *science* of the inquiry into the nature of man's chief good and into finding out how to become good. For Aristotle, educational matters turn on the nature of ethical and political inquiry; indeed, an explicit treatment of education is part of this inquiry.

18. Nichomachean Ethics

Aristotle

Every art and every inquiry, and similarly every action and pursuit, is thought to aim at some good; and for this reason the good has rightly been declared to be that at which all things aim. But a certain difference is found among ends; some are activities, others are products apart from the activities that produce them. Where there are ends apart from the actions, it is the nature of the products to be better than the activities. Now, as there are many actions, arts, and sciences, their ends also are many; the end of the medical art is health, that of shipbuilding a vessel, that of strategy victory, that of economics wealth. But where such arts fall under a single capacity —as bridle-making and the other arts concerned with the equipment of horses fall under the art of riding, and this and every military action under strategy, in the same way other arts fall under yet others—in all of these the ends of the master arts are to be preferred to all the subordinate ends; for it is for the sake of the former that the latter are pursued. It makes no difference whether the activities themselves are the ends of the actions, or something else apart from the activities, as in the case of the sciences just mentioned.

If, then, there is some end of the things we do, which we desire for its own sake (everything else being desired for the sake of this), and if we do not choose everything for the sake of something else (for at that rate the process would go on to infinity, so that our desire would be empty and vain), clearly this must be the good and the chief good. Will not the knowledge of it, then, have a great influence on life? Shall we not, like archers who have a mark to aim at, be more likely to hit upon what is right? If so, we must try, in outline at least to determine what it is, and of which of the sciences or capacities it is the object. It would seem to belong to the most authoritative art and that which is most truly the master art. And politics appears to be of this nature; for it is this that ordains which of the sciences should be studied in a state, and which each class of citizens should learn and up to what point they should learn them; and we see even the most highly esteemed of capacities to fall under this, e.g. strategy, economics, rhetoric; now, since politics uses the rest of the sciences, and since, again,

From Aristotle, *Nichomachean Ethics,* translated by W. D. Ross, from *The Basic Works of Aristotle,* edited by Richard McKeon. Copyright 1941 and renewed 1969 by Random House, Inc. Reprinted by permission of the publisher. Original source *The Oxford Translation of Aristotle,* ed. W. D. Ross, 1925. Reprinted by permission of The Clarendon Press, Oxford. This selection is from Book I, Chapters 1-4 (pp. 935-938); Chapter 7 (pp. 941-944); Chapter 9 (pp. 945-946). The translator's notes are not included here.

it legislates as to what we are to do and what we are to abstain from, the end of this science must include those of the others, so that this end must be the good for man. For even if the end is the same for a single man and for a state, that of the state seems at all events something greater and more complete whether to attain or to preserve; though it is worth while to attain the end merely for one man, it is finer and more godlike to attain it for a nation or for city-states. These, then, are the ends at which our inquiry aims, since it is political science, in one sense of that term.

Our discussion will be adequate if it has as much clearness as the subject-matter admits of, for precision is not to be sought for alike in all discussions, any more than in all the products of the crafts. Now fine and just actions, which political science investigates, admit of much variety and fluctuation of opinion, so that they may be thought to exist only by convention, and not by nature. And goods also give rise to a similar fluctuation because they bring harm to many people; for before now men have been undone by reason of their wealth, and others by reason of their courage. We must be content, then, in speaking of such subjects and with such premises to indicate the truth roughly and in outline, and in speaking about things which are only for the most part true and with premises of the same kind to reach conclusions that are no better. In the same spirit, therefore, should each type of statement be *received;* for it is the mark of an educated man to look for precision in each class of things just so far as the nature of the subject admits; it is evidently equally foolish to accept probable reasoning from a mathematician and to demand from a rhetorician scientific proofs.

Now each man judges well the things he knows, and of these he is a good judge. And so the man who has been educated in a subject is a good judge of that subject, and the man who has received an all-round education is a good judge in general. Hence a young man is not a proper hearer of lectures on political science; for he is inexperienced in the actions that occur in life, but its discussions start from these and are about these; and, further, since he tends to follow his passions, his study will be vain and unprofitable, because the end aimed at is not knowledge but action. And it makes no difference whether he is young in years or youthful in character; the defect does not depend on time, but on his living, and pursuing each successive object, as passion directs. For to such persons, as to the incontinent, knowledge brings no profit; but to those who desire and act in accordance with a rational principle knowledge about such matters will be of great benefit.

These remarks about the student, the sort of treatment to be expected, and the purpose of the inquiry, may be taken as our preface.

Let us resume our inquiry and state, in view of the fact that all knowledge and every pursuit aims at some good, what it is that we say political science aims at and what is the highest of all goods achievable by action. Verbally there is very general agreement; for both the general run of men and people of superior refinement say that it is happiness, and identify living well and doing well with being happy; but with regard to what happiness is they differ, and the many do not give the same account as the wise. For the former think it is some plain and obvious thing, like pleasure, wealth, or honour; they differ, however, from one another—and often even the same man identifies it with different things, with health when he is ill, with wealth when he is poor; but, conscious of their ignorance, they admire those who proclaim some great ideal that is above their comprehension. Now some thought that apart from these many goods there is another which is self-subsistent and causes the goodness of all these as well. To examine all the opinions that have been held were perhaps somewhat fruitless; enough to examine those that are most prevalent or that seem to be arguable.

Let us not fail to notice, however, that there is a difference between arguments from and those to the first principles. For Plato, too, was right in raising this question and asking, as he used to do, "are we on the way from or to the first principles?" There is a difference, as there is in a race-course between the course from the judges to the turning-point and the way back. For, while we must begin with what is known, things are objects of knowledge in two senses—some to us, some without qualification. Presumably, then, *we* must begin with things known to *us*. Hence any one who is to listen intelligently to lectures about what is noble and just and, generally, about the subjects of political science must have been brought up in good habits. For the fact is the starting-point, and if this is sufficiently plain to him, he will not at the start need the reason as well; and the man who has been well brought up has or can easily get starting-points. And as for him who neither has nor can get them, let him hear the words of Hesiod:

> Far best is he who knows all things himself;
> Good, he that hearkens when men counsel right;
> But he who neither knows, nor lays to heart
> Another's wisdom, is a useless wight.

.   .   .

Let us again return to the good we are seeking, and ask what it can be. It seems different in different actions and arts; it is different in medicine, in strategy, and in the other arts likewise. What then is the good of each? Surely that for whose sake everything else is done. In medicine this is health, in strategy victory, in architecture a house, in any other sphere something else, and in every action and pursuit the end; for it is for the sake of this that all men do whatever else they do. Therefore, if there is an end for all that we do, this will be the good achievable by action, and if there are more than one, these will be the goods achievable by action.

So the argument has by a different course reached the same point; but we must try to state this even more clearly. Since there are evidently more than one end, and we choose some of these (e.g., wealth, flutes, and in general instruments) for the sake of something else, clearly not all ends are final ends; but the chief good is evidently something final. Therefore, if there is only one final end, this will be what we are seeking, and if there are more than one, the most final of these will be what we are seeking. Now we call that which is in itself worthy of pursuit more final than that which is worthy of pursuit for the sake of something else, and that which is never desirable for the sake of something else more final than the things that are desirable both in themselves and for the sake of that other thing, and therefore we call final without qualification that which is always desirable in itself and never for the sake of something else.

Now such a thing happiness, above all else, is held to be; for this we choose always for itself and never for the sake of something else, but honour, pleasure, reason, and every virtue we choose indeed for themselves (for if nothing resulted from them we should still choose each of them), but we choose them also for the sake of happiness, judging that by means of them we shall be happy. Happiness, on the other hand, no one chooses for the sake of these, nor, in general, for anything other than itself.

From the point of view of self-sufficiency the same result seems to follow; for the final good is thought to be self-sufficient. Now by self-sufficient we do not mean that which is sufficient for a man by himself, for one who lives a solitary life, but also for parents, children, wife, and in general for his friends and fellow citizens, since man is born for citizenship. But some limit must be set to this; for if we extend our requirement to ancestors and descendants and friends' friends we are in for an infinite series. Let us examine this question, however, on another occasion; the self-sufficient we now define as that which when isolated makes life desirable and lacking in nothing; and such we think happiness to be; and further we think it most desirable of all things, without being counted as one good thing among others—if it were so counted it would clearly be made more desirable by the addition of even the least of goods; for that which is added becomes an excess of goods, and of goods the greater is always more desirable. Happiness, then, is something final and self-sufficient, and is the end of action.

Presumably, however, to say that happiness is the chief good seems a platitude, and a clearer account of what it is is still desired. This might perhaps be given, if we could first ascertain the function of man. For just as for a flute-player, a sculptor, or any artist, and, in general, for all things that have a function or activity, the good and the "well" is thought to reside in the function, so would it seem to be for man, if he has a function. Have the carpenter, then, and the tanner certain functions or activities, and has man none? Is he born without a function? Or as eye, hand, foot, and in general each of the parts evidently has a function, may one lay it down that man similarly has a function apart from all these? What then can this be? Life seems to be common even to plants, but we are seeking what is peculiar to man. Let us exclude, therefore, the life of nutrition and growth. Next there would be a life of perception, but *it* also seems to be common even to the horse, the ox, and every animal. There remains, then, an active life of the element that has a rational principle; of this, one part has such a principle in the sense of being obedient to one, the other in the sense of possessing one and exercising thought. And, as "life of the rational element" also has two meanings, we must state that life in the sense of activity is what we mean; for this seems to be the more proper sense of the term. Now if the function of man is an activity of soul which follows or implies a rational principle, and if we say "a so-and-so" and "a good so-and-so" have a function which is the same in kind, e.g., a lyre-player and a good lyre-player, and so without qualification in all cases, eminence in respect of goodness being added to the name of the function (for the function of a lyre-player is to play the lyre, and that of a good lyre-player is to do so well): if this is the case, [and we state the function of man to be a certain kind of life, and this to be an activity or actions of the soul implying a rational principle, and the function of a good man to be the good and noble performance of these, and if any action is well performed when it is performed in accordance with the appropriate excellence: if this is the case,] human good turns out to be activity of soul in accordance with virtue, and if there are more than one virtue, in accordance with the best and most complete.

But we must add "in a complete life." For one swallow does not make a summer, nor does one day; and so too one day, or a short time, does not make a man blessed and happy.

Let this serve as an outline of the good; for we must presumably first sketch it roughly, and then later fill in the details. But it would seem that any one is capable of carrying on and articulating what has once been well outlined, and that time is a good discoverer or partner in such a work; to which facts the advances of the arts are due; for any one can add what is lacking. And we must also remember what has been said before, and not look for precision in all things alike, but in each class of things such precision as accords with the subject-matter, and so much as is appropriate to the inquiry. For a carpenter and a geometer investigate the right angle in different ways; the former does so in so far as the right angle is useful for his work, while the latter inquires what it is or what sort of thing it is; for he is a spectator of the truth. We must act in the same way, then, in all other matters as well, that our main task may not be subordinated to minor questions. Nor must we demand the cause in all matters alike; it is enough in some cases that the *fact* be well established, as in the case of the first principles; the fact is the primary thing or first principle. Now of first principles we see some by induction, some by perception, some by a certain habituation, and others too in other ways. But each set of principles we must try to investigate in the natural way, and we must take pains to state them definitely, since they have a great influence on what follows. For the beginning is thought to be more than half of the whole, and many of the questions we ask are cleared up by it.

.   .   .

For this reason also the question is asked, whether happiness is to be acquired by learning or by habituation or some other sort of training, or comes in virtue of some divine providence or again by chance. Now if there is *any* gift of the gods to men, it is reasonable that happiness should be god-given, and most surely god-given of all human things inasmuch as it is the best. But this question would perhaps be more appropriate to another inquiry; happiness seems, however, even if it is not god-sent but comes as a result of virtue and some process of learning or training, to be among the most god-like things; for that which is the prize and end of virtue seems to be the best thing in the world, and something godlike and blessed.

It will also on this view be very generally shared; for all who are not maimed as regards their potentiality for virtue may win it by a certain kind of study and care. But if it is better to be happy thus than by chance, it is reasonable that the facts should be so, since everything that depends on the action of nature is by nature as good as it can be, and similarly everything that depends on art or any rational cause, and especially if it depends on the best of all causes. To entrust to chance what is greatest and most noble would be a very defective arrangement.

The answer to the question we are asking is plain also from the definition of happiness; for it has been said to be a virtuous activity of soul, of a certain kind. Of the remaining goods, some must necessarily pre-exist as conditions of happiness, and others are naturally co-operative and useful as instruments. And this will be found to agree with what we said at the outset; for we stated the end of political science to be the best end, and political science spends most of its pains on making the citizens to be of a certain character, viz. good and capable of noble acts.

It is natural, then, that we call neither ox nor horse nor any other of the animals happy; for none of them is capable of sharing in such activity. For this reason also a boy is not happy; for he is not yet capable of such acts, owing to his age; and boys who are called happy are being congratulated by reason of the hopes we have for them. For there is required, as we said, not only complete virtue but also a complete life, since many changes occur in life, and all manner of chances, and the most prosperous may fall into great misfortunes in old age, as is told of Priam in the Trojan Cycle; and one who has experienced such chances and has ended wretchedly no one calls happy.

.   .   .

Virtue, then, being of two kinds, intellectual and moral, intellectual virtue in the main owes both its birth and its growth to teaching (for which reason it requires experience and time), while moral virtue comes about as a result of habit, whence also its name *ethike* is one that is formed by a slight variation from the word *ethos* (habit). From this it is also plain that none of the moral virtues arises in us by nature; for nothing that exists by nature can form a habit contrary to its nature. For instance the stone which by nature moves downwards cannot be habituated to move upwards, not even if one tries to train it by throwing it up ten thousand times; nor can fire be habituated to move downwards, nor can anything else that by nature behaves in one way be trained to behave in another. Neither by nature, then, nor contrary to nature do the virtues arise in us; rather we are adapted by nature to receive them, and are made perfect by habit.

Again, of all the things that come to us by nature we first acquire the potentiality and later exhibit the activity (this is plain in the case of the senses; for it was not by often seeing or often hearing that we got these senses, but on the contrary we had them before we used them, and did not come to have them by using them); but the virtues we get by first exercising them, as also happens in the case of the arts as well. For the things we have to learn before we can do them, we learn by doing them, e.g., men become builders by building and lyre-players by playing the lyre; so too we become just by doing just acts, temperate by doing temperate acts, brave by doing brave acts.

This is confirmed by what happens in states; for legislators make the citizens good by forming habits in them, and this is the wish of every legislator, and those who do not effect it miss their mark, and it is in this that a good constitution differs from a bad one.

From Aristotle, *Nichomachean Ethics*, translated by W. D. Ross, from *The Basic Works of Aristotle*, edited by Richard McKeon. Copyright 1941 and renewed 1969 by Random House, Inc. Reprinted by permission of the publisher. Original source *The Oxford Translation of Aristotle*, ed. W. D. Ross, 1925. Reprinted by permission of The Clarendon Press, Oxford. This selection is from Book II, Chapters 1-2 (pp. 952-954); Chapter 4 (pp. 955-956); Chapter 6 (pp. 957-959). The translator's notes are not included here.

Again, it is from the same causes and by the same means that every virtue is both produced and destroyed, and similarly every art; for it is from playing the lyre that both good and bad lyre-players are produced. And the corresponding statement is true of builders and of all the rest; men will be good or bad builders as a result of building well or badly. For if this were not so, there would have been no need of a teacher, but all men would have been born good or bad at their craft. This, then, is the case with the virtues also; by doing the acts that we do in our transactions with other men we become just or unjust, and by doing the acts that we do in the presence of danger, and being habituated to feel fear or confidence, we become brave or cowardly. The same is true of appetites and feelings of anger; some men become temperate and good-tempered, others self-indulgent and irascible, by behaving in one way or the other in the appropriate circumstances. Thus, in one word, states of character arise out of like activities. This is why the activities we exhibit must be of a certain kind; it is because the states of character correspond to the differences between these. It makes no small difference, then, whether we form habits of one kind or of another from our very youth; it makes a very great difference, or rather *all* the difference.

Since, then, the present inquiry does not aim at theoretical knowledge like the others (for we are inquiring not in order to know what virtue is, but in order to become good, since otherwise our inquiry would have been of no use), we must examine the nature of actions, namely how we ought to do them; for these determine also the nature of the states of character that are produced, as we have said. Now, that we must act according to the right rule is a common principle and must be assumed—it will be discussed later, i.e., both what the right rule is, and how it is related to the other virtues. But this must be agreed upon beforehand, that the whole account of matters of conduct must be given in outline and not precisely, as we said at the very beginning that the accounts we demand must be in accordance with the subject-matter; matters concerned with conduct and questions of what is good for us have no fixity, any more than matters of health. The general account being of this nature, the account of particular cases is yet more lacking in exactness; for they do not fall under any art or precept but the agents themselves must in each case consider what is appropriate to the occasion, as happens also in the art of medicine or of navigation.

But though our present account is of this nature we must give what help we can. First, then, let us consider this, that it is the nature of such things to be destroyed by defect and excess, as we see in the case of strength and of health (for to gain light on things imperceptible we must use the evidence of sensible things); both excessive and defective exercise destroys the strength, and similarly drink or food which is above or below a certain amount destroys the health, while that which is proportionate both produces and increases and preserves it. So too is it, then, in the case of temperance and courage and the other virtues. For the man who flies from and fears everything and does not stand his ground against anything becomes a coward, and the man who fears nothing at all but goes to meet every danger becomes rash; and similarly the man who indulges in every pleasure and abstains from none becomes self-indulgent, while the man who shuns every pleasure, as boors do, becomes in a way insensible; temperance and courage, then, are destroyed by excess and defect, and preserved by the mean.

But not only are the sources and causes of their origination and growth the same as those of their destruction, but also the sphere of their actualization will be the same; for this is also true of the things which are more evident to sense, e.g., of strength; it is produced by taking much food and undergoing much exertion, and it is the strong man that will be most able to do these things. So too is it with the virtues; by abstaining from pleasures we become temperate, and it is when we have become so that we are most able to abstain from them; and similarly too in the case of courage; for by being habituated to despise things that are terrible and to stand our ground against them we become brave, and it is when we have become so that we shall be most able to stand our ground against them.

.   .   .

The question might be asked, what we mean by saying that we must become just by doing just acts, and temperate by doing temperate acts; for if men do just and temperate acts, they are already just and temperate, exactly as, if they do what is in accordance with the laws of grammar and of music, they are grammarians and musicians.

Or is this not true even of the arts? It is possible to do something that is in accordance with the laws of grammar, either by chance or at the suggestion of another. A man will be a grammarian, then, only when he has both done something grammatical and done it grammatically; and this means doing it in accordance with the grammatical knowledge in himself.

Again, the case of the arts and that of the virtues are not similar; for the products of the arts have their goodness in themselves, so that it is enough that they should have a certain character, but if the acts that are in accordance with the virtues have themselves a certain character it does not follow that they are done justly or temperately. The agent also must be in a certain condition when he does them; in the first place he must have knowledge, secondly he must choose the acts, and choose them for their own sakes, and thirdly his action must proceed from a firm and unchangeable character. These are not reckoned in as conditions of the possession of the arts, except the bare knowledge; but as a condition of the possession of the virtues knowledge has little or no weight, while the other conditions count not for a little but for everything, i.e., the very conditions which result from often doing just and temperate acts.

Actions, then, are called just and temperate when they are such as the just or the temperate man would do; but it is not the man who does these that is just and temperate, but the man who also does them *as* just and temperate men do them. It is well said, then, that it is by doing just acts that the just man is produced, and by doing temperate acts the temperate man; without doing these no one would have even a prospect of becoming good.

But most people do not do these, but take refuge in theory and think they are being philosophers and will become good in this way, behaving somewhat like patients who listen attentively to their doctors, but do none of the things they are ordered to do. As the latter will not be made well in body by such a course of treatment, the former will not be made well in soul by such a course of philosophy.

.   .   .

We must, however, not only describe virtue as a state of character, but also say what sort of state it is. We may remark, then, that every virtue or excellence both brings into good condition the thing of which it is the excellence and makes the work of that thing be done well; e.g., the excellence of the eye makes both the eye and its work good; for it is by the excellence of the eye that we see well. Similarly the excellence of the horse makes a horse both good in itself and good at running and at carrying its rider and at awaiting the attack of the enemy. Therefore, if this is true in every case, the virtue of man also will be the state of character which makes a man good and which makes him do his own work well.

How this is to happen we have stated already, but it will be made plain also by the following consideration of the specific nature of virtue. In everything that is continuous and divisible it is possible to take more, less, or an equal amount, and that either in terms of the thing itself or relatively to us; and the equal is an intermediate between excess and defect. By the intermediate in the object I mean that which is equidistant from each of the extremes, which is one and the same for all men; by the intermediate relatively to us that which is neither too much nor too little—and this is not one, nor the same for all. For instance, if ten is many and two is few, six is the intermediate, taken in terms of the object; for it exceeds and is exceeded by an equal amount; this is intermediate according to arithmetical proportion. But the intermediate relatively to us is not to be taken so; if ten pounds are too much for a particular person to eat and two too little, it does not follow that the trainer will order six pounds; for this also is perhaps too much for the person who is to take it, or too little—too little for Milo, too much for the beginner in athletic exercises. The same is true of running and wrestling. Thus a master of any art avoids excess and defect, but seeks the intermediate and chooses this—the intermediate not in the object but relatively to us.

If it is thus, then, that every art does its work well—by looking to the intermediate and judging its works by this standard (so that we often say of good works of art that it is not possible either to take away or to add anything, implying that excess and defect destroy the goodness of works of art, while the mean preserves it; and good artists, as we say, look to this in their work), and if, further, virtue is more exact and better than any art, as nature also is, then virtue must have the quality of aiming at the intermediate. I mean moral virtue; for it is this that is concerned with passions and actions, and in these there is excess, defect, and the intermediate. For instance, both fear and confidence and appetite and anger and pity and in general pleasure and pain may be felt both too much and too little, and in both cases not well; but to feel them at the right times, with reference to the right objects, towards the right people, with the right motive, and in the right way, is what is both intermediate and best, and this is characteristic of virtue. Similarly with regard to actions also there is excess, defect, and the intermediate. Now virtue is concerned with passions and actions, in which excess is a form of failure, and so is defect, while the intermediate is praised and is a form of success; and being praised and being successful are both characteristics of virtue. Therefore virtue is a kind of mean, since, as we have seen, it aims at what is intermediate.

Again, it is possible to fail in many ways (for evil belongs to the class of the unlimited, as the Pythagoreans conjectured, and good to that of the limited), while to succeed is possible only in one way (for which reason also one is easy and the other difficult—to miss the mark easy, to hit it difficult); for these reasons also, then, excess and defect are characteristic of vice, and the mean of virtue;

For men are good in but one way, but bad in many.

Virtue, then, is a state of character concerned with choice, lying in a mean, i.e., the mean relative to us, this being determined by a rational principle, and by that principle by which the man of practical wisdom would determine it. Now it is a mean between two vices, that which depends on excess and that which depends on defect; and again it is a mean because the vices respectively fall short of or exceed what is right in both passions and actions, while virtue both finds and chooses that which is intermediate. Hence in respect of its substance and the definition which states its essence virtue is a mean, with regard to what is best and right an extreme.

But not every action nor every passion admits of a mean; for some have names that already imply badness, e.g., spite, shamelessness, envy, and in the case of actions adultery, theft, murder; for all of these and such-like things imply by their names that they are themselves bad, and not the excesses or deficiencies of them. It is not possible, then, ever to be right with regard to them; one must always be wrong. Nor does goodness or bad-ness with regard to such things depend on committing adultery with the right woman, at the right time, and in the right way, but simply to do any of them is to go wrong. It would be equally absurd, then, to expect that in unjust, cowardly, and voluptuous action there should be a mean, an excess, and a deficiency; for at that rate there would be a mean of excess and of deficiency, an excess of excess, and a deficiency of deficiency. But as there is no excess and deficiency of temperance and courage because what is in-termediate is in a sense an extreme, so too of the actions we have mentioned there is no mean nor any excess and deficiency, but however they are done they are wrong; for in general there is neither a mean of excess and deficiency, nor excess and deficiency of a mean.

.   .   .

If happiness is activity in accordance with virtue, it is reasonable that it should be in accordance with the highest virtue; and this will be that of the best thing in us. Whether it be reason or something else that is this element which is thought to be our natural ruler and guide and to take thought of things noble and divine, whether it be itself also divine or only the most divine element in us, the activity of this in accordance with its proper virtue will be perfect happiness. That this activity is contemplative we have al-ready said.

Now this would seem to be in agreement both with what we said before and with the truth. For, firstly, this activity is the best (since not only is reason the best thing in us, but the objects of reason are the best of know-able objects); and secondly, it is the most continuous, since we can con-template truth more continuously than we can *do* anything. And we think happiness has pleasure mingled with it, but the activity of philosophic

From Aristotle, *Nichomachean Ethics,* translated by W. D. Ross, from *The Basic Works of Aristotle,* edited by Richard McKeon. Copyright 1941 and renewed 1969 by Random House, Inc. Reprinted by permission of the publisher. Original source *The Oxford Translation of Aristotle,* ed. W. D. Ross, 1925. Reprinted by permission of The Clarendon Press, Oxford. This selection is from Book X, Chapter 7 (pp. 1104-1105). The translator's notes are not in-cluded here.

wisdom is admittedly the pleasantest of virtuous activities; at all events the pursuit of it is thought to offer pleasures marvellous for their purity and their enduringness, and it is to be expected that those who know will pass their time more pleasantly than those who inquire. And the self-sufficiency that is spoken of must belong most to the contemplative activity. For while a philosopher, as well as a just man or one possessing any other virtue, needs the necessaries of life, when they are sufficiently equipped with things of that sort the just man needs people towards whom and with whom he shall act justly, and the temperate man, the brave man, and each of the others is in the same case, but the philosopher, even when by himself, can contemplate truth, and the better the wiser he is; he can perhaps do so better if he has fellow-workers, but still he is the most self-sufficient. And this activity alone would seem to be loved for its own sake; for nothing arises from it apart from the contemplating, while from practical activities we gain more or less apart from the action. And happiness is thought to depend on leisure; for we are busy that we may have leisure, and make war that we may live in peace. Now the activity of the practical virtues is exhibited in political or military affairs, but the actions concerned with these seem to be unleisurely. Warlike actions are completely so (for no one chooses to be at war, or provokes war, for the sake of being at war; any one would seem absolutely murderous if he were to make enemies of his friends in order to bring about battle and slaughter); but the action of the statesman is also unleisurely, and — apart from the political action itself — aims at despotic power and honours, or at all events happiness, for him and his fellow citizens — a happiness different from political action, and evidently sought as being different. So if among virtuous actions political and military actions are distinguished by nobility and greatness, and these are unleisurely and aim at an end and are not desirable for their own sake, but the activity of reason, which is contemplative, seems both to be superior in serious worth and to aim at no end beyond itself, and to have its pleasure proper to itself (and this augments the activity), and the self-sufficiency, leisureliness, unweariedness (so far as this is possible for man), and all the other attributes ascribed to the supremely happy man are evidently those connected with this activity, it follows that this will be the complete happiness of man, if it be allowed a complete term of life (for none of the attributes of happiness is *in*complete).

But such a life would be too high for man; for it is not in so far as he is man that he will live so, but in so far as something divine is present in him; and by so much as this is superior to our composite nature is its activity superior to that which is the exercise of the other kind of virtue. If reason is divine, then, in comparison with man, the life according to it is divine in comparison with human life. But we must not follow those who advise us, being men, to think of human things, and, being mortal, of mortal things, but must, so far as we can, make ourselves immortal, and strain every nerve to live in accordance with the best thing in us; for even if it be small in bulk, much more does it in power and worth surpass everything. This would seem, too, to be each man himself, since it is the authoritative and better part of him. It would be strange, then, if he were to choose not the life of his self but that of something else. And what we said before will apply now; that which is proper to each thing is by nature best and most pleasant for each thing; for man, therefore, the life according to reason is best and pleasantest, since reason more than anything else *is* man. This life therefore is also the happiest.

19. Politics

Aristotle

Every state is a community of some kind, and every community is established with a view to some good; for mankind always act in order to obtain that which they think good. But, if all communities aim at some good, the state or political community, which is the highest of all, and which embraces all the rest, aims at good in a greater degree than any other, and at the highest good.

Some people think that the qualifications of a statesman, king, householder, and master are the same, and that they differ, not in kind, but only in the number of their subjects. For example, the ruler over a few is called a master; over more, the manager of a household; over a still larger number, a statesman or king, as if there were no difference between a great household and a small state. The distinction which is made between the king and the statesman is as follows: When the government is personal, the ruler is a king; when, according to the rules of the political science, the citizens rule and are ruled in turn, then he is called a statesman.

But all this is a mistake; for governments differ in kind, as will be evident to any one who considers the matter according to the method which has

From Aristotle, *Politics,* translated by Benjamin Jowett, from *The Basic Works of Aristotle,* edited by Richard McKeon. Copyright 1941 and renewed 1969 by Random House, Inc. Original source *The Oxford Translation of Aristotle,* ed. W. D. Ross, 1925. Reprinted by permission of The Clarendon Press, Oxford. This selection is from Book I, Chapters 1-2 (pp. 1127-1130). The translator's notes are not included here.

hitherto guided us. As in other departments of science, so in politics, the compound should always be resolved into the simple elements or least parts of the whole. We must therefore look at the elements of which the state is composed, in order that we may see in what the different kinds of rule differ from one another, and whether any scientific result can be attained about each one of them.

He who thus considers things in their first growth and origin, whether a state or anything else, will obtain the clearest view of them. In the first place there must be a union of those who cannot exist without each other; namely, of male and female, that the race may continue (and this is a union which is formed, not of deliberate purpose, but because, in common with other animals and with plants, mankind have a natural desire to leave behind them an image of themselves), and of natural ruler and subject, that both may be preserved. For that which can foresee by the exercise of mind is by nature intended to be lord and master, and that which can with its body give effect to such foresight is a subject, and by nature a slave; hence master and slave have the same interest. Now nature has distinguished between the female and the slave. For she is not niggardly, like the smith who fashions the Delphian knife for many uses; she makes each thing for a single use, and every instrument is best made when intended for one and not for many uses. But among barbarians no distinction is made between women and slaves, because there is no natural ruler among them: they are a community of slaves, male and female. Wherefore the poets say—

"It is meet that Hellenes should rule over barbarians";

as if they thought that the barbarian and the slave were by nature one.

Out of these two relationships between man and woman, master and slave, the first thing to arise is the family, and Hesiod is right when he says—

"First house and wife and an ox for the plough,"

for the ox is the poor man's slave. The family is the association established by nature for the supply of men's everyday wants, and the members of it are called by Charondas "companions of the cupboard," and by Epimenides the Cretan, "companions of the manager." But when several families are united, and the association aims at something more than the supply of daily needs, the first society to be formed is the village. And the most natural form of the village appears to be that of a colony from the family, composed of the children and grandchildren, who are said to be "suckled with the same milk." And this is the reason why Hellenic states were originally governed by kings; because the Hellenes were under royal rule before they came together, as the barbarians still are. Every family is ruled by the eldest, and therefore in the colonies of the family the kingly form of government prevailed because they were of the same blood. As Homer says:

"Each one gives law to his children and to his wives."

For they lived dispersedly, as was the manner in ancient times. Wherefore men say that the Gods have a king, because they themselves either are or were in ancient times under the rule of a king. For they imagine, not only the forms of the Gods, but their ways of life to be like their own.

When several villages are united in a single complete community, large enough to be nearly or quite self-sufficing, the state comes into existence, originating in the bare needs of life, and continuing in existence for the sake of a good life. And therefore, if the earlier forms of society are natural, so is the state, for it is the end of them, and the nature of a thing is its end. For what each thing is when fully developed, we call its nature, whether we are speaking of a man, a horse, or a family. Besides, the final cause and end of a thing is the best, and to be self-sufficing is the end and the best.

Hence it is evident that the state is a creation of nature, and that man is by nature a political animal. And he who by nature and not by mere accident is without a state, is either a bad man or above humanity; he is like the

"Tribeless, lawless, hearthless one,"

whom Homer denounces—the natural outcast is forthwith a lover of war; he may be compared to an isolated piece at draughts.

Now, that man is more of a political animal than bees or any other gregarious animals is evident. Nature, as we often say, makes nothing in vain, and man is the only animal whom she has endowed with the gift of speech. And whereas mere voice is but an indication of pleasure or pain, and is therefore found in other animals (for their nature attains to the perception of pleasure and pain and the intimation of them to one another, and no further), the power of speech is intended to set forth the expedient and inexpedient, and therefore likewise the just and the unjust. And it is a characteristic of man that he alone has any sense of good and evil, of just and unjust, and the like, and the association of living beings who have this sense makes a family and a state.

Further, the state is by nature clearly prior to the family and to the individual, since the whole is of necessity prior to the part; for example, if the whole body be destroyed, there will be no foot or hand, except in an equivocal sense, as we might speak of a stone hand; for when destroyed the hand will be no better than that. But things are defined by their working and power; and we ought not to say that they are the same when they no longer have their proper quality, but only that they have the same name. The proof that the state is a creation of nature and prior to the individual is that the individual, when isolated, is not self-sufficing; and therefore he is like a part in relation to the whole. But he who is unable to live in society, or who has no need because he is sufficient for himself, must be either a beast or a god: he is no part of a state. A social instinct is implanted in all men by nature, and yet he who first founded the state was the greatest of benefactors. For man, when perfected, is the best of animals, but, when separated from law and justice, he is the worst of all; since armed injustice is the more dangerous, and he is equipped at birth with arms, meant to be used by intelligence and virtue, which he may use for the worst ends. Wherefore, if he have not virtue, he is the most unholy and the most savage of animals, and the most full of lust and gluttony. But justice is the bond of men in states, for the administration of justice, which is the determination of what is just, is the principle of order in political society.

.   .   .

Returning to the constitution itself, let us seek to determine out of what and what sort of elements the state which is to be happy and well-governed should be composed. There are two things in which all well-being consists: one of them is the choice of a right end and aim of action, and the other the discovery of the actions which are means towards it; for the means and the end may agree or disagree. Sometimes the right end is set before men, but in practice they fail to attain it; in other cases they are successful in all the means, but they propose to themselves a bad end; and sometimes they fail in both. Take, for example, the art of medicine; physicians do not always understand the nature of health, and also the means which they use may not effect the desired end. In all arts and sciences both the end and the means should be equally within our control.

The happiness and well-being which all men manifestly desire, some have the power of attaining, but to others, from some accident or defect of nature, the attainment of them is not granted; for a good life requires a supply of external goods, in a less degree when men are in a good state, in a greater degree when they are in a lower state. Others again, who possess

From Aristotle, *Politics*, translated by Benjamin Jowett, from *The Basic Works of Aristotle*, edited by Richard McKeon. Copyright 1941 and renewed 1969 by Random House, Inc. Original source *The Oxford Translation of Aristotle*, ed. W. D. Ross, 1925. Reprinted by permission of The Clarendon Press, Oxford. This selection is from Book VII, Chapters 13-15 (pp. 1294-1301). The translator's notes are not included here.

the conditions of happiness, go utterly wrong from the first in the pursuit of it. But since our object is to discover the best form of government, that, namely, under which a city will be best governed, and since the city is best governed which has the greatest opportunity of obtaining happiness, it is evident that we must clearly ascertain the nature of happiness.

We maintain, and have said in the *Ethics,* if the arguments there adduced are of any value, that happiness is the realization and perfect exercise of virtue, and this not conditional, but absolute. And I used the term "conditional" to express that which is indispensable, and "absolute" to express that which is good in itself. Take the case of just actions; just punishments and chastisements do indeed spring from a good principle, but they are good only because we cannot do without them — it would be better that neither individuals nor states should need anything of the sort — but actions which aim at honour and advantage are absolutely the best. The conditional action is only the choice of a lesser evil; whereas these are the foundation and creation of good. A good man may make the best even of poverty and disease, and the other ills of life; but he can only attain happiness under the opposite conditions (for this also has been determined in accordance with ethical arguments, that the good man is he for whom, because he is virtuous, the things that are absolutely good are good; it is also plain that his use of these goods must be virtuous and in the absolute sense good). This makes men fancy that external goods are the cause of happiness, yet we might as well say that a brilliant performance on the lyre was to be attributed to the instrument and not to the skill of the performer.

It follows then from what has been said that some things the legislator must find ready to his hand in a state, others he must provide. And therefore we can only say: May our state be constituted in such a manner as to be blessed with the goods of which fortune disposes (for we acknowledge her power): whereas virtue and goodness in the state are not a matter of chance but the result of knowledge and purpose. A city can be virtuous only when the citizens who have a share in the government are virtuous, and in our state all the citizens share in the government; let us then inquire how a man becomes virtuous. For even if we could suppose the citizen body to be virtuous, without each of them being so, yet the latter would be better, for in the virtue of each the virtue of all is involved.

There are three things which make men good and virtuous; these are nature, habit, rational principle. In the first place, every one must be born a man and not some other animal; so, too, he must have a certain character, both of body and soul. But some qualities there is no use in having at birth, for they are altered by habit, and there are some gifts which by nature are made to be turned by habit to good or bad. Animals lead for the most part a life of nature, although in lesser particulars some are influenced by habit as well. Man has rational principle, in addition, and man only. Wherefore nature, habit, rational principle must be in harmony with one another; for they do not always agree; men do many things against habit and nature, if rational principle persuades them that they ought. We have already determined what natures are likely to be most easily moulded by the hands of the legislator. All else is the work of education; we learn some things by habit and some by instruction.

Since every political society is composed of rulers and subjects let us consider whether the relations of one to the other should interchange or be permanent. For the education of the citizens will necessarily vary with the answer given to this question. Now, if some men excelled others in the same degree in which gods and heroes are supposed to excel mankind in general (having in the first place a great advantage even in their bodies, and secondly in their minds), so that the superiority of the governors was undisputed and patent to their subjects, it would clearly be better that once for all the one class should rule and the others serve. But since this is unattainable, and kings have no marked superiority over their subjects, such as Scylax affirms to be found among the Indians, it is obviously necessary on many grounds that all the citizens alike should take their turn of governing and being governed. Equality consists in the same treatment of similar persons, and no government can stand which is not founded upon justice. For if the government be unjust every one in the country unites with the governed in the desire to have a revolution, and it is an impossibility that the members of the government can be so numerous as to be stronger than all their enemies put together. Yet that governors should excel their subjects is undeniable. How all this is to be effected, and in what way they will respectively share in the government, the legislator has to consider. The subject has been already mentioned. Nature herself has provided the distinction when she made a difference between old and young within the same species, of whom she fitted the one to govern and the other to be governed. No one takes offence at being governed when he is young, nor does he think himself better than his governors, especially if he will enjoy the same privilege when he reaches the required age.

We conclude that from one point of view governors and governed are identical, and from another different. And therefore their education must be the same and also different. For he who would learn to command well must, as men say, first of all learn to obey. As I observed in the first part of this treatise, there is one rule which is for the sake of the rulers and another rule which is for the sake of the ruled; the former is a despotic, the latter a free government. Some commands differ not in the thing commanded, but in the intention with which they are imposed. Wherefore, many apparently menial offices are an honour to the free youth by whom they are performed;

for actions do not differ as honourable or dishonourable in themselves so much as in the end and intention of them. But since we say that the virtue of the citizen and ruler is the same as that of the good man, and that the same person must first be a subject and then a ruler, the legislator has to see that they become good men, and by what means this may be accomplished, and what is the end of the perfect life.

Now the soul of man is divided into two parts, one of which has a rational principle in itself, and the other, not having a rational principle in itself, is able to obey such a principle. And we call a man in any way good because he has the virtues of these two parts. In which of them the end is more likely to be found is no matter of doubt to those who adopt our division; for in the world both of nature and of art the inferior always exists for the sake of the better or superior, and the better or superior is that which has a rational principle. This principle, too, in our ordinary way of speaking, is divided into two kinds, for there is a practical and a speculative principle. This part, then, must evidently be similarly divided. And there must be a corresponding division of actions; the actions of the naturally better part are to be preferred by those who have it in their power to attain to two out of the three or to all, for that is always to every one the most eligible which is the highest attainable by him. The whole of life is further divided into two parts, business and leisure, war and peace, and of actions some aim at what is necessary and useful, and some at what is honourable. And the preference given to one or the other class of actions must necessarily be like the preference given to one or other part of the soul and its actions over the other; there must be war for the sake of peace, business for the sake of leisure, things useful and necessary for the sake of things honourable. All these points the statesman should keep in view when he frames his laws; he should consider the parts of the soul and their functions, and above all the better and the end; he should also remember the diversities of human lives and actions. For men must be able to engage in business and go to war, but leisure and peace are better; they must do what is necessary and indeed what is useful, but what is honourable is better. On such principles children and persons of every age which requires education should be trained. Whereas even the Hellenes of the present day who are reputed to be best governed, and the legislators who gave them their constitutions, do not appear to have framed their governments with a regard to the best end, or to have given them laws and education with a view to all the virtues, but in a vulgar spirit have fallen back on those which promised to be more useful and profitable. Many modern writers have taken a similar view: they commend the Lacedaemonian constitution, and praise the legislator for making conquest and war his sole aim, a doctrine which may be refuted by argument and has long ago been refuted by facts.

For most men desire empire in the hope of accumulating the goods of fortune; and on this ground Thibron and all those who have written about the Lacedaemonian constitution have praised their legislator, because the Lacedaemonians, by being trained to meet dangers, gained great power. But surely they are not a happy people now that their empire has passed away, nor was their legislator right. How ridiculous is the result, if, while they are continuing in the observance of his laws and no one interferes with them, they have lost the better part of life! These writers further err about the sort of government which the legislator should approve, for the government of freemen is nobler and implies more virtue than despotic government. Neither is a city to be deemed happy or a legislator to be praised because he trains his citizens to conquer and obtain dominion over their neighbours, for there is great evil in this. On a similar principle any citizen who could, should obviously try to obtain the power in his own state—the crime which the Lacedaemonians accuse king Pausanias of attempting, although he had so great honour already. No such principle and no law having this object is either statesmanlike or useful or right. For the same things are best both for individuals and for states, and these are the things which the legislator ought to implant in the minds of his citizens. Neither should men study war with a view to the enslavement of those who do not deserve to be enslaved; but first of all they should provide against their own enslavement, and in the second place obtain empire for the good of the governed, and not for the sake of exercising a general despotism, and in the third place they should seek to be masters only over those who deserve to be slaves. Facts, as well as arguments, prove that the legislator should direct all his military and other measures to the provision of leisure and the establishment of peace. For most of these military states are safe only while they are at war, but fall when they have acquired their empire; like unused iron they lose their temper in time of peace. And for this the legislator is to blame, he never having taught them how to lead the life of peace.

Since the end of individuals and of states is the same, the end of the best man and of the best constitution must also be the same; it is therefore evident that there ought to exist in both of them the virtues of leisure; for peace, as has been often repeated, is the end of war, and leisure of toil. But leisure and cultivation may be promoted, not only by those virtues which are practised in leisure, but also by some of those which are useful to business. For many necessaries of life have to be supplied before we can have leisure. Therefore a city must be temperate and brave, and able to endure: for truly, as the proverb says, "There is no leisure for slaves," and those who cannot face danger like men are the slaves of any invader. Courage and endurance are required for business and philosophy for leisure, temperance and justice for both, and more especially in times of peace and leisure, for war compels men to be just and temperate, whereas the enjoyment of good fortune and the leisure which comes with peace tend to make them insolent. Those then who seem to be the best-off and to be in the possession of every good, have special need of justice and temperance—for example, those (if such there be, as the poets say) who dwell in the Islands of the Blest; they above all will need philosophy and temperance and justice, and all the more the more leisure they have, living in the midst of abundance. There is no difficulty in seeing why the state that would be happy and good ought to have these virtues. If it be disgraceful in men not to be able to use the goods of life, it is peculiarly disgraceful not to be able to use them in time of leisure—to show excellent qualities in action and war, and when they have peace and leisure to be no better than slaves. Wherefore we should not practise virtue after the manner of the Lacedaemonians. For they, while agreeing with other men in their conception of the highest goods, differ from the rest of mankind in thinking that they are to be obtained by the practice of a single virtue. And since [they think] these goods and the enjoyment of them greater than the enjoyment derived from the virtues . . . and that [it should be practised] for its own sake, is evident from what has been said; we must now consider how and by what means it is to be attained.

We have already determined that nature and habit and rational principle are required, and, of these, the proper *nature* of the citizens has also been defined by us. But we have still to consider whether the training of early life is to be that of rational principle or habit, for these two must accord, and when in accord they will then form the best of harmonies. The rational principle may be mistaken and fail in attaining the highest ideal of life, and there may be a like evil influence of habit. Thus much is clear in the first place, that, as in all other things, birth implies an antecedent beginning, and that there are beginnings whose end is relative to a further end. Now, in men rational principle and mind are the end towards which nature strives, so that the birth and moral discipline of the citizens ought to be ordered with a view to them. In the second place, as the soul and body are two, we see also that there are two parts of the soul, the rational and the irrational, and two corresponding states—reason and appetite. And as the body is prior in order of generation to the soul, so the irrational is prior to the rational. The proof is that anger and wishing and desire are implanted in children from their very birth, but reason and understanding are developed as they grow older. Wherefore, the care of the body ought to precede that of the soul, and the training of the appetitive part should follow: none the less our care of it must be for the sake of the reason, and our care of the body for the sake of the soul.

.   .   .

No one will doubt that the legislator should direct his attention above all to the education of youth; for the neglect of education does harm to the constitution. The citizen should be moulded to suit the form of government under which he lives. For each government has a peculiar character which originally formed and which continues to preserve it. The character of democracy creates democracy, and the character of oligarchy creates oligarchy; and always the better the character, the better the government.

Again, for the exercise of any faculty or art a previous training and habituation are required; clearly therefore for the practice of virtue. And since the whole city has one end, it is manifest that education should be one and the same for all, and that it should be public, and not private—not as at present, when every one looks after his own children separately, and gives them separate instruction of the sort which he thinks best; the training in things which are of common interest should be the same for all. Neither must we suppose that any one of the citizens belongs to himself, for they all belong to the state, and are each of them a part of the state, and the care of each part is inseparable from the care of the whole. In this particular as in some others the Lacedaemonians are to be praised, for they take the greatest pains about their children, and make education the business of the state.

That education should be regulated by law and should be an affair of state is not to be denied, but what should be the character of this public education, and how young persons should be educated, are questions which remain to be considered. As things are, there is disagreement about the subjects. For mankind are by no means agreed about the things to be taught, whether we look to virtue or the best life. Neither is it clear whether education is more concerned with intellectual or with moral virtue. The existing practice is perplexing; no one knows on what principle we should proceed—should the useful in life, or should virtue, or should the higher knowledge, be the aim of our training; all three opinions have been entertained. Again, about the means there is no agreement; for different persons, starting with different ideas about the nature of virtue, naturally disagree about the practice of it. There can be no doubt that children should be taught those useful things which are really necessary, but not all useful things; for occupations are divided into liberal and illiberal; and to young children should be imparted only such kinds of knowledge as will be useful to them without vulgarizing them. And any occupation, art, or science,

From Aristotle, *Politics*, translated by Benjamin Jowett, from *The Basic Works of Aristotle*, edited by Richard McKeon. Copyright 1941 and renewed 1969 by Random House, Inc. Original source *The Oxford Translation of Aristotle*, ed. W. D. Ross, 1925. Reprinted by permission of The Clarendon Press, Oxford. This selection is from Book VIII, Chapters 1-3 (pp. 1305-1308); Chapter 7 (pp. 1314-1316). The translator's notes are not included here.

which makes the body or soul or mind of the freeman less fit for the practice or exercise of virtue, is vulgar; wherefore we call those arts vulgar which
tend to deform the body, and likewise all paid employments, for they ab-
sorb and degrade the mind. There are also some liberal arts quite proper
for a freeman to acquire, but only in a certain degree, and if he attend to
them too closely, in order to attain perfection in them, the same evil effects will follow. The object also which a man sets before him makes a
great difference; if he does or learns anything for his own sake or for the
sake of his friends, or with a view to excellence, the action will not appear
illiberal; but if done for the sake of others, the very same action will be
thought menial and servile. The received subjects of instruction, as I have
already remarked, are partly of a liberal and partly of an illiberal character.

The customary branches of education are in number four; they are—
(1) reading and writing, (2) gymnastic exercises, (3) music, to which is
sometimes added (4) drawing. Of these, reading and writing and drawing
are regarded as useful for the purposes of life in a variety of ways, and gymnastic exercises are thought to infuse courage. Concerning music a doubt
may be raised—in our own day most men cultivate it for the sake of pleasure, but originally it was included in education, because nature herself, as
has been often said, requires that we should be able, not only to work well,
but to use leisure well; for, as I must repeat once again, the first principle
of all action is leisure. Both are required, but leisure is better than occupation and is its end; and therefore the question must be asked, what ought
we to do when at leisure? Clearly we ought not to be amusing ourselves,
for then amusement would be the end of life. But if this is inconceivable,
and amusement is needed more amid serious occupations than at other
times (for he who is hard at work has need of relaxation, and amusement
gives relaxation, whereas occupation is always accompanied with exertion
and effort), we should introduce amusements only at suitable times, and
they should be our medicines, for the emotion which they create in the soul
is a relaxation, and from the pleasure we obtain rest. But leisure of itself
gives pleasure and happiness and enjoyment of life, which are experienced,
not by the busy man, but by those who have leisure. For he who is occupied
has in view some end which he has not attained; but happiness is an end,
since all men deem it to be accompanied with pleasure and not with pain.
This pleasure, however, is regarded differently by different persons, and
varies according to the habit of individuals; the pleasure of the best man is
the best, and springs from the noblest sources. It is clear then that there are
branches of learning and education which we must study merely with a
view to leisure spent in intellectual activity, and these are to be valued for
their own sake; whereas those kinds of knowledge which are useful in business are to be deemed necessary, and exist for the sake of other things. And

therefore our fathers admitted music into education, not on the ground either of its necessity or utility, for it is not necessary, nor indeed useful in the same manner as reading and writing, which are useful in money-making, in the management of a household, in the acquisition of knowledge and in political life, nor like drawing, useful for a more correct judgment of the works of artists, nor again like gymnastic, which gives health and strength; for neither of these is to be gained from music. There remains, then, the use of music for intellectual enjoyment in leisure; which is in fact evidently the reason of its introduction, this being one of the ways in which it is thought that a freeman should pass his leisure; as Homer says—

"But he who alone should be called to the pleasant feast,"

and afterwards he speaks of others whom he describes as inviting

"The bard who would delight them all."

And in another place Odysseus says there is no better way of passing life than when men's hearts are merry and

"The banqueters in the hall, sitting in order, hear the voice of the minstrel."

It is evident, then, that there is a sort of education in which parents should train their sons, not as being useful or necessary, but because it is liberal or noble. Whether this is of one kind only, or of more than one, and if so, what they are, and how they are to be imparted, must hereafter be determined. Thus much we are now in a position to say, that the ancients witness to us; for their opinion may be gathered from the fact that music is one of the received and traditional branches of education. Further, it is clear that children should be instructed in some useful things—for example, in reading and writing—not only for their usefulness, but also because many other sorts of knowledge are acquired through them. With a like view they may be taught drawing, not to prevent their making mistakes in their own purchases, or in order that they may not be imposed upon in the buying or selling of articles, but perhaps rather because it makes them judges of the beauty of the human form. To be always seeking after the useful does not become free and exalted souls. Now it is clear that in education practice must be used before theory, and the body be trained before the mind; and therefore boys should be handed over to the trainer, who creates in them the proper habit of body, and to the wrestling-master, who teaches them their exercises.

We have also to consider rhythms and modes, and their use in education.

Shall we use them all or make a distinction? and shall the same distinction be made for those who practise music with a view to education, or shall it be some other? Now we see that music is produced by melody and rhythm, and we ought to know what influence these have respectively on education, and whether we should prefer excellence in melody or excellence in rhythm. But as the subject has been very well treated by many musicians of the present day, and also by philosophers who have had considerable experience of musical education, to these we would refer the more exact student of the subject; we shall only speak of it now after the manner of the legislator, stating the general principles.

We accept the division of melodies proposed by certain philosophers into ethical melodies, melodies of action, and passionate or inspiring melodies, each having, as they say, a mode corresponding to it. But we maintain further that music should be studied, not for the sake of one, but of many benefits, that is to say, with a view to (1) education, (2) purgation (the word "purgation" we use at present without explanation, but when hereafter we speak of poetry, we will treat the subject with more precision); music may also serve (3) for intellectual enjoyment, for relaxation and for recreation after exertion. It is clear, therefore, that all the modes must be employed by us, but not all of them in the same manner. In education the most ethical modes are to be preferred, but in listening to the performances of others we may admit the modes of action and passion also. For feelings such as pity and fear, or, again, enthusiasm, exist very strongly in some souls, and have more or less influence over all. Some persons fall into a religious frenzy, whom we see as a result of the sacred melodies—when they have used the melodies that excite the soul to mystic frenzy—restored as though they had found healing and purgation. Those who are influenced by pity or fear, and every emotional nature, must have a like experience, and others in so far as each is susceptible to such emotions, and all are in a manner purged and their souls lightened and delighted. The purgative melodies likewise give an innocent pleasure to mankind. Such are the modes and the melodies in which those who perform music at the theatre should be invited to compete. But since the spectators are of two kinds—the one free and educated, and the other a vulgar crowd composed of mechanics, labourers, and the like—there ought to be contests and exhibitions instituted for the relaxation of the second class also. And the music will correspond to their minds; for as their minds are perverted from the natural state, so there are perverted modes and highly strung and unnaturally coloured melodies. A man receives pleasure from what is natural to him, and therefore professional musicians may be allowed to practise this lower sort of music before an audience of a lower type. But, for the purposes of education, as I have already said, those modes and melodies should be employed which are ethical, such as the Dorian, as we said before; though we may include any others which are approved by philosophers who have had a musical education. The Socrates of the *Republic* is wrong in retaining only the Phrygian mode along with the Dorian, and the more so because he rejects the flute; for the Phrygian is to the modes what the flute is to musical instruments—both of them are exciting and emotional. Poetry proves this, for Bacchic frenzy and all similar emotions are most suitably expressed by the flute, and are better set to the Phrygian than to any other mode. The dithyramb, for example, is acknowledged to be Phrygian, a fact of which the connoisseurs of music offer many proofs, saying, among other things, that Philoxenus, having attempted to compose his *Mysians* as a dithyramb in the Dorian mode, found it impossible, and fell back by the very nature of things into the more appropriate Phrygian. All men agree that the Dorian music is the gravest and manliest. And whereas we say that the extremes should be avoided and the mean followed, and whereas the Dorian is a mean between the other modes, it is evident that our youth should be taught the Dorian music.

Two principles have to be kept in view, what is possible, what is becoming: at these every man ought to aim. But even these are relative to age; the old, who have lost their powers, cannot very well sing the high-strung modes, and nature herself seems to suggest that their songs should be of the more relaxed kind. Wherefore the musicians likewise blame Socrates, and with justice, for rejecting the relaxed modes in education under the idea that they are intoxicating, not in the ordinary sense of intoxication (for wine rather tends to excite men), but because they have no strength in them. And so, with a view also to the time of life when men begin to grow old, they ought to practise the gentler modes and melodies as well as the others, and, further, any mode, such as the Lydian above all others appears to be, which is suited to children of tender age, and possesses the elements both of order and of education. Thus it is clear that education should be based upon three principles—the mean, the possible, the becoming, these three.

Summary

THE main purpose of this work has been to illustrate the relationship between the development of certain Greek cultural and educational ideals from the time of the Homeric epic to fourth century philosophy and rhetoric. The educational ideals which took shape during that period had been influenced first by the ideal Homeric hero, a noble warrior and noble orator, unenlightened except by his "inborn noble nature"; later by the ideal Periclean democrat, who could serve both himself and his Athens by meeting whatever difficulties the situation called for nobly; and, later still, in an increasingly enlightened Sophistic culture, by the ideal philosopher, who strove to know the highest excellence by which anything whatsoever may be known and so came to possess the kind of knowledge which is not apart from right activity but which is needed to direct that activity; or, in the same Sophistic culture, by the ideal orator who was not a mere speechmaker but a good man speaking well, using his acquired wisdom to suggest right courses of action.

The earliest "educational literature" of the Greeks was their poetry, which portrayed men as embodying eternal forms of heroic dimensions rather than as ordinary human beings. By the second half of the fifth century, the drama of Euripides had ordinary men and women coping with ordinary life problems rather than tragic heroes living out themes of eternal significance; such drama was made popular by the conditions which brought the Sophists into being and led to an age of enlightenment. In creating alternatives to the old culture and the old drama, the increasingly self-critical and intellectualized culture created a new education which challenged the traditional athletic and poetic education that dated back to the Homeric knightly ideals. The possibility that an acquired, "learned" wisdom, taught by the Sophists, might stand alongside the "natural" wisdom of the nobly born would lead to a fundamental revision of the ideal of the educated man.

Not only in poetry, drama, rhetoric, and philosophy, but strikingly in Thucydides' conception of the purpose of history writing, the view is evident that men express in their activities a purpose of things which is natural and, as such, limited, but limited in a way which men may understand. There is a sort of tragedy in history which finds that perceiving what man has achieved through time is but one way of understanding what his limits are. The idea that man's mind is in harmony with the rest of nature, and that all of his arts and sciences constitute his attempt to know the nature of that harmony, finds expression in the sometimes poetic, sometimes inquiring philosophizing of Plato, and in the more systematic, but no less inquiring philosophy of Aristotle.

From the "poetic wisdom" of Homeric epics to the "philosophic wisdom" of Plato and Aristotle; from the earlier orator-warrior to the later wise man of affairs (be he philosopher or orator); the basic assumption among the Greeks was that the wise should rule. This assumption might be called the central idea around which Greek education, first largely unconsciously and later quite deliberately, oriented itself. The Homeric hero, the Pericles-like man of affairs, the enlightened philosopher and orator—these were the figures on which were based, in both theory and practice, the ideals which directed educators in their endeavours to shape educated leaders.

The asking of explicit educational questions led to a serious consideration of the kinds of arts and sciences which should be studied in the education of leaders. Thus the process by which heroic, aristocratic, and, finally, enlightened leaders are supposed to have taken shape became the point of departure for the deliberate study of educational ends and means.

How human beings might be shaped according to ideals of heroic stature; how human beings who work out their inescapable human tragedies in brief spans of time might deliberately learn how to make use of eternal ideas; how man might finally learn how best to be happy in the face of destiny; and how that harmony is sought by which an individual lives not by himself in the universe apart from others, but in situations that are naturally and necessarily social as well—these were, for the Greeks, aesthetic, political, and educational matters; and the way in which they were unified is the Greeks' most enduring contribution to educational thinking.

Bibliographic Note

THOSE who want introductions to the mind and character of the ancient Greeks might well begin with H.D.F. Kitto, *The Greeks* (Baltimore: Penguin Books, 1951) or C.E. Robinson, *Hellas* (Boston: Beacon Press, 1955).

There is one work which treats, at some length, most aspects of the development illustrated in this book of readings. It is Werner Jaeger, *Paideia: The Ideals of Greek Culture,* 3 volumes, translated by Gilbert Highet (New York: Oxford University Press, 1945, 1943, 1944). Jaeger's study is the most provocative interpretation, available in English, of Greek educational ideals from Archaic Greece to the days of Plato and Isocrates. The best work available on Greek educational institutions is H. I. Marrou, *A History of Education in Antiquity,* translated by George Lamb (New York: A Mentor Book, 1964).

In addition to the *Republic,* the following dialogues by Plato are particularly valuable for the student of the history of education: *Meno, Protagoras, Gorgias,* and *Laws;* one who has training in philosophy can also read *Theatetus* and *The Sophist* with profit. For studies of Plato that are aimed at a wide scope of his thought, see A. E. Taylor, *Plato, The Man and His Work* (London: Methuen, 1960) or G. M. A. Grube, *Plato's Thought* (Boston: Beacon Press, 1958). Gilbert Ryle, in *Plato's Progress* (Cambridge: The University Press, 1966), reconstructs Plato's career in such a way as to suggest a reinterpretation of his educational work and philosophical development.

Isocrates is considered at some length by both Jaeger and Marrou in the studies already mentioned. Two other essays on Isocrates are George Norlin's introduction to Volume I of *Isocrates* (New York: G. P. Putnam's, 1928); and Costas M. Proussis, "The Orator: Isocrates," in Nash, Kazamias, and Perkinson, editors, *The Educated Man* (New York: John Wiley & Sons, 1965).

The student of the history of education who is interested in additional reading in the works of Aristotle will find *Prior Analytics, Posterior Analytics, Topics, Metaphysics,* and *On the Soul* of especial interest. For a brief introduction to Aristotle's philosophy, see A. E. Taylor's *Aristotle* (New York: Dover Publications, 1955). For a more elaborate interpretation, see John Herman Randall, Jr., *Aristotle* (New York: Columbia University Press, 1960).

Index